# Mastering
The business environment

# Palgrave Master Series

Accounting
Accounting Skills
Advanced English Language
Advanced English Literature
Advanced Pure Mathematics
Arabic
Basic Management
Biology
British Politics
Business Administration
Business Communication
Business Environment
C Programming
C++ Programming
Chemistry
COBOL Programming
Communication
Computing
Counselling Skills
Customer Relations
Database Design
Delphi Programming
Desktop Publishing
Economic and Social History
Economics
Electrical Engineering
Electronic and Electrical Calculations
Electronics
English Grammar
English Language
English Literature
Fashion Buying and Merchandising
  Management
Fashion Styling
French

Geography
German
Global Information Systems
Human Resource Management
Information Technology
Internet
Italian
Java
Mathematics
Microsoft Office
Microsoft Windows, Novell NetWare and
  UNIX
Modern British History
Modern European History
Modern US History
Modern World History
Networks
Organisational Behaviour
Pascal and Delphi Programming
Philosophy
Photography
Physics
Practical Criticism
Psychology
Shakespeare
Skills of Management
Social Welfare
Sociology
Spanish
Statistics
Strategic Management
Systems Analysis and Design
Theology
Visual Basic
World Religions

**Palgrave Master Series**
**Series Standing Order ISBN 0–333–69343–4**
*(outside North America only)*

You can receive future titles in this series as they are published by placing a standing order. Please contact your bookseller or, in case of difficulty, write to us at the address below with your name and address, the title of the series and the ISBN quoted above.

Customer Services Department. Macmillan Distribution Ltd
Houndmills, Basingstoke, Hampshire RG21 6XS, England

# Mastering
## The Business Environment

Roger I. Cartwright, MA

*Business Series Editor*
Richard Pettinger

palgrave

First published 2001 by
PALGRAVE
Houndmills, Basingstoke, Hampshire RG21 6XS and
175 Fifth Avenue, New York, N.Y. 10010
Companies and representatives throughout the world

PALGRAVE is the new global academic imprint of St. Martin's Press LLC
Scholarly and Reference Division and Palgrave Publishers Ltd (formerly
Macmillan Press Ltd).

ISBN 0–333–92937–3

A catalogue record for this book is available from the British Library.

This book is printed on paper suitable for recycling and
made from fully managed and sustained forest sources.

10   9   8   7   6   5   4   3   2   1
10  09  08  07  06  05  04  03  02  01

Printed and bound in Great Britain by
Creative Print & Design (Wales), Ebbw Vale

# ■ ▼ Contents

# ▾  Preface

This is a book of analyses, the key analyses that need to be carried out as part of the decision-making processes of any organisation, be it in the private, public or voluntary sectors.

All organisations operate within two environments. Firstly, there is the internal environment unique to the particular organisation and secondly, the wider external environment which is shared with other organisations and stakeholders. It is the latter that is the subject of this book and its importance lies in the fact that actions by others, be they individuals, customers, competitors, governments etc., may have a profound effect on the way an organisation operates, irrespective of its internal strengths and weaknesses.

During a career, especially in management, the further up an organisational hierarchy one progresses, the more like the god Janus one needs to become. Janus is depicted as having two faces, one looking one way (back to the old year) and the other forward into the new one. This is not to suggest that managers should be two-faced in a relationship context but they do need to have an eye on both the internal and external environments of the organisation.

The analyses in this book are designed to allow you to decide which pieces of information are important to a particular organisation and which are not. As more and more information becomes freely available through advances in information and communications technology (ICT), the more important it is to recognise what information is actually important and which may just serve to muddy the waters. It can be just as dangerous to be overloaded with information as it is not to have enough.

In the 1980s, students on business and management courses were introduced to an external analysis known as PEST, standing for Political, Economic, Social and Technological. By the early 1990s, Environmental was added, reflecting the growing importance of environmental issues, thus changing the acronym to STEEP and by the late 1990s many authorities had added Legal, again changing the acronym, this time to PESTLE.

This book seeks to widen the scope of the analyses that need to be carried out in order to include a more detailed consideration of the culture within which the organisation must operate: the customer base, competition within the sector and the aesthetic implications both physical and behavioural of the organisation on its external operating environment. To this end the set of analyses presented in this book can be known as SPECTACLES (Social, Political, Economic, Cultural, Technological, Aesthetic, Customers, Legal, Environmental and Sectoral). Given that the concept revolves around examining the organisation's environment, an acronym associated with sight is not inappropriate.

A study of the external environment is a crucial part of business planning and, as such, forms a part of the planning processes in most organisations. Business planning and a consideration of micro- and macro-economics also form important parts of many programmes of study from A-level/Higher Still (the Scottish equivalent) through HNC/HND/BA courses in Business Administration and on to Certificate/Diploma in Management and MBA programmes.

The use of such analyses as covered in this book is not confined to students. As mentioned earlier, an analytical review forms a major component in business planning, and thus the book will be of use to both those studying business and those who are actually involved in decision-making within organisations.

This is not a linear book where a requirement of understanding a particular chapter involves an understanding of preceding chapters. All of the factors contained within SPECTACLES are important to every organisation to a greater or lesser extent, depending upon its particular circumstances, and all need to be considered when examining that organisation within its business environment. However, the relative importance may change from organisation to organisation and from business sector to business sector. For example, an examination of cultural practices within the Far East may be of immense importance to an organisation that trades extensively with the region or which has competitors based there, whilst this may be of less importance to a UK local authority for whom national/European political factors may be of more importance. As mentioned earlier, one of the skills of modern management is deciding which information is important. In analysing an organisation you need to ask the right questions in order to decide the relative importance of the factors influencing that organisation's operations. By the end of this book you should be competent to ask those questions and then to select the information you require to build up as complete a picture as possible of the way that the organisation interfaces with its operating environment.

The book is laid out to take you through the various components of the SPECTACLES analysis, following an introductory chapter that examines the various typologies of organisations and the sectors within which they operate. Wherever possible, examples are taken from the operations of real organisations.

Business uses many terms and acronyms that have become part of a fairly specialised language. A Glossary of these terms and acronyms is provided immediately after this Preface.

At the end of each chapter, following the Chapter summary, is a set of questions. If you are undertaking a set course of study, you may be required to answer the questions as part of an assignment. If you are not engaged in an actual course of study, you will find the questions of use as part of your reflection on the content of the chapter.

There is also, at the end of each chapter covering the SPECTACLES analysis (Chapters 3–12) a section called Analysis that can be used by those carrying out an environmental analysis for an organisation as an *aide-mémoir* of the important aspects to consider.

No book of a general nature can hope to cover every topic in depth. In addition to the Bibliography at the end of this book, each chapter concludes with suggestions for Further reading for you to undertake in order to gain a more detailed appreciation of the chapter topic. The Bibliography also includes some Web page references (URLs) that were current at the time of writing and which may be useful to you. As the World Wide Web changes constantly, no responsibility can be taken for any changes to URLs etc., although the references given have been confined to official and semi-official pages that should still be available.

The author of this books lives and works in Scotland, a country which although an integral part of the UK has had its own parliament since 1999 and which, since the Act of Union in 1707, has retained its own legal and education systems together with the issuing of its own currency. Further details of the political changes brought about by devolution in 1999 are contained in Chapter 4 of this book. There are a number of references to Scottish institutions in this book although the use of Scottish idioms has been kept to a minimum. There is one exception. The word **outwith**, as the opposite of within, is used on a number of occasions because it is such a useful word and one which appears on official notices and documents in Scotland – hopefully this book will help introduce the word to a wider English-speaking audience.

This book does not seek to provide detailed statistics, as these become rapidly outdated, but rather to provide you with the questions to ask when conducting an external analysis relevant to an organisation, and ideas and suggestions as to where relevant information may be found and how it should be used. By the start of the 21st Century, a wealth of data had become easily accessible via the Internet, with an increasing percentage of the global population having Internet access either at work or at home. Governments, regions and organisations, both large and small, have web pages that can provide up-to-date facts and figures. The days of books such as this one needing to include masses of statistics are, in the main, past. The role of books is likely to become what it was in the earliest days of printing – a vehicle for stimulating thought.

# ▪ ☑  Acknowledgements

Many thanks to all those people who have provided information for this book. Especial gratitude to my wife June for her patience and encouragement.

The author and publishers wish to thank the following for permission to use copyright material:

Berlitz Publishing Company, Inc for Fig. 13.1 which includes data abstracted from the 1994 to 2000 editions of the *Berlitz Complete Guide to Cruising & Cruise Ships*. Copyright © 1994–2000 Berlitz Publishing Company, Inc.

Pearson Education for Figs. 1.2, 1.3, 1.4 for data from Mintzberg, Quinn and James, *The Strategy Process*, Prentice Hall (1988) Figs. 1, 11, 14; and Fig. 6.1 from G Johnson and K Scholes, *Exploring Corporate Strategy, 3rd ed.*, Prentice Hall, (1993) Fig. 2.10.

Every effort has been made to trace the copyright holders but if any have been inadvertently overlooked the publishers will be pleased to make the necessary arrangement at the first opportunity.

# ■ ⋎ Glossary

| | |
|---|---|
| ACM | Association of College Managers (UK) |
| AM | Assembly Member (Wales) |
| ASA | Advertising Standards Authority (UK) |
| ATM | Automatic Teller Machine |
| BA | British Airways |
| BACK | Baggage, Aspirations, Culture and Knowledge |
| BoE | Bank of England |
| CAP | Common Agricultural Policy (of the EU) |
| CEO | Chief Executive Officer |
| CFC | Chlorofluorocarbon |
| CPS | Crown Prosecution Service |
| CV | *Curriculum Vitae* |
| DBT | Design–Build Team |
| DfEE | Department for Education and Employment (UK) |
| DGFT | Director General of Fair Trading |
| DNA | Deoxyribonucleic acid |
| DOS | Disk Operating System |
| DTI | Department of Trade and Industry (UK) |
| ECB | European Central Bank |
| EEC | European Economic Community (now EU) |
| EFTA | European Free Trade Association |
| EIB | European Investment Bank |
| EMU | European Monetary Union |
| EPA | Environmental Protection Agency (USA) |
| EPOS | Electronic Point of Sale |
| ETF | Electronic Transfer of Funds |
| ETOPS | Extended Range Twin Operations |
| EU | European Union |
| FAA | Federal Aviation Administration |
| FMEA | Failure Modes and Effects Analysis |
| GATT | General Agreements on Tariffs and Trade |
| GDP | Gross Domestic Product |
| GM | Genetically modified |
| HMG | Her (His) Majesty's Government |
| ICT | Information and Communications Technology |
| IMF | International Monetary Fund |
| M0/1/2/3/4/5 | Measures of money supply |
| MEP | Member of the European Parliament |
| MOD | Ministry of Defence |
| MP | Member of Parliament |

| | |
|---|---|
| MSP | Member of the Scottish Parliament |
| NHS | National Health Service |
| OFT | Office of Fair Trading |
| OU | Open University |
| PEST | Political, Economic, Social and Technological |
| PESTLE | Political, Economic, Social, Technological, Legal and Environmental |
| QMV | Qualified Majority Voting |
| RNA | Ribonucleic acid |
| SEC | Securities and Exchange Commission (USA) |
| SMEs | Small and Medium sized Enterprises |
| SPECTACLES | Social, Political, Economic, Cultural, Technological, Aesthetic, Customers, Legal, Environmental and Sectoral |
| SSSI | Site of Special Scientific Interest (UK) |
| STEEP | Social, Technological, Economic, Environmental and Political |
| SWOT | Strengths, Weaknesses, Opportunities and Threats |
| TES | *Times Educational Supplement* |
| TURER | Trade Union Reform and Employment Rights (UK) |
| UHI | University of the Highlands and Islands |
| UN | United Nations |
| UNK-UNKs | Unknown, unknowns |
| USP | Unique Selling Point |

# ▮ **1** Introduction

The world of business at the start of the 21st Century is paradoxically more simple and yet at the same time more complex than at any time in the past. The paradox is due to the rate, quantity and speed of information available not only to managers and owners (the decision-makers) but also to other employees and customers.

Even the word 'business' itself is often misunderstood. Many people use the word to describe the interactions between organisations that trade with each other for profit, and thus business has come to be equated with some form of profit motive. As will be demonstrated later in this chapter, in this book 'business' is used to refer to all interactions between organisations whether they are prompted by a profit or a public service/charity motive.

In the latter years of the 20th Century much was made of the dangers of 'information overload', the phenomenon that can paralyse decision-making when there is so much information available that making decisions becomes increasingly harder. In earlier times the problem was one of 'information underload'. There was in fact often not enough information available to make a rational decision. John Keegan (1998), writing about the origins of the First World War (1914–18), comments on the decisions that were made by the governments of Britain, France, Russia, Austria and Germany in the Summer of 1914 based on fragments of unco-ordinated information. Perhaps the four years of carnage that followed could have been prevented if there had been a clearer view of what was actually happening in the chancelleries and military installations of Europe at the time.

It is difficult to imagine the slowness of communication of two hundred years ago. Apart from rudimentary line-of-sight signalling devices that could only send simple messages along a set route, the speed of communication was that of a horse or a person. Warships sailing into battle did so at just four or five miles an hour and communicated with each other by means of signal flags. It was not until the practical application of the steam engine to mass transportation that speeds of communication improved dramatically. Steam trains could travel at speeds in excess of thirty miles per hour. When the Liverpool and Manchester Railway opened in 1830 as the world's first steam operated public railway designed for timetabled passenger and goods transport, it did more than speed up communications between the two cities. Long-distance transport was brought within reach of ordinary people and this began a social revolution that saw workers being able to live further and further from their place of employment. No longer did they need to live within walking distance of work. Suburbs grew up alongside the railways and tramways, their ribbon-like growth being still discernible today and echoed in the developments on either side of newly built roads and motorways.

It took people some time to come to terms with the safety implications of faster means of travel. On the opening day of the Liverpool and Manchester Railway, 15 September 1830, the President of the Board of Trade, Huskisson was run down and fatally injured by George Stephenson's famous *Rocket*, having failed to move out of the way quickly enough. A railway locomotive cannot turn away and even the puny locomotives of 1830 needed considerable distance to stop, especially given their relatively inefficient brakes. It was not until the 1870s that the use of the electric telegraph to control the movement of trains and provide communications between signalmen was developed throughout the UK rail network. Before then a system based on time intervals was used and if the preceding train broke down, there was no way of letting the driver of a following train know. The development of the telegraph also brought about a massive increase in the speed of communication. A shout travels at the speed of sound, approximately 700 mph at sea level whereas an electric impulse moves at the speed of light, 186 281 miles per second, i.e. 670 611 600 mph, nearly a million times faster than a shout and a hundred million times faster than walking!

By the end of the 20th Century, the Internet and the vast amounts of communication that it contained, coupled with the ease with which information could be communicated, were leading to a revolution in business relationships. Distance and time were no longer issues. The computer had become a regular fixture not only at work but also in the home and, for an increasing number of people, the home was also fast becoming the workplace.

At the start of the 20th Century, a key managerial problem was how to acquire enough information; by the start of the 21st Century, this was no longer the problem. Information is available in abundance – the key issues centre around the sifting and analysis of information; it is often more a problem of knowing what to ignore!

One of the disadvantages of the increased speed of communication has been what may be described as 'the immediacy of effect'. This is often seen in the currency and stock markets where traders in one place are able to react almost immediately to a slight change in the value of a currency or share in another marketplace. There is little or no time for reflection. Increased communications have led to a danger of over-centralisation as the central control can send out instantaneous instructions to its outlying operations or branches. Max Hastings & Simon Jenkins (1983), in their account of the 1982 conflict between Britain and Argentina after the latter's invasion of the Falkland Islands in the South Atlantic, make the point that the commander of the first wave of British troops to go ashore on the Islands, Major General

Jeremy Moore, Royal Marines, spent much of his time on the satellite link to London, a link that allowed his commanders the opportunity to direct the battle from 8000 miles away. Unfortunately, cold, damp and the true feelings of people on the ground cannot be sent over a communications link – only raw statistics. In a previous era, Moore would have received his basic instructions and been allowed to get on with it. It would have been impossible for the BBC to announce the attack on Goose Green before the operation had started, an act that Colonel 'H' Jones of the Parachute Regiment (and who was killed in the attack) and others claimed endangered lives.

Information and Communications Technology (ICT) can ensure that the headquarters of a supermarket could, if it so wished, knew the exact moment in real time when a tin of baked beans was sold. Such information may be very relevant to those responsible for placing orders and ensuring that branches do not run out of stock, but such detail could be a hindrance to those making strategic decisions who require to see a bigger picture rather than a succession of tactical details. In essence this book is about undertaking the analyses that enable a view of the big picture to be obtained and then used as a basis for decision-making.

## The importance of scanning the external environment

'No man is an island,' wrote John Dunne in the 17th Century and no organisation exists in a vacuum. Whatever the function of an organisation it has to co-exist with other organisations in a complex external environment. In many cases it is actions taken by those outside the organisation that are a major influence on organisational decisions, and for this reason it is important that decision-makers have as clear a picture as possible as to what is happening in the external environment. This book separates the various components of the external environment and examines each in turn. It will also be self-apparent to anybody who has experienced the world of work that the boundaries between the internal and external environments can be blurred. Whilst this book is mainly concerned with the external environment, nevertheless many of the concepts will also be as applicable to the internal environment of an organisation.

## Types of businesses and organisations

'Organisations', as a term is one that is freely used and yet one that is not easy to define. Argyris (1960) defined organisations as:

> '[Organisations are] intricate human strategies designed to achieve certain objectives.'

Whilst a later writer, Pugh (1971), considered that:

'Organisations are systems of inter-dependent human beings.'

Pugh's definition as it stands is all-embracing. As Cartwright *et al.* (1993) have pointed out, Pugh's definition covers everything from the UK Government and British Airways to even a family, all of which depend for their success on people working with and relying on each other. With a little imagination, even Argyris's definition could encompass the family as an organisation, because the family has developed biologically and socially as an excellent method of ensuring the survival of children to maturity. It should be noted that this is not a way of saying that the Western concept of the nuclear family is the only acceptable form as there are many variations of family structure in the world, each suited to a particular culture and way of life and each of equal importance.

Business can be described as the relationship between organisations. All business relationships involve some form of trade or exchange, goods for money, services for money, goods for services etc. Money, that apparently all-important factor in our lives, is nothing more than a convenient common denominator that allows a trade to take place.

A whole chapter of this book is related to the type of economic analyses of the external environment carried out by organisations but it is important to realise at the outset that money has no intrinsic value. When a person goes into a shop to buy an item priced at £9.95 and pays for it with a £10 note and receives 5p change, a number of assumptions are made:

- The seller values the item at £9.95 (or less)
- The buyer also values the item at £9.95 (or more)
- The seller recognises the exchange value of a £10 note
- The buyer recognises the exchange value of 5p.

The addition of the words 'or less' and 'or more' to the £9.95 is a recognition of a simple economic fact. Unless they are forced to by circumstances outwith their control, people will sell something at a price equal to or higher than its lowest value, whilst people will want to buy something at a price equal to or lower than the value they place on it – a bargain is something for which we pay less than we expected.

The £10 note is itself just a piece of paper but, because a huge number of people are prepared to recognise it as having a certain value in trade, it can be given in exchange, the seller knowing that it can be used later to purchase other goods and services. Trade has developed so that there are agreements relating to the relative value of one currency against another. The difference between hard currencies such as sterling, the US dollar, the deutschmark, the franc and the yen etc. and soft currencies such as the rouble and many third world currencies, is that other countries recognise the value of the hard currencies and will exchange them freely for their own currency whilst the value of soft currencies is not recognised.

There are four basic typologies of organisations, defined by ownership and prime function, be it for-profit or not-for-profit, as shown in Figure 1.1.

In terms of size, the current position in the UK is that the for-profit/ private ownership and the not-for-profit/public ownership sectors are in fact by far the biggest components in terms of economic activity. The former includes the majority of all commercial activities and the latter the entire public sector including national and local government, the National Health Service, education and the armed forces. Prior to the 1980s, the not-for-profit/public ownership sector was very large and contained some huge monopoly or near monopoly organisations. These included the steel, coal, gas, electricity and ship-building industries, railways, British Airways and other nationalised concerns. Under privatisation many of them have moved into the for-profit/private ownership quadrant. In an increasing number of countries the not-for-profit/public ownership sector is decreasing rapidly as governments divest themselves of commercial interests through privatisation.

In the private ownership quadrant, organisations may be owned by a single or small number of individuals or a large group of shareholders. Whilst most organisations that are owned solely by an individual are small, there are some very large examples, Stagecoach being a well-known example. Although most people in the UK would say that they do not own the organisation they work for, they may through shareholding have an ownership interest in a number of organisations. Anybody who holds shares, however few, in a company has an ownership interest in that company.

It is important not to be confused between the term plc (public limited company) and a publicly owned organisation. The former is an organisation whose shares are offered on the stockmarket and are thus available to the public, whilst the latter is an organisation that is part of the operation of the central or local government and in effect owned by all citizens.

|  | Public ownership | Private ownership |
|---|---|---|
| For-profit | Nationalised industry | Commercial organisations |
| Not-for-profit | National/local government | Voluntary sector |

*Figure 1.1 Typologies of organisations.*

# Sectors of business and organisations

The world of business used to be divided into two main sectors – private and public as discussed above – with a third, the so-called voluntary sector (charities etc.) gaining in prominence in the second half of the 20th Century. As was shown earlier, these are really descriptions of the typologies of organisations and actually describe ownership. 'Sector' is a description of the type of core activity the organisation is engaged on. Whilst the list can be never-ending, the main business sectors may be described as:

- Government
- Financial service (banks, insurance etc.)
- Information services
- Manufacturing
- Building
- Transportation (airlines, bus companies, taxis, railways, shipping)
- Hospitality
- Tourism
- Care (hospitals, nursing homes etc.)
- Entertainment
- Education
- Services (including plumbers, electricians etc.).

Each sector can have further subsectors as illustrated in the brackets. For example, the transportation sector includes railways, shipping, airlines, road transport etc. It is not always clear without a careful study exactly which sector or sectors an organisation belongs to. The huge P&O Group in the UK has operations within the transportation sector through its shipping interests but has also been involved in building. However a proportion of the shipping is engaged in the cruise industry and as an area of operation that industry may be considered to have major components within the tourism and entertainment sectors (Cartwright & Baird, 1999). One method of ascertaining which sector or sectors an organisation is in, is to see which sector or sectors their major competitors are in. In the case of P&O's cruising interests, where they hold the world number 3 position, its competitors are not only other cruise companies with their ships but also package holidays and hotels, thus giving P&O a firm footing in the tourism sector. The company also operates bulk freighters and car ferries, and in these cases these parts of the operation clearly fit directly into the transportation sector, as did their original passenger liner shipping operation which took passengers from the UK to India, Australia and the Far East.

# Mission and objectives

All organisations have been set up to do something, whether it is to run a country, to provide a holiday or to manufacture a motor car. Whilst the ultimate objective of a for-profit organisation may be just that – profit, in order to achieve that objective the organisation needs to deliver a product or service to its customers. Modern organisations usually produce a statement of their mission which encapsulates what business they are in and where they see themselves positioned within the particular market or markets that they serve. Unfortunately many mission statements, originally intended to motivate staff and to inspire customers, have become, in the words of Clutterbuck *et al.* (1993) 'woolly platitudes' that do reflect actual performance. Many, as Clutterbuck and his colleagues report, do not even mention service.

## Structure

Before commencing the formal external analyses of factors affecting the relationship of an organisation with its external environment, it is possible, on close study of any organisation, to say which typology it fits into based on ownership (public or private) and operational motive (for-profit or not-for-profit). The size of an organisation can be small, medium or large, usually defined by the number of employees (small, under 50; medium, 51 up to 249; large, 250+).

As will be seen in the next section, organisational structures have been developed to serve the particular needs of the individual organisation. This is not a text on organisational design, books such as Richard Pettinger's (1996) *Introduction to Organisational Behaviour* providing comprehensive coverage of this topic. It is necessary, however, for those examining an organisation to consider the relation between design and function. Is the organisation a compact one operating on a single site or is it diverse with a need to standardise quality and performance over a wide geographic range, e.g. Marks and Spencer, Dixons, high street banks and building societies, Ford? Towards the end of the 20th Century another type of organisation has begun to develop, one that has two major centres of operation, i.e. a **bi-polar** organisation. Scottish and Southern Electricity, formed from a merger between Hydro Electric serving the North of Scotland and Southern Electric in the South of England, was one of the early examples. It is useful to consider the reporting links and the degree of autonomy provided at the customer interface – how much authority does a branch manager have to solve a problem before having to seek permission from head office? Cartwright (2000) has divided organisations into those that are concentrated, e.g. a village shop or a single factory unit, and those which are diffuse, and makes the point that consistency of product and especially service will always be more difficult for the latter. Diffuse organisations operating across regional and national borders may also need to carry out separate parts of the SPECTACLES analysis, especially in the economic, political, environmental and sociological fields as these may be radically different for some parts of the organisation. As a simple example, the safety and emission regulations for motor cars may be different in various parts of the world, requiring different national specifications.

That there are a science and logic to organisational structure is shown in the next section where the developments that have led to the recognisable forms of organisational structure present today are described.

# A brief history of organisational development

Television documentaries depicting the lives of gorillas, chimpanzees and other great apes never cease to be popular, perhaps because the behaviour of such animals reminds us uncannily of our own. Given that we have a large number of genes in common with these species it should not be surprising that we also share certain aspects of social behaviour, not least in the way we organise our activities. Human beings, like other advanced primates, are social animals whose groupings have a distinct hierarchy and are territorial in nature. Desmond Morris (1969) the well-known anthropologist, in his book *The Human Zoo*, described the similarities in social behaviour and structure between all of the great apes including humans, and Robert Ardrey (1967) has compared the similarities between humankind's territorialism and that of our primate relatives in his study entitled *The Territorial Imperative*.

If the anthropologists are correct, then the development of organisational structures goes back to the very dawn of primate development. Living and working in groups with clearly defined membership, shared tasks, an agreed hierarchy and 'space to call the group's own', i.e. its territory appears to be the natural form of primate social organisation, it is thus not surprising that these aspects are reflected in the structure of most work and social organisations.

Up to the early 1800s, most organisations were small because of the difficulty in communications mentioned at the beginning of this chapter. There were however exceptions, the Church, the Royal Navy and the Honourable East India Company being three good examples. Widely diffuse, these organisations had very clear hierarchical structures, that of the Church having survived for nearly two millennia relatively unchanged. Even when the Reformation led to the setting up of new Christian sects, these still tended to reflect to some degree the organisational structures of the Roman Catholic Church. The structure of the Catholic Church has proved remarkably resilient. As far as human involvement is concerned, and meaning no disrespect, comparing the Church to any other organisation it has a CEO (the Pope at the head office in Rome), senior management both in Rome and at its principal branches in other countries (the Cardinals), a set of branch managers (the parish priests) and even sales staff (missionaries). A similar structure is found in a traditional family, with a clear hierarchy and promotion from within. Whilst the mission of any religious movement is spiritual rather than profit oriented, the same structures that have proved useful for religious movements have also been adopted by business.

Leadership is also a key role; indeed one of Morris's observations in *The Human Zoo* concerns the similarity between leadership roles within primates including man. It appears that, as a species, we need leaders and leadership and that any organisation without a clearly defined leader, even if just a figurehead, is doomed to failure.

Biblical stories relating to such projects as Noah's Ark clearly show that an organisation, recognisable in structure, was set up to achieve the required objectives. Even the earliest annals of military history show a command structure similar to that of today's highly technical armed forces – commander, senior officers, junior officers, NCOs, ordinary soldiers, sailors etc.

Because of the difficulties of communications, organisations were forced, in the main to remain small. Those that did become large, such as the Church, Royal Navy etc. mentioned earlier, set up for their time quite complex communications systems and developed extremely detailed operating instructions. The 18th Century Royal Navy maintained an extensive courier brig system taking despatches from the Admiralty (today part of the Ministry of Defence – MOD) to flag officers (admirals) who commanded each station, the Channel Fleet, the Mediterranean Fleet, various West Indies commands etc., who in turn briefed or sent out despatches to the captains of the ships under their flag. There was also a set of detailed fighting instructions telling each captain how a particular set of battle circumstances should be approached, in effect detailing the tactics a captain should use. If, like Nelson, the captain ignored the instructions and gained a victory then little was said (although the instructions were rarely amended). If the captain ignored the instructions and suffered a defeat then a court martial and severe penalty (which could and in the case of Admiral Byng in 1757 did include execution!) was the norm. It should also be noted that if the captain obeyed the instructions to the letter and still lost the fight, they would also face a court martial and again severe penalties. Their Lordships of the Board of Admiralty could not lose!

Once the railway began to develop, firstly in the UK and then in the rest of Europe and the USA, communications were eased and it became possible to set up various branches of organisations in different towns. The removal of the need for workers to live within immediate walking distance of their place of work meant that organisations could grow bigger without having to provide housing next to the workplace. This in turn led to the growth of management and supervision as a distinct work role. As more and more people began to be employed in any one organisation, it became apparent that there was a limit to the number of individuals one person can supervise effectively. Urwick (1947) believed that the 'span of control' was as few as one person supervising no more than five or six others. This was not a new concept, just an elucidation of something that had been recognised, especially by the military, for some time.

The classic writers on management and supervision of the late 19th and early 20th Centuries, who include Taylor (1911) and Fayol (1916), were considering organisations where there was not just a distinction between workers and management in terms of tasks but also of education. They believed in the necessity for the same form of detailed operational instructions as covered earlier when discussing the fighting instructions of the Royal Navy. Clearly, as educational standards rose in the Western world throughout the 20th Century, it became possible to loosen the span of control by allowing for initiative. This brought about a new component to organisational structure, that of the technician.

Henry Mintzberg (1983) has developed a simple model to examine organisational structures. His basic model has three components (see Figure 1.2).

The **strategic apex**, which may be just one person in a small organisation or a group of very senior managers in a larger one, is where the major decisions are taken. Given the previous discussion on human behaviour, there is normally a figurehead at the very top of the apex, often with a senior operating individual immediately below him or her in the chain of command. In many organisations, and indeed governments, the chairperson, president or monarch may be purely ceremonial, the real power lying with the CEO or Managing Director, or Prime Minister, immediately below them on the structure chart. Linking the strategic apex with the **operating core**, the people who carry out the majority of the organisation's immediate tasks, is the **middle line** of management.

The basic Mintzberg model can be applied to many small organisations. In the very smallest there may be no middle line, with the individual or individuals in the strategic apex also carrying out direct supervision of the operating core and, if the organisation consists of just a very small number of people, there may be little distinction between any of the components although there will always be one 'final' decision-maker who forms the strategic apex.

Mintzberg's more comprehensive model has two additions that reflect the situation in medium to large organisations. Firstly there are the **support staff** who carry out those tasks required to support the operating core but who are not directly involved in the production of the core product or delivery of the core service. Such functions include finance, staffing, administration, facilities management etc. Recent trends have been to reduce the size of this component, managers being expected to carry out their own budgeting, staffing, administration etc., with advice being provided from specialists within the support staff.

The second addition to the model for many medium to large organisations is the **technostructure** which houses those technical experts who support the organisation. Advancements in Information and Communications Technology (ICT) and improved robotics and machine tools have led to a similar growth in the technical support required, hence the requirement for a defined technostructure.

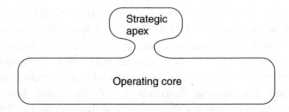

*Figure 1.2   The basic Mintzberg model* (after Mintzberg, 1983).

The comprehensive Mintzberg model thus takes on the configuration shown in Figure 1.3.

Mintzberg's work looks at the relative sizes of the various components within organisations. In some the technostructure may be small or even missing, in others the support side may be very small; every organisation is different. A current trend has been to remove much of the support staff and technostructure from the organisation but then to outsource those roles, allowing the organisation to concentrate on its core business. In organisations that have done this, the support staff and technostructure components may be very small indeed but will have to be carried out within another organisation, where they form part of the operating core as here they will be the primary objective, i.e. the core product of that organisation as in, for example, a company formed to provide personnel for other companies or, as another example, outside caterers providing canteen facilities for organisations.

Whilst early management writers like Fayol (1916) stressed the benefits of centralising planning and control using the rapidly improving communications systems, modern trends have been to decentralise. Peters & Waterman (1982) in their treatise on excellent organisations, *In Search of Excellence*, stressed the importance of giving staff the autonomy to make decisions and to demonstrate initiative and entrepreneurship by decentralising decision-making as close to the point of customer contact as possible. They also made the point that consistency demands that some aspects of an organisation's operations need to be controlled centrally, e.g. quality standards and overall financial management. It would be of little comfort to the customer if different branches of the same organisation worked to different quality standards!

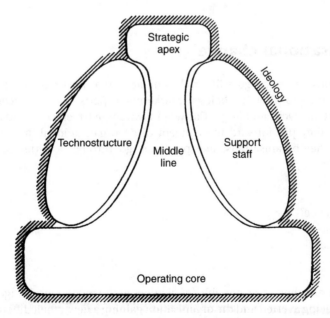

*Figure 1.3    The comprehensive Mintzberg model* (after Mintzberg, 1983).

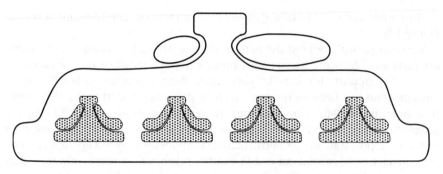

*Figure 1.4    The Mintzberg divisionalised model* (after Mintzberg, 1983).

What tends to happen, in terms of the Mintzberg model, when an organisation decentralises or adopts a divisional form is shown in Figure 1.4.

Each division of the organisation tends to adopt a mini-version of the main model. If you examine any large organisation that has a divisionalised or a branch structure – British Airways, Marks and Spencer, Tesco, the faculty structure within colleges and universities, Boeing etc. – a similar arrangement is found, suggesting that this may be the 'natural' structure for organisations to take. All possess a strategic apex, a middle line, an operating core, support staff and a techno-structure or, in the case of the latter two, if they are not there at branch or divisional level there is access to those components either at corporate headquarters or through outsourcing.

## Organisational change

Organisations can undergo a life cycle similar to that for products and indeed similar to that for human beings. Marketing experts use a concept called the product life cycle, and Roger Cartwright & George Green (1997) adapted this idea when they put forward the concept of an organisational life cycle. They suggested that organisations, like products, go through a series of changes (Figure 1.5):

- Birth
- Adolescence
- Maturity
- Menopause
- Decline.

They suggested that it was possible for changes at the menopausal stage to result in decline being averted and the organisation gaining a new, albeit different, lease of life.

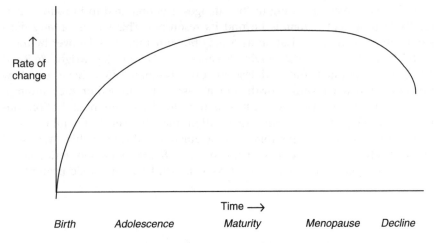

*Figure 1.5    Organisational life cycle basic model* (Cartwright & Green, 1997 with permission).

# Birth

At this stage a newly formed organisation will be keen to gain customers and establish itself within the marketplace. There may be launch offers and prices may be kept low in an attempt to gain market share. This is often the strategy adopted by car manufacturers when entering a new market or market segment, examples being Proton and Chrysler in the UK. There is a danger that the organisation may promise more than it can deliver, either in terms of quality or demand exceeding supply. A new company may be relatively naive but may well be dealing with sophisticated customers. Customers are likely to be new and the gaining of further new customers is all-important. Such an organisation can change very rapidly but may attempt changes that are beyond its resources. Customers may demand more and more in an attempt to gain greater value for less cost, and the organisation may well attempt to respond with the resultant possible drain on its cashflows. An organisation that wishes to survive into adolescence needs to realise which changes it can encompass and which it cannot.

# Adolescence

The adolescent organisation is usually gaining both in confidence and sophistication. Competitors and existing/potential customers may see it as a growing force. The customer base will be growing and the keeping of repeat customers becomes as important as gaining new ones (Cartwright, 2000). Because the organisation has begun to develop a history and culture, it can be more discriminating in the changes it is prepared to introduce. It is less likely to accept demands beyond its resources. This can be a very dangerous time for the organisation as it may be vulnerable to take-over by more established players, as Cartwright & Green (1997) and Cartwright & Baird (1999) have pointed out. Adolescent organisations often have cashflow problems associated with growth and a cash-rich competitor may attempt to gain control or use the cash situation to force the organisation out of the market. An adolescent organisation may be very vulnerable when faced with mature competitors. The acquisition of the highly successful but relatively young Princess Cruises (of *Love Boat*® television series fame) by the much older UK-based P&O Group in 1974 was a classic example of this.

# Maturity

This is the time of greatest stability and thus a period when the organisation may not want to make changes unless they are forced upon it. Markets are known and there is likely to be a strong customer base. There is a danger that the organisation may begin to take its customers for granted and be reluctant to accept the changes they require.

# Menopause

Medically, Dr Miriam Stoppard (1980) says of menopause that it may cause no problems at all or at its extreme be characterised by hot flushes, tearfulness, anxiety, profound depression, inability to concentrate, inability to deal with problems and inability to make decisions. Biologically, menopause is a condition built into the endocrine (hormonal) system of the body and that it will occur is inevitable. Menopause is often referred to in Western society as 'the change'. It is not necessarily a change for the worse. Cartwright & Green used the concept to equate a natural part of the human life cycle to that of organisations to aid understanding of organisational behaviour.

It is reported that many women find that they acquire new interests after menopause and, in a similar fashion, many organisations develop in new and exciting ways.

Cartwright & Green believed that there is a menopausal stage in many organisations where after a period of relative maturity, outside forces (the equivalent of the body's hormones) cause alterations to markets, available technologies and customer requirements and perceptions. Just like hormones in the body, the organisation cannot control these forces and this may bring about inabilities in decision-making, a failure to deal with problems,

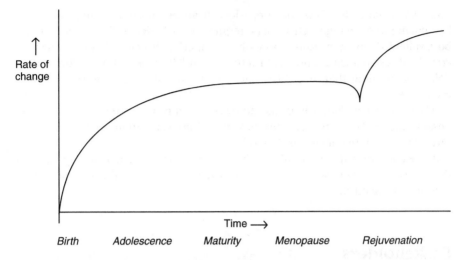

*Figure 1.6 Organisational life cycle expanded model* (Cartwright & Green, 1997, with permission).

organisation anxiety and depression. The organisation becomes more interested in its own internal problems rather than those of its customers, and any changes tend to be inwardly focused on systems and especially organisational structures rather than on the products, services and customers. Lethargy becomes a danger, a paradoxical danger because lethargy is what will destroy the organisation and yet, just when the organisation needs to concentrate on its position and survival, it becomes lethargic. The main dangers are ultimate decline following a loss of customer base or else a take-over by a competitor. Indeed menopausal organisations may be at risk from predatory adolescent ones that have the energy but require the respectability of an older player in the market. Rates of change are often very low.

An organisation that recognises the menopausal stage can often take steps to rejuvenate itself and this may mean hard decisions. The aim is to become vibrant again but the organisation must ensure that the changes it makes are the ones its customers want. Often this is referred to as 'the organisation re-inventing itself'.

The model an organisation should be aiming for is shown in Figure 1.6.

## Decline

Organisations hope that they never decline but Pan Am, the Passenger Shipping Industry and many retail stores that were household names have gone, some like Pan Am to reappear as smaller scale operations, others never to be heard of again; often they have been acquired by a more vibrant organisation and the name has been lost. If an organisation cannot compete by making the changes customers require, it will decline and die or else be swallowed up by a more successful competitor. Decline is often characterised by restructuring upon restructuring, and there is a frantic attempt to deliver something that, even if it does not make much money, at least pays the wages.

Where an organisation is in its life cycle will affect its strengths and weaknesses, and make some opportunities more important than others and some threats much more dangerous than others.

It must be stressed that examining the external environment of an organisation is a fairly useless exercise unless it is done with a knowledge of the internal factors within that organisation.

## Stakeholders

A stakeholder in an organisation can be defined as an individual or a group having a vested interest in the operation of that organisation.

Many stakeholders are easy to identify: the employees of an organisation and in the case of a for-profit organisation its owners including shareholders all have a vested interest in its success as their income depends on it. As Cartwright (2000) has stressed in a companion volume to this one, customers are always stakeholders. However there may be other stakeholders who do not have such a direct financial interest. To illustrate the point, consider the example of a company deciding to develop a light engineering works in a small town where unemployment is at a fairly high level.

Assuming the company brings in a small number of key staff from its existing operation, who else will benefit or be disadvantaged by the development of the new operation?

- The government – the development will have a beneficial effect on employment and may encourage other companies to move into the area
- The local government – local taxes will be raised
- The local population – jobs will be available directly in the company and also indirectly through the use of local suppliers
- The local housing market – staff brought in from other parts of the company will need to be housed
- The local economy – more people working means more disposable income.

All of the above benefit. If the company produces waste products there may be a disadvantage. Similarly if there is an increase in noise, those living near the factory may see the value of their property decline. There may be a need to develop infrastructure changes, new roads etc. Whilst these may ultimately benefit the area, there may be short-term increases in traffic with attendant pollution and safety dangers.

It is not unusual when a large organisation closes down for there to be concerns about the knock-on effects beyond immediate job losses, as seen in the West Midlands of the UK after an announcement in Spring 2000 that BMW intended to divest itself of the Rover car-making concern – the major West Midland's employer. All organisations have suppliers and if they are highly dependent on one large manufacturer, then job losses there may well lead to further job losses down what is known as the supply chain. Suppliers seek, wherever possible, to reduce their dependence on a single customer. This is one reason why the Customer section of the SPECTACLES analysis is so important. The supply chain is a very important component in organisational planning. Manufacturers may obtain their raw materials and even preassembled parts from a wide geographic area. In his book and television documentary series for the UK's Channel 4/USA's KCTS, *21st Century Jet*, detailing the planning and building of the Boeing 777, Karl Sabbach (1995) shows how pre-assembled components for the aircraft came from all over the world to be assembled in Everett near Seattle on the USA's Pacific Coast. A few examples of the wide geographic range of manufacturer (not an exhaustive list) is given in Figure 1.7.

P&O Cruises (1995) have produced an interesting book and video on the building of their cruise liner *Oriana* (see Chapter 13) which had components manufactured all over Europe for assembly at the Pappenberg (Germany) yard of Myer Weft.

Both the *Oriana* and the Boeing 777 were able to benefit from computer aided design where the computers at the main contractor could be linked to those at their suppliers. Boeing pioneered the concept of 'Working Together' where Design–Build Teams (DBTs) consisting of the main contractor, subcontractors, designers and customers worked together to solve problems, a good example of including stakeholders in the design and planning processes.

The views of stakeholders always need to be taken into account. If the factory in the example given earlier was the source of complaints from local residents during the process of gaining planning permission, then the whole project could be delayed. As will be shown in the next section, early consideration of stakeholder reaction may prevent later problems.

| Component | Where built |
|---|---|
| Outboard flaps | Italy |
| Passenger doors | Japan |
| In-spar ribs | Japan |
| Elevators | Australia |
| Rudder | Australia |
| Engines (for first aircraft) | East Hartford, Connecticut, USA |
| Automated Spar Assembly Tool | Wisconsin, USA |
| Some fuselage sections | Japan |
| Fuel gauges | UK |
| Nose | Kansas, USA |
| Entertainment system | UK |

*Figure 1.7   Sources of supply for a sample of Boeing 777 components.*

# Planning

All of the analyses that follow in this book are designed to inform the strategic and tactical planning processes within an organisation. They provide a comprehensive list of those items that should be considered as part of such processes.

As Hastings *et al.* (1986) have pointed out, it is necessary to plan for things that you *know* are likely to happen but it also necessary to have contingencies in place to deal with the *unknowns*. There are five states to the knowledge needed for planning:

- Known
- Likely
- Possible
- Unknown
- Unk-Unks.

## Known

Much of the known will come from organisational experience and research. It is known that toy sales increase at Christmas and production and distribution schedules can be planned accordingly. In the UK, until 1999, it had been the practice to change the year registration letter of new cars in August, thus leading to a peak of sales in the summer. These factors are known from the first part of any planning process.

## Likely

Any organisation that is carrying out a proper analysis of its environment will know those things that are likely to happen. If a political party has announced certain legislative changes that will affect an organisation and the opinion polls show a strong likelihood of that party winning an election due to be held in the next couple of months, then it would be a foolish not to consider that such a change was likely and to plan accordingly. However, as was shown in the 1992 UK General Election, opinion polls can be wrong!

Manufacturing organisations know the anticipated lifespan of components and thus know when it is likely that a replacement will be required. In the aircraft manufacturing industry, certification of a new model by the regulatory authorities requires the manufacturer to show the likelihood of certain events. For the Boeing 777, which has only two engines, to gain approval to fly ETOPS (Extended Range Twin Operations) it was necessary to demonstrate to the Federal Aviation Authority (FAA) in the USA and other similar authorities in other countries that, firstly, the plane could fly safely on only one engine for up to three hours and, secondly, that the possibility of two engines shutting down in flight was so remote as to be very, very unlikely to happen. As Karl Sabbach (1995) has detailed, extensive testing showed that the Boeing 777 met these requirements and thus became the first twin-engined aircraft to be certified for extended range operations from the outset. Previous aircraft had been required always to fly within 60 minutes of a suitable airport, which precluded many trans-ocean routes. The ability to operate a long-range twin-engined aircraft brought considerable cost benefits to airlines, both in terms of purchase prices and operating costs. Obviously where safety is a concern, all eventualities must be considered and the FAA require manufacturers to draft a Failure Modes and Effects Analysis (FMEA) to show that a particular occurrence is unlikely and what the consequences would be if it actually occurred. Such a process was carried out when Convair began work on the rear cargo door for the Douglas (later McDonnell Douglas DC10). Unfortunately, because of a design fault it was not only possible that the door might open in flight but that it was extremely likely to do so. As Eddy *et al.* (1976) showed in their book *Destination Disaster*, the manufacturers even received a stark warning when a door fell off in flight and the aircraft floor collapsed without any fatalities. A less-than-satisfactory remedy was applied and some months later a DC10 crashed outside Paris following the loss of a rear cargo door, all 346 people on board being killed.

It is salutary to note that the captain of the *Titanic* knew that there was a likelihood (indeed a fairly high probability) of meeting ice on the ship's route, indeed he is quoted as predicting the time at which this would happen. Unfortunately, perceived wisdom of the day did not include planning for a speed reduction nor for the unusual but not unknown visual problems of that night (despite its size, the iceberg was not seen until the last moment), with results that have become well known.

## Possible

It is possible that London or Edinburgh may suffer a devastating earthquake but the likelihood is very low. If an organisation is planning to set up in those cities, earthquake contingencies may not be part of the planning process. Were they setting up in California or Japan, such contingencies would need to be taken into account, indeed there may well be a legal requirement to do so before planning permission would be granted.

The Hegelist Principle, named after the German Philosopher Georg Wilhelm Friedrich Hegel (1770–1831), in a simplistic form states that if something can be thought about then it must in some ways exist (if it can happen – it will!). Hegel was concerned about the nature of reality! In the context of this book, whatever may be possible must be considered if the probability of it happening makes it sensible to do so. No company on earth could be justly criticised for failing to build major earthquake protection into their London buildings, where it is known from historical data that the danger is very slight, but that would not be the case in Los Angeles or Tokyo.

A key task of those carrying out an analysis of the external environment is to determine what is possible and then what is the probability of it occurring. Such an analysis can only really be carried out using historical data. This is part of the role of actuaries who use data on human lifespans to calculate life insurance premiums.

Just because there is a high probability of something happening does not mean that it will, but the organisation should have a plan in place.

Possibility is also affected by time considerations; the further into the future one looks, the less easy it is to assign a probability. The media in December 1999 was full of articles etc. on what had been predicted in 1899 for the 20th Century and predictions for the 21st Century. If one had said in December 1903, when the Wright Brothers made the first powered flight, that just over 60 years later it would be possible to fly from London to New York on *Concorde* in three and a half hours and that people would have walked on the moon, it might have been difficult to be taken seriously – such fancies may have attracted the readers of H. G. Wells or Jules Verne but no organisation appears to have written such developments into their planning. Even in 1914 the British War Office were still disputing whether there was any use for military aircraft at all!

Unfortunately, hindsight is a wonderful thing. All an organisation can realistically do in its planning process is to take account of what is known, what is likely and draw up a contingency for possibilities with a fairly high probability.

There is a management accounting technique called **cost–benefit analysis**, often used as part of the planning process, which is utilised to ascertain the benefits for any given investment set against the cost. The more likely something is to happen, then the more **not** planning for it may cost the organisation.

## Unknown

In the ideal world there should be no such thing as an unknown; if everything is possible, however remotely, then it should be known. However managers and planners are human and are caught out by unexpected events. 'Unexpected' is perhaps a better word than 'unknown'. Again it is easy to be wise after an event, but part of any environmental scanning should be the encouragement of those involved to undertake some brainstorming based on unexpected but possible factors.

## Unk-Unks

Unk-Unks (Unknown Unknowns) were quoted by Karl Sabbach (1995) as part of the study into the Boeing 777. These are events that are so unlikely that nobody has even considered them. Often they are things that somebody should have dealt with but didn't, often through the vagaries of human nature. The loss of the *Herald of Free Enterprise* in 1987 might be considered an Unk-Unk, as it was unimaginable that the vessel would sail with its bow door open. The spread of AIDS in the late 20th Century came as a surprise to many, as did the popularity of the home computer; even in the 1970s it was not believed that there would be a domestic market for such computing power. The Unk-Unk was the versatility of the human mind that found so many uses for the microchip.

Barry Minkin, a US-based best-selling author, consultant and futurologist (there is such a word in the USA!) was one of the people who first realised the potential of linked computers – the forerunner of the Internet, and he has spoken about 'two-steppers' in his seminars. Many people can see the one step, say from the mainframe to smaller computers, but it takes a very imaginative mind to see the next step. H. G. Wells and Jules Verne were two-steppers. Few organisations possess such people and even fewer know how to use them to their full potential, but companies such as British Telecom are beginning to employ such people to aid their forward planning and push back the boundaries of longer term forecasting.

## Summary

This chapter has considered the importance of scanning the external environment, the use of a SWOT analysis, the typologies of organisations, i.e. private, public, voluntary, for-profit, not-for-profit, the various business sectors, a brief history of organisational development, organisational changes, what is meant by stakeholders and planning for both the known and the unknown, and then considered the imponderable Unk-Unks.

## Concepts covered

- The complex, contemporary world of business
- The importance of the external environment
- Types of businesses and organisations
- Organisational typologies
- Business sectors
- Mission and objectives
- Organisational structures
- Organisational development
- Organisational change
- Organisational life cycle
- Stakeholders
- Planning

QUESTIONS

1. Consider a group of organisations that you are familiar with. Classify them according to their typology and sector. What is the main objective of each of the organisations and who are its stakeholders?
2. Put yourself 5, 10, 25 and 100 years from now. Taking one particular product or service, try to advise an organisation dealing with that field on what the future in respect of that product or service will look like 5, 10, 25 and 100 years from now. Be imaginative but sensible!

# Further reading

For a more detailed consideration of organisational structures you are advised to read Charles Handy's (1976) *Understanding Organisations*, published by Penguin, and James Quinn, Henry Mintzberg and Robert M. James (1988) *The Strategy Process*, published by Prentice Hall.

# ▣ ⊻ 2 Internal and external analyses

*The links between internal and external analyses – Relevant internal analyses – BACK analysis – SWOT analysis – Product portfolio – Introduction of SPECTACLES analysis (Social, Political, Economic, Cultural, Technological, Aesthetic, Customers, Legal, Environmental, Sectoral) – The importance of links between the components of a SPECTACLES analysis.*

## The links between internal and external analyses

As was mentioned in the previous chapter, it is important that both the internal and the external environments of an organisation are considered as part of any planning period. In Chapter 9 where customers and Chapter 12 where the sectoral analysis and competition are considered, the importance of carrying out such analyses on customers and competitors will be demonstrated.

There is nothing magical about the structure of the analyses used in this book. They comprise the key areas that planners and those studying an organisation need to consider. They are by nature holistic. It is important to carry out the full analysis. A political analysis that did not have all the other components, social, economic, technological etc., would be meaningless on its own. It is the holistic picture that provides the analyst with the information needed for future progress.

Whilst this book is primarily concerned with the external environment within which organisations operate, it is also necessary to consider those critical internal analyses that the organisation needs to carry out to support the analysis of the external environment. Internal financial analyses are beyond the scope of this text but any organisation's accountants will be constantly analysing and monitoring budgets, cashflows, investments, costs etc. The financial health of an organisation and its relationship to the external economy receives consideration in Chapter 5.

Three internal analyses are considered in this chapter: first a BACK (Baggage, Aspirations, Culture and Knowledge) analysis, followed by a SWOT (Strengths, Weaknesses, Opportunities and Threats) analysis and finally an analysis of the product/service portfolio offered by the organisation.

Just as every organisation is unique in terms of its history, culture, product/ service mix, staff etc., so it follows that the results of any analysis will be unique for the organisation in question, in effect producing an organisational fingerprint.

# BACK analysis

This is a recently devised analysis by Cartwright *et al.* (1994), initially to support personal development programmes but then used by a number of organisations with considerable success as an aid to understanding organisational behaviour. The analysis was further refined in a companion book to this volume, *Mastering Customer Relations* (Cartwright, 2000), from which this section is adapted with permission. The analysis is designed to provide an overall picture of an organisation. The acronym stands for: Baggage, Aspirations, Culture and Knowledge.

## Baggage

Imagine a person, with suitcases and hand baggage and souvenirs trying to exit a hotel through a set of revolving doors. In order to make progress they are going to have to put down one or more pieces of baggage. So it is with both organisational and personal life. 'Baggage' is collected as the organisation or individual moves through life. Life also presents a series of revolving doors which, being fixed in time, means that unlike the holidaymaker above, baggage once set down may not always be retrieved. Often it is the case that some baggage must be relinquished in order to make progress. The problem with baggage is that both individuals and organisations become very attached to it even when it no longer serves a practical purpose. How many lofts, garages and garden sheds are filled with those things that people cannot bear to throw away, just in case they might be useful! In organisation terms, baggage can include procedures that were once relevant but are no longer needed.

Procedures, policies, rules and even products themselves all need to be looked at when considering baggage. Much baggage is necessary but organisations should review on a regular basis if they are still doing things that, at best, are of no practical use and, at worse, actually impede the relationship with the customer or supplier. Surplus baggage always consumes organisational energy and should be dropped as soon as possible. The best way to ascertain the baggage that an organisation carries with it is to talk to members of staff, not only about what they do but why they do it. If they don't know the answer to the second question, then this may indicate a piece of baggage that should be dropped.

Organisations need to be careful about dropping any baggage that may identify them positively to their customer base. British Airways provoked an outcry in the late 1990s when the company decided to change the traditional tailfin logo for a set of non-country-specific designs in an attempt to express the global nature of the operation. Unfortunately many in the UK did not agree with this decision and a reversal of policy ensued.

## Aspirations

If baggage is about where the organisation has been, then Aspirations are about where it wants to go. In conducting a BACK analysis, it is useful to ask staff at various levels within the organisation as to what they see as the main aspirations. Mission statements and statements relating to organisational objectives may also provide valuable clues.

Aspirations can only be realised if they are unhindered by baggage, fit into the culture of the organisation (to be covered under the next heading) and if the organisation possesses the necessary knowledge. This shows the interlocking nature of the four components of the BACK analysis. It is important that an organisation and all who work for it have an idea of its aspirations and that they are realistic. It is only if one knows where one wants to go that proper plans can be made and implemented.

## Culture

Chapter 6 on Culture within the SPECTACLES analysis will consider both organisational and national cultures. Organisational culture is an internal factor and is thus considered first in this section and will be re-considered in Chapter 6. Culture, when referring to organisations, is a function of 'the way we do things around here'. As in definitions of national cultures, it is made up of a set of underlying values, assumptions and beliefs.

It is possible to write whole books about organisational culture, as has indeed been done. Charles Handy (1976, 1978) has produced a simple-to-understand but highly effective descriptive method for illustrating organisational cultures. Handy has identified four types of organisational cultures each with its own distinctive behaviours.

## Role culture

The Role culture that Handy depicted as a Greek temple (Figure 2.1), a highly stable structure, represents the typical bureaucratic organisation.

Such organisations often have a plethora of rules and regulations with departmental boundaries clearly defined. They are often slow to change, seeing in stability their means of survival. The Role culture places great emphasis on stating what a person's job title is, rather than what the person actually does. There tend to be barriers to inter-departmental communication across the pillars of the temple. Communication tends to be up and down individual pillars. Such a structure is typical of many large organisations and has often been identified with the traditional public sector/governmental organisations. In recent times, many organisations have been trying to move away from the inflexibility that such a structure produces. Handy ascribes the god Apollo to this type of culture, as Apollo was the Greek god of order and rules.

## Club/Power

The god Zeus is ascribed by Handy to the spider's web of the Club/Power culture (Figure 2.2). Power rests in the centre, often with a single individual with a strong personality. It is not unusual for that person to be the founder of the organisation. Power flows outwards from the centre. This is a culture that suits the

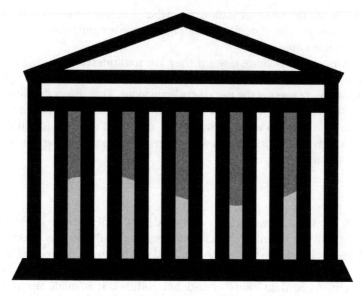

*Figure 2.1    Role culture.*

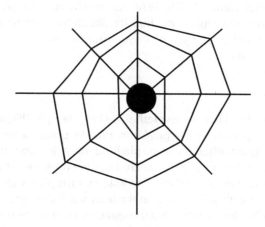

*Figure 2.2    Club/Power culture.*

entrepreneur who can keep an eye on operations. Club cultures can respond very quickly but only in the direction personally favoured by those at the centre. The UK-based Virgin Group with Richard Branson in the centre became a byword for entrepreneurship in the 1990s, with operations that included an airline, rail travel, music, personal finance and publishing – all interests of Sir Richard.

## Task culture

In the 1980s and 1990s many larger organisations began to adopt a Task culture approach as they moved away from the Role culture discussed earlier. The Task

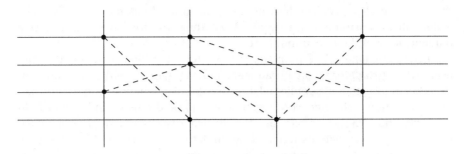

*Figure 2.3    Task culture.*

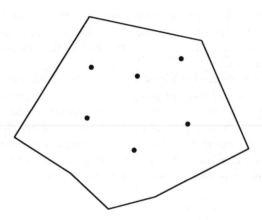

*Figure 2.4    Existential culture.*

culture has been ascribed by Handy to Athena, the goddess of craftsmen. Power in a Task culture lies in expertise and creativity. Handy represents Task cultures as a matrix (Figure 2.3). Whilst in a Role culture, promotion and advancement are regulated by rules relating to position in the hierarchy and time served, for those in a Task culture advancement is purely on ability. Task cultures actively break down departmental barriers and thus are much more flexible organisations to deal with.

## Existential culture

Represented in Handy's work by the god Dionysus, the god of wine and song, Handy (1978) points out that the Role, Power/Club and Task cultures all have one thing in common: the individual employee is there to serve the organisation (it might be argued that this does not apply to the individual or the small group at the centre of a Power/Club culture). In the Existential culture (Figure 2.4), the organisation exists to serve the needs of those in it. A partnership of doctors, architects, lawyers etc. is an example of an Existential culture. Such organisations suit professionals who may well appoint a manager to oversee the day-to-day running of the organisation but the professionals themselves operate on the basis that they are all equal. The lack of rules and procedures may actually make it difficult for customers and suppliers but they will not have to negotiate a bureaucracy in order to communicate.

Cartwright (2000) has demonstrated the interesting inter-reactions that can occur when two different organisational cultures interact in either a competitor situation or a customer–supplier relationship. Similar situations can occur when different national cultures work together, as will be discussed in Chapter 6. In the 1980s and 1990s, the rivalry between British Airways and Virgin Atlantic led to a series of court actions initiated by the latter (Gregory, 1994). In terms of organisational culture, what was actually happening was that a Role culture (as BA was at the time) was competing with a Power/Club culture (Virgin Atlantic), with interesting results.

It is not difficult to imagine the frustration that those in a Role culture might experience if they become the customers of an Existential supplier; the former's rules may well be alien to the latter. One can look at the possibilities of a whole range of combinations.

There is a useful concept from George Bernard Shaw and used by Handy in 1989: Shaw remarked that all progress depends on unreasonable people. Reasonable people adapt themselves to the world whilst those who are unreasonable persist in trying to adapt the world to themselves. A successful organisation will attempt to adapt itself and thus its culture to the customers and not force customers to adapt to its methods and procedures. The two ends of this continuum are known as *product led* and *customer driven*.

## Knowledge

It is common sense that certain things cannot be accomplished without prior knowledge and experience. If an organisation wishes to pursue a particular strategy or set of goals it needs people with the relevant knowledge. This is one area where consultancy has grown, as that allows the organisation to obtain the knowledge and skills when needed without long-term payroll costs.

Organisations that value the knowledge held by their people and which have the development of people as a clear part of their overall strategy can be termed 'learning organisations'. An organisation that develops its staff also acquires organisational knowledge, which permeates through the organisation. As part of the BACK analysis it is important to consider those aspects of organisational knowledge that can form entries in the SWOT analysis that follows this section.

## SWOT

A SWOT (Strengths, Weaknesses, Opportunities and Threats) analysis is a common component of organisational planning.

A SWOT analysis is a two-part analysis, the first part looking at the strengths and weaknesses of the organisation and is thus an *internal* analysis, while the second part considers the threats and opportunities facing the organisation from

| STRENGTHS | WEAKNESSES |
|---|---|
| OPPORTUNITIES | THREATS |

*Figure 2.5   SWOT analysis.*

the external environment which are derived from the *external* analyses that form the subject of this book.

The *strengths* of an organisation are those things it does particularly well, especially when viewed against the operations of its competitors, whereas its *weaknesses* are areas in which it is less strong than the competition.

*Opportunities* are those external factors where the organisation can use its strengths to outclass the competition and *threats* are those factors from the external environment from which the organisation may suffer because of its weaknesses.

The goal should always be to aim for strategies that build on strengths, minimise weaknesses, exploit opportunities and defend against threats.

A SWOT analysis is usually displayed as a quadrant, as shown in Figure 2.5.

Items may appear in more than one quadrant. The large size of an organisation may be seen as a strength when it comes to economies of scale but as a weakness in respect of communications. It is perfectly legitimate to place it in both quadrants.

To achieve maximum effect, a SWOT analysis should be carried out at a minimum on an annual basis. It is best done as a group activity involving people from across the organisation and at differing positions within the hierarchy. Different views may thus be represented. In large organisations it is not unusual for individual departments, sections etc. to complete their own SWOT analysis on their part of the operation. When this is done, what one part of the organisation may see as a strength may be regarded as a weakness by another; again this is perfectly legitimate if it aids discussion. To give an example, a large transport concern carried out such an exercise with groups of its employees. Those in engineering saw the highly competitive nature of the then Chief Executive as a weakness, because it affected their professional relationship with engineers who worked for other, competing organisations and who were sometimes less willing to provide information to help solve problems. (The balance between helping as a fellow professional and not helping because you are a competitor is one that can bedevil professional relationships.) The staff in the customer services department, however, saw the CEO's approach as a major strength, because they relished the cut and thrust of competition. Different views of the same issue can produce different perceptions.

It must be stressed that there is no point in undertaking an analysis of strengths and weaknesses, i.e. an internal analysis, without then going on to link that analysis to one of the external opportunities and threats.

# Product portfolio

All organisations exist to offer some form of product or service. In this section, the word 'product' will be used to describe both product and service. Most organisations have more than one such product, they have in fact a *product portfolio*. A vehicle manufacturer may offer a range of cars and vans but also, through its dealers, a servicing product. Banks offer a deposit product but also loan, investment etc. products.

The importance of the product portfolio in terms of the analyses considered in this book is that successful organisations only offer those products that a comprehensive study of the external environment has shown the market requires. Such organisations also have an eye to the future and actively develop those products and services that their analyses indicate will be required in the future.

# The product life cycle

When thinking about the product, it is important to consider its life cycle, and this is done using the concept of the product life cycle, a fairly orthodox marketing idea, and the more recent and sophisticated 'dynamic product life progression' of Cartwright & Green (1997).

Products and services go through a life cycle from birth to decline and it is important for you to be aware of this life cycle in order to understand the behaviour of the market, and therefore the decisions that organisations make about the introduction and removal of products in their portfolio.

Life cycles can be short, as in the fashion industry or some of the more esoteric products that appear, for example hula hoops or those linked to other products, toys associated with films etc.; or they may be very long, P&O's Cruise Liner *Canberra* (1961–97), the Boeing 747 and KitKat chocolate bars being good examples.

The classic but perhaps too simplistic view of the product life cycle is as shown in Figure 2.6.

## Introduction

Assume that an organisation has developed a new product. At the moment it is not available in the marketplace but the organisation believes that it will be successful as a result of analysing potential market demand.

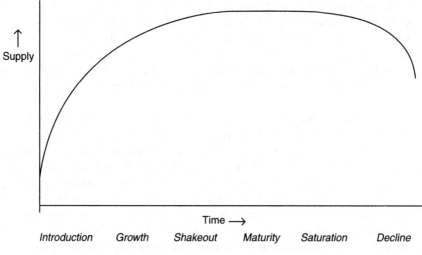

Figure 2.6   *The product life cycle (simplified).*

At the point of introduction, this particular organisation may be the only player in the market although others may be working on a similar product or service. There are considerable advantages in being the first into the market but there are also some disadvantages.

A good example of this is the Comet airliner developed in the UK. The Comet was the first commercial jet airliner in service and in theory should have given its makers, De Havilland, a considerable advantage. Unfortunately the problems of pressurisation and jet operations were only just being understood when the Comet made its first flight in 1949. The early Comet variants were too small for viable, long-term commercial service and suffered from a hitherto unknown form of metal fatigue, which caused a series of accidents that dented airline and public confidence. Boeing, who came into the market with the 707 at a later date, the first flight of the prototype being in 1954, were able to learn from the teething problems of the Comet and delivered a product that, in the words of Stout quoted in Eddy *et al.* (1976), 'could support itself both financially and aerodynamically.' In Boeing's case, being second proved to be an advantage, not a disadvantage. Their great rival, the Douglas Aircraft Corporation (now McDonnell Douglas) had as part of their philosophy a couplet (from Pope):

> 'Never be the first by whom the new is tried, nor the last to cast the old aside'                                                              (quoted in Eddy *et al.*, 1976)

In the Western world Douglas was third into the market with the DC8 and never caught up with Boeing. Boeing built 917 civil 707s; Douglas only built 556 DC8s. Of the smaller jetliners that followed, the UK built 117 Tridents (introduced in 1962), Boeing a massive 1832 versions of the similar Boeing 727 introduced in 1963, and Douglas 976 DC9s introduced in 1965. Boeing seems to have done very well out of being second in the market. Their biggest gamble came with the introduction of the 'jumbo', the Boeing 747 in 1969 where they were the first into the market. No other manufacturer at that time decided to build such a large aircraft and Boeing gained the whole of the market, although by the end of the century they were being actively challenged by the Airbus A330/340 series.

If, at introduction, the organisation can make sufficient impact, a long-lasting set of advantages can occur. If the product is of high quality, then customer loyalty can be enhanced and subsequent purchases will be of the organisation's products. Repeat business is a very important market indicator and organisations need a range of products to offer both existing and new customers. Existing customers can be encouraged to trade up to new replacements. Of equal importance is making the product synonymous with your name. Many Britons 'hoover' the floor but the vacuum cleaner they use may have been made by any one of a number of manufacturers; the verb 'to hoover' has entered the language and provides free advertising and reinforcement for the Hoover Company each time it is used.

## Growth

Assume now that the introduction phase has gone well and that the product is selling well. Not-for-profit organisations do not necessarily 'sell' products but they still need customers to use their products and services. In their case, uptake may be a satisfactory substitute for a sale.

As the success becomes apparent, others will enter the market. If a product or service is very successful, it is often the case that demand will be greater than supply and this will allow others to enter the market with similar products. Growth markets are often characterised by a large number of small organisations in competition with each other.

## Shakeout

As growth begins to peak, the weaker organisations leave the market. Demand is reaching a plateau and the tendency is for the smaller organisations to merge or be taken over by one of the bigger existing players or a large organisation using the shakeout to acquire an entry into a new market. P&O acquired Princess Cruises (see Chapter 1) at this point in the Princess organisational life cycle when P&O was having difficulty establishing its own identity in the cruise market on the West Coast of the USA. Smaller organisations are vulnerable at this time to raids by cash-rich predators.

Larger organisations, it is claimed, can produce at lower cost and can benefit from economies of scale; what they have to be careful of is that they don't reduce quality and service along with costs. Service is a very important part of the product and there is evidence that customers will pay that little bit more for good service and higher quality as disposable incomes increase.

## Maturity

As growth slows, the market becomes more mature and possibly dominated by fewer but larger suppliers. Entry is difficult as the existing suppliers will know the market well and will have developed considerable customer loyalty. It requires true entrepreneurship and considerable resources to break into a mature market; Richard Branson and his Virgin Atlantic airline is one of the rare examples of a newcomer successfully entering a mature market. The issues relating to market entry are discussed in Chapter 12.

As the marketplace becomes saturated, organisations need to be in a position to bring new products or adaptations of existing products to the marketplace. In the automobile market, there are normally a number of versions of each vehicle introduced over time, with a completely new model being introduced every so often.

The product life cycle for a series of related products looks like that depicted in Figure 2.7.

The new variant is introduced just about the time that uptake of its predecessor has begun to decline.

## Saturation and decline

When the market is saturated, supply often begins to exceed demand, possibly because of changing tastes. As demand drops, so profits shrink and competition becomes even fiercer. As decline sets in, players leave the market, or are forced out, or old products are removed from the product portfolio. If you are buying a car and you don't want the latest model, this can be a good time to buy, as the manufacturers will cut prices to clear stocks and free up production facilities.

For an airframe or a ship, the product life cycle is measured in years or even decades; for the latest fashion it may be measured in weeks. Successful organisations monitor the market carefully because a demand for a product or service today does not mean that it will be required next year or even next week.

One of the most dramatic illustrations of the product life cycle is the facsimile machine – the fax. Virtually unknown at the beginning of the 1980s, there was hardly an office in the world that did not have fax facilities by the 1990s. Indeed

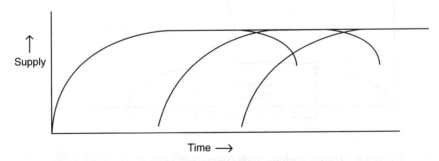

*Figure 2.7   Product succession.*

the market for straightforward commercial fax machines was probably saturated by 1995. However, clever marketing has produced a rejuvenation through selling to the domestic market.

Most models of the product life cycle show saturation leading into decline, but there is an alternative model described by Cartwright & Green (1997) which may, perhaps more correctly, reflect the reality of the situation. They called this refinement **the dynamic product life progression**, because it provides for a series of alternatives, with *progression* indicating that there is life after apparent decline for many products.

## Dynamic product life progression

This concept is slightly more complex than the simple product life cycle model and a slightly different graph with two decision points is used.

When a product or service first enters the market, there always seem to be some people who must have the latest. Thus whilst initial take-up figures may be very encouraging, they may not point to a continuation of success. Demand may plateau whilst the bulk of the potential customer population makes up its mind. Some of the more esoteric products of the technological age (electric bicycles, the electric mini-mini car etc.) seem never to pass this point. If the product is acceptable to the mass of potential buyers, the growth phase is resumed; if not, then the product will go into decline. The critical success factor for any new product or service is whether demand picks up after a short time at the growth plateau (Figure 2.8).

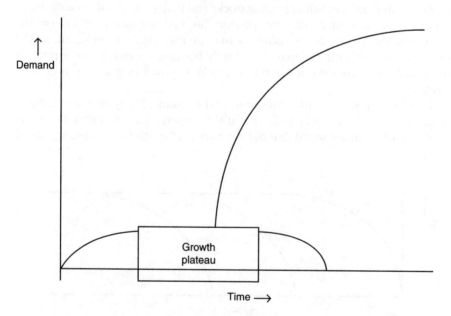

*Figure 2.8   Dynamic product life progression – growth phase* (taken from Cartwright & Green, 1997, with permission).

The next adaptation to the simple product life cycle model *can* occur at the shakeout phase. It is possible that one supplier or product gains such ascendancy as to **blastout** its competitors. Examples of this have happened in the video-cassette market, VHS blasting out Betamax, Windows computer operating system gaining the major market share and, in the UK satellite television market, the major dominance of BSkyB.

The final adaptation to the classic model occurs towards the end of saturation and the beginning of decline (Figure 2.9). As we shall see from the examples, not all products decline.

There are six possibilities and it is possible that decline *per se* can be avoided and a product or service can be rejuvenated.

## Residual markets

In the 1960s, the British Leyland 'Mini' was a revolutionary small car that carried with it considerable customer loyalty. Many UK citizens had a Mini as their first car. The replacement, the Metro (later renamed Rover 100), was intended to serve the whole of the Mini market. There was, however, enough of a residual market for the Mini to justify Rover re-starting the production line, albeit with reduced capacity and fewer models. Therefore, in the early 1990s both models were available, catering for similar but slightly differing markets. Enough people wanted to buy the Mini to make it profitable for production to continue even after the Rover 100 was discontinued. Indeed, in Spring 2000 when BMW, who had acquired Rover, announced that they wished to divest themselves of the Rover brand, they made it clear that they wished to retain production of the replacement to the Mini as an important part of their operation.

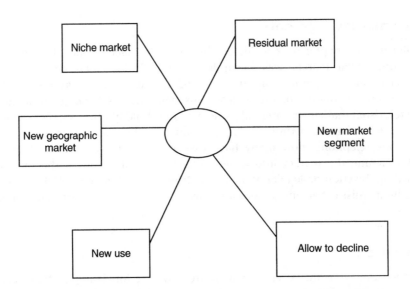

*Figure 2.9   Dynamic product life progression – decline and alternatives* (taken from Cartwright & Green, 1997, with permission).

## Niche markets

Niche markets are small and specialised. Niche markets develop either by being set up especially to cater for that market or by a larger company selling off part of its product/service portfolio. Because niche markets are small, they often don't have the economies of scale that larger organisations require and may not fit into corporate plans. Selling an apparent loss-making product to somebody who is prepared to put in the hard work that a niche market requires can be a better alternative than the product leaving the market altogether. Almost by definition, niche products command a premium price as low volumes normally require higher returns.

## New geographic markets

The Morris Oxford motor car, popular in the UK in the 1960s, found a ready market as a new product in India from the 1980s up to the present day as the Hindustan Ambassador. Easy to maintain and well suited to Indian conditions, the vehicle has been a big success. The British Aircraft Corporation (BAC) sold the jigs etc. for making their highly successful BAC1-11 airliner to Romania after UK production ceased. Honda has set up an operation in India based on the Honda 50 motorcycle that was a best seller in the USA and Europe in the 1960s.

As most of the production snags will have been ironed out and staff will be well advanced up the production learning curve, the introduction of an established but declining product into a new geographic market can be very profitable. It may (as in the case of BAC and the Morris Oxford) be possible to sell the whole production plant to an indigenous manufacturer.

## New market segments

Earlier in this chapter we considered the facsimile machine and the fact that the commercial market was becoming saturated. The manufacturers and the telephone companies started marketing the fax machine as a domestic product in the middle of the 1990s. Thus demand has been re-stimulated. The television market was originally one per household but now smaller models are available for the bedrooms, kitchen and even for boats! Homes used to have one telephone, now many have two or three, all stimulating demand and widening the market into a new segment as witnessed by the massive growth in the UK mobile telephone market from the middle of the 1990s. It may well be a truism that one generation's luxuries become the next generation's necessities!

## New use

Products that were once used for baking are now used for cleaning refrigerators! One way of stimulating demand for a declining product is to find a new use for it. Redundant British buses, no longer suitable for the rigours of the rush hour, appear as sightseeing vehicles on the streets of New York. A new use for a product can put it right back at the start of the product life cycle, which it can then work through again (and earn profits) over a period of time.

## Allow to decline

Some products and services have, of course, outlived their usefulness. New developments and customer expectations have changed the market. In these cases, a swift end is better than a long drawn out one; organisations do not want a declining product affecting their image.

# The product matrix

In the 1960s the Boston Consulting Group developed a model for examining the portfolio of products for a company. This model, known as the **Boston matrix**, looks at the position of products against the two factors of *market share* and *market growth* (see Figure 2.10).

To illustrate the matrix, imagine that an organisation has just introduced a brand new product. To be successful, that product will need to capture a certain percentage of market share either by attracting customers from rival companies or brand new customers to the market. Until sales or uptake starts, the product will have no market share at all. Assuming that the organisation has done its homework, it will be launching the product into a high-growth market – it would be very foolish to launch a new product into a low-growth or declining market

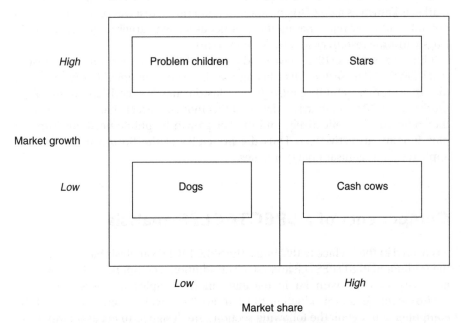

*Figure 2.10   The Boston matrix.*

unless the organisation was very sure that demand could be stimulated sufficiently to guarantee success. If growth is slow, then the introduction of a new product needs to coincide with the removal of an old one.

Until uptake increases, the organisation will have a combination of a low market share in a high-growth regime, which is known as a *problem child* – a problem because there are start-up costs, new customers to attract, perhaps large numbers of staff to train and an infrastructure to build; a child because with proper nurturing children grow to become adults earning their way in the world.

Some companies never make it past the problem-child state; the initial start-up costs may be too high and, if it is to progress beyond the growth plateau of the dynamic life progression model shown earlier, there needs to be constant demand.

If the product progresses past the point of low market share and begins to pick up new and repeat business at profitable load factors, there is the possibility of becoming a star. A *star* exists when the organisation/product has a high market share of a growing market, i.e. the best of both worlds.

Nothing can remain a star forever but, provided that market share can be held, profits can still be maintained even when growth rates slow. The whole operation is 'debugged' to become routine and then becomes a *cash cow*. It is cash cows that generate profits for shareholders and future expansion. Cash cows include many well-known and well-respected products. Cash cows may not produce dramatic profits but they provide a constant stream of reliable income.

Everything comes to an end: even the most well-known product, having a finite life, sooner or later experiences decline in demand. Some are never seen again, others become somebody else's stars and cash cows, as shown in the alternatives to decline discussed earlier. A product with low market share in a declining market is known as a *dog*. Organisations should rid themselves of dogs as soon as possible, either by rejuvenating the product as shown earlier or getting rid of it. Dogs consume resources for little or no reward.

Johnson & Scholes (1993) have produced a public-sector version of the Boston matrix with *public sector stars* (Boston matrix – stars), *political hot box* (Boston matrix – problem child), *golden fleece* (Boston matrix – cash cows) and *back drawer issues* (Boston matrix – dogs). In this model, market share is replaced by the ability to serve effectively, and market growth by public need and support plus funding attractiveness. Thus the principles of the Boston matrix can be applied to all organisational typologies.

# Components of a SPECTACLES analysis

As covered in the Preface to this book, the SPECTACLES analysis has grown out of the traditional PEST/PESTLE analyses. The additional components have become necessary to cope with an increasingly more complex business and social environment. As an introduction to Chapters 3–12, which consider each of the components in detail, the following sections are designed to act as an introduction to those components and to show the interrelationships between them.

Not only do each of the components of the analysis impact upon the organisation, they also impact upon each other as will be shown in the final section of this chapter.

## Social analysis

Sociology is the study of the organisation and functioning of human societies. Margaret Thatcher, the UK Prime Minister from 1979 until 1990, is reputed to have remarked that 'there is no such thing as society, there are only individuals and their families.' Part of the Thatcher philosophy was to stress the rights and responsibilities of the individual and that in many respects we are all responsible for our own destiny. However, in the main we all live and work in close proximity to other human beings whom we rely on for certain services and products. It is these relationships that form society.

The social analysis component of SPECTACLES is concerned with examining the changes in the societies with which the organisation interfaces and what trends within those societies are likely to have implications for the organisation. Included within this part of the analysis is a consideration of the phenomenon known as *consumerism*, a concept that will also be used as part of the customer analysis and the role of the media in communicating with society and influencing societal views and changes. The recent trends in priority accorded to green/environmental issues are considered so important as to merit a chapter of this text to themselves; however, it must be noted that it is society itself that has raised these issues as a priority and thus the growth of green issues is a rightful part of the social analysis, although the addressing of those issues forms part of the environmental analysis.

The social analysis of Chapter 3 also includes a consideration of the demographic changes (size, age etc. of populations) that may impact upon an organisation.

## Political

Politics is the art and science of government. As will be demonstrated in Chapter 4 on political analysis, the citizens of every country are normally subject to a complex series of governmental layers. In Scotland the lowest level of government may be a Community Council, followed by a District Council, the Scottish Parliament and the UK Parliament at Westminster. As the UK is a member of the European Union, Scots as UK citizens are also governed to an extent by the European Parliament.

Each layer of government has its own responsibilities and normally some form of revenue-raising. As the various layers may well be controlled by parties with differing political ideologies, this can make any analysis by an organisation fairly complex.

Governments produce legislation and legal issues form a separate chapter of this book (Chapter 10). The political discussion in Chapter 4 is concerned with those external policy developments that affect the organisation. As even the smallest organisations begin to trade globally, it is not enough to consider indigenous political policies but also to have due regard for policies in the national regions of customers and suppliers.

Chapter 10 is concerned with UK and European political issues, together with those of the USA. A full study of the politics of the world would be beyond this, or possibly any book. What the chapter seeks to achieve is an awareness in the reader of analysing political policy in terms of its impacts upon the organisation.

## Economic

All organisations depend on sources of finance. Economics is always the source of much debate and has been the subject of countless books. Chapter 5 on the economic environment considers the sources of finance for organisations and then the effects of regional, national and international economies, including exchange rates, interest rates and inflation.

Money does make the world go around but it must be stressed that there are considerable interrelationships between political and economic factors. Governments have a vested interest in managing their economies and some may be much more interventionist in the economic field than others.

## Cultural

Much human and therefore organisational behaviour can be traced back to culture. As has already been discussed, there are distinct types of organisational culture, each of which needs to inter-react with organisations displaying different cultures. An understanding of the culture of suppliers, customers and competitors forms an important part of the analysis of the environment in Chapter 11.

There are also national cultures and as the world of business becomes increasingly global in nature so organisations need to take much more cognisance of the cultures they will encounter. As will be demonstrated in Chapter 6, good products can fail because those supplying them have not carried out a sufficiently in-depth analysis of the culture of the target market.

## Technological

It almost seems as if last year's technological miracle is this year's major best-seller. Technology has been moving at an almost exponential pace. The aircraft industry has been mentioned earlier in this book; a brief chronology of manned flight is very illuminating and is presented in Chapter 7 to show just how fast the pace of technological change has been, especially in the 20th Century.

The development of the use of computers, from purely scientific through business and then domestic markets, also receives consideration in Chapter 7, followed by the implications of the Internet and ecommerce, developments that affect nearly every organisation worldwide.

Chapter 7 does not seek to be a technical treatise but to show the types of technological issues that organisations need to include in an effective environmental analysis.

## Aesthetic

Modern technology allows organisations to produce even the most mundane products and services at very high levels. Quality is becoming almost a given. In such an environment, those involved externally with an organisation, especially customers and potential customers, become more and more influenced by the intangibles that surround product and service delivery.

The aesthetic analysis in Chapter 8 considers the way in which those in the external environment respond to organisational image and design – design of products, packaging design and even building design. In a link to culture it is a fact that many organisations from the Far East would not consider the design of a new building without the assistance of a Feng Shui consultant, so important is this aspect of culture.

This chapter also considers how organisations need to analyse the message they put out to the external environment through the Organisational Body Language (Cartwright & Green, 1997; Cartwright, 2000) that they display.

## Customers

Every organisation, no matter what its type or products/services, has customers. Indeed customers are the most important stakeholders (see Chapter 1) of any organisation. No customers eventually equals no organisation.

Organisations need to analyse the needs of current and, most importantly, potential customers. What are the needs and wants of customers and how can they be met in a cost-effective way? Chapter 9 tackles this question.

The customer base for many organisations is growing not only in geographic and number terms but also in sophistication, and this provides a useful link to Chapter 3 on social analysis.

## Legal

All organisations need to be aware of and take account of the law in those areas where they operate. Each national jurisdiction has its own set of laws and whilst many of them may be based on the same principles, there will be national and even local differences, as seen between the states making up the United States of America.

Whilst a detailed analysis of legal aspects in the external environment is rightly a subject for specialist lawyers, it is important that all those involved in carrying out an analysis of the external environment are aware of current legal practices and proposed legislative changes that may impact upon the organisation.

Chapter 10 considers the sources and application of law, and looks at the types of issues facing organisations at the current time. Whilst the chapter concentrates on British and European law, it is not to the exclusion of a consideration of other jurisdictions.

## Environmental

One of the major movements of the late 20th Century was that of environmentalism. No longer can organisations ignore the environmental implications of their actions and the effects these may have on waste disposal, pollution, biodiversity etc.

An environmental analysis is rightly accorded its own chapter in consideration of the factors affecting an organisation. Indeed, an environmental impact analysis may well be a condition of planning permission or funding for new projects.

Chapter 11 considers not only 'green' issues but also those relating to health and safety, both of which link to the political and social sections of the SPECTACLES analysis.

## Sectoral

The final component of the SPECTACLES analysis concerns other organisations operating in similar markets. These include collaborators and competitors. The actions of both of these can have a dramatic effect on an organisation.

Analysis of the competition (and collaborators) in Chapter 12 includes looking at their strengths and weaknesses, plus analysing the competitive forces that are operating within the marketplace.

## Links

The ten components of the SPECTACLES analysis plus the organisation itself provide for no fewer than 55 possible interactions (the number of pathways that join 11 points together).

To give an example of the complexity of the relationships between the analytical components of SPECTACLES, consider the case of a UK supermarket that decided in 1999 to offer a range of genetically modified (GM) foods.

In 1999 there was a massive debate about the safety of such foods ongoing in the UK. Such a decision would require an analysis not just of the *technological* possibilities but also an analysis of *social, legal, environmental* and *customer* aspects at a minimum. It would not be enough to look at the opportunities that the technology had provided but in addition at the threats that the other components may present.

That simple example shows how important the interrelationships are and also the criticality of ensuring that all are represented in an analysis of the external operating environment.

# Summary

The chapter commenced by stressing the links between internal and external analyses that an organisation needs to carry out. Three important internal analyses – BACK (Baggage, Aspirations, Culture and Knowledge) analysis, SWOT (Strengths, Weaknesses, Opportunities and Threats) analysis and a consideration of the product portfolio – were introduced with examples. A brief introduction to the importance of SPECTACLES analysis (Social, Political, Economic, Cultural, Technological, Aesthetic, Customers, Legal, Environmental and Sectoral) was provided. The chapter concluded with an illustration of the importance of links between the components of a SPECTACLES analysis.

# Concepts covered

- The links between internal and external analyses
- Relevant internal analyses
- BACK analysis
- SWOT analysis
- Product portfolio
- SPECTACLES analysis
- The importance of links between the components of a SPECTACLES analysis

QUESTIONS

1. Using an organisation you are familiar with, carry out a strengths and weaknesses analysis of the internal operations of the organisation. Are there any items that appear as both strengths and weaknesses? Overall, what are the three greatest strengths and the three greatest weaknesses of the organisation and how could the latter be addressed? What point in the Organisational Life Cycle has the organisation reached?

2. Using a well-known organisation, detail its product/service portfolio showing where each product or service is on the product life cycle and how it fits into the concepts of the Boston matrix.

3. Describe two organisations (demonstrating different organisational cultures) in terms of Handy's organisational culture typology. How does the culture manifest itself in the way the organisation behaves?

# Further reading

For further consideration of organisational cultures you are advised to read *Gods of Management* by Charles Handy (1978).

Information about product portfolios, product life cycles, the dynamic life progression and organisational life cycles can be found in *In Charge of Customer Satisfaction* by Roger Cartwright and George Green (1997).

# ☒ 3 Social analysis

*Social classification – Changes in society and societal trends – Demographic trends and influences*

As with all the analyses in this book, the actual importance of any particular component will depend on the specific organisation being studied. What is an important social trend for a retail organisation may be less important or even irrelevant to an organisation in another business sector. The skill of those engaged in scanning the external environment is in considering as wide a range of factors as possible and then picking those that are relevant. Remember, if it hasn't been considered then no objective judgement as to relevancy can be made.

The similarity between human societies and those of other primates is mentioned in Chapter 1 of this book. Belonging is a fairly basic human need, as described in the much quoted but still relevant work of Abraham Maslow (1970).

Abraham Maslow suggested that human needs were hierarchical in nature and that a need can only be truly satisfied when the ones below it have been dealt with. He proposed that human beings have five levels of needs, as shown in Figure 3.1.

Maslow's concept was that humans (and other animals) would put physiological needs – food, water etc. – before safety, which comes before belonging. Esteem needs are only met when the needs up to and including belonging have been met, and self-actualisation only becomes a motivator when all other needs have been fulfilled. The Maslow model has some inconsistencies, it fails to explain how an artist or poet can starve in an attic whilst working on their masterpiece – the model postulates that such self-actualisation should not take precedent over physiological needs. It does however explain the risks that animals will take to obtain food and water even in the face of apparent danger. A human equivalent is that of sailors who have been shipwrecked and have taken to the lifeboats drinking seawater which can be fatal because the need for water (physiological) overrides that for safety.

Maslow's hierarchy is useful in that it allows us to distinguish between levels of needs. In respect of human beings, physiological and safety can be described as *lower-level* or *basic* needs, belonging as a *middle-level* need, and esteem and self-actualisation as *higher-level* needs.

Belonging, as a middle-level need, is very important to humans. The punishment of 'sending people to Coventry' is a good example of how important it is for us to be accepted into the society within which we live or work – most people would find being a hermit very difficult. People, in fact, do need other people.

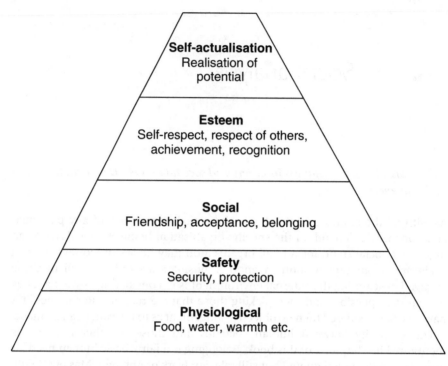

*Figure 3.1    Maslow's hierarchy of needs.*

Many models based on Maslow are shown as a pointed triangle. The model in Figure 3.1, first used in *Mastering Customer Relations* (Cartwright, 2000) cuts off the top of self-actualisation to reflect the fact that there are things that will never be totally achieved. Part of human motivation is to strive for the unreachable. In effect, the top part of the model would stretch; as one target is reached, so another one will appear. A life that had nothing to strive for may well be a very unfulfilled one.

## Social classification

No society is homogeneous. From earliest times there have been attempts made to place people into set categories. Early methods included dividing British society into the Monarchy, the Aristocracy, the Clergy and the Commoners. Such a system would be very difficult to use today, as well as being irrelevant to 21st Century social organisation.

The UK currently uses a system based primarily on occupational area (which has a loose connection with income). The UK system (other countries use similar methods) is based upon six categories, with a grade and category based upon the occupation of the nominal head of the household, as detailed in Figure 3.2.

| Grade | Category | Occupation of the nominal head of the household |
|-------|----------|--------------------------------------------------|
| A | Upper and Upper middle class | Senior professional/higher managerial |
| B | Middle class | Junior professional/managerial/senior administrative |
| C1 | Lower middle class | Supervisory/middle administration |
| C2 | Skilled working class | Skilled manual |
| D | Working class | Semi or unskilled manual |
| E | Subsistence | Low-paid workers, unwaged or living on basic pension |

*Figure 3.2    UK social groups (simplified).*

The use of categories such as lower working class has been attacked as being politically incorrect and patronising but the gradings do provide a basis for segmenting society.

There may have been a time when one could see a clear correlation between progression up the social grades (if that were possible, but for much of history such progression has been actively discouraged) and income. However today it is perfectly possible for somebody in C2 to earn as much, if not more, than somebody in B.

The surveys one is often asked to contribute to on the street or when returning from a package holiday seek, in addition to gaining information about experience of a product or service, to determine the type of person using that product or service. Thus there are usually questions relating to occupation, household income, house ownership and newspapers read. The latter is very important information to an organisation as it can help determine advertising strategy. Certain groups of people tend to read certain types of newspapers. If you are involved in marketing an executive price motor car in the UK, then advertising in a tabloid newspaper may bring less favourable results than advertising in one of the respected broadsheets. Similarly cut-price holidays to the Costa del Sol may be more effectively advertised in the tabloids. In Lynn & Jay's brilliant satire *Yes Prime Minister* (1989) there is an explanation of exactly who reads each particular UK newspaper, an analysis that whilst humorous is probably not far from the truth!

Different groups of people have different interests, perhaps even different aspirations, and a knowledge of this can assist organisations in ensuring that the products and services they develop meet the demands of those parts of society they wish to form their customer base.

# Changes in society

For much of human history, the society people lived in was ascribed to them by their birth. Even in the early 20th Century there were still people living in the UK who had never travelled more than a few miles from their place of birth.

It is true to say that up to the start of the 19th Century, the lives of the vast majority of people were bounded by the family, the village or town (and the latter were small by today's standards), the tribe etc. Communities were much smaller than those seen in today's vast cities and urban areas.

To give an example, according to Hall (1995) the population of Manchester (England) had increased eightfold between 1760 and 1830 and had then doubled again by 1850. Such massive increases in population had far-reaching social implications on housing, health, education, work patterns and leisure. As far as urban areas were concerned, the growth in population comprised both an increase in the birth rate plus people living relatively longer, and the migration of former agricultural workers into urban areas.

Based on a variety of sources it can be shown that in respect of the UK, the percentage of the workforce engaged in agriculture, for instance, has dropped from 58% in 1700 to less than 1% in 2000, and that from a peak of nearly 40% in 1900, the percentage of those engaged in manufacturing is now only 2 or 3% and falling. Conversely, nearly 80% (and rising) of the UK workforce is involved with service delivery and the information industry.

Paradoxically, despite the fact that in the UK and the whole of the developed world the number of people as a percentage of the workforce employed in manufacturing is falling, the number of manufactured products is rising. The paradox is explained in two ways. Firstly, much manufacturing has been moved to lower wage economies where increased transportation and import costs are offset by lower wage rates (and in some cases lower health and safety requirements). Secondly, automation has removed many of the repetitive jobs that existed in the pre-computer age. In respect of the former, by 2000 there was a groundswell of public opinion expressing concern at the conditions experienced by workers in developing countries and the exploitation of children.

Sociologists state that the developed world is in a state of post-Fordism. Fordism is characterised by the assembly lines of Henry Ford and dates from the period immediately before World War I. Management specialists might describe this era as Taylorist, after F. W. Taylor, the 'Father of Scientific Management' who developed the concept of breaking industrial operations into small tasks and using scientific means to set payment rates based on a prescribed amount of time for the completion of a task.

In the developed world, the number of mundane, unskilled jobs has (and continues) to decrease and this has major implications for education. For the individual, a high standard of education is no longer just desirable; in order to obtain employment it is rapidly becoming a necessity and, as will be shown later, this is reflected in the growth of further and higher education.

In scanning the external environment, organisations need to take account of the following factors, details of which follow in this chapter:

- Work patterns
- Education
- Leisure
- Health
- Demographics.

Environmental concerns within society have become so important that they are accorded a separate chapter later in this book.

The factors are important because they impinge on the services and products developed by the organisation and on the nature of the organisation's workforce.

## Work patterns

In any part of the world, prior to a degree of industrialisation, work has tended to commence at dawn and finish at sunset. In the UK, that was the pattern throughout the agriculture age which began to decline with the Industrial Revolution in the early 1800s.

Natural light was no longer sufficient to illuminate the huge factories that began to spring up in the growing industrial landscape. Indeed, the vagaries of natural light required the development of some form of artificial illumination whose constancy could be assured.

Firstly oil and gas and then electricity freed the factory owners and managers from the need to operate during daylight hours only; where necessary, night shift operations could be carried out.

However, no human being can work without rest. In 1841, a railway signalman, a highly responsible position requiring considerable concentration, on the London, Brighton and South Coast Railway was expected to work eighteen hours per day. In order to gain a full day off per week, it was not unusual for a full twenty-four hour shift to be worked (Rolt, 1955). Not surprisingly, Rolt reports this fact as part of the study of a serious accident on that railway. However, even as late as 1992, he reports the case of a signalman whose child had died during the previous night but for whom the North Eastern Railway could find no replacement and insisted that he work a full shift the next night – and again a serious accident occurred.

Governments have slowly legislated to control the time without rest spent at work. Firstly, in the UK and other developed countries legislation was enacted restricting the working hours of children. This was before the enactment of legislation making firstly primary and then secondary education compulsory, as covered later in this chapter. Next was the enactment of legislation restricting working hours for those involved in safety-related occupations. Thus train drivers, lorry drivers and, with the development of air transport, cockpit and cabin crew have had their working hours regulated. Interestingly, in the UK and other countries, junior doctors still work exceptionally long hours.

In 1998, despite reservations by some members, the European Union enacted the Working Time Directive that, for a great many occupations, regulated the compulsory working hours, although it is still possible for workers to undertake overtime etc. on a voluntary basis.

Whenever an organisation is making its plans, it is important to calculate staffing requirements based on the numbers available and the hours that those people are able to work. Once allowance has been made for holidays, sickness etc., which, as will be shown later, are also a statutory requirement in most countries, this allows work utilisation rates to be calculated. In the UK in 1999, the government announced that in addition to the statutory maternity leave arrangements already in force, employees would also be entitled to a certain number of permitted, unpaid absences during their children's early years to cope with domestic emergencies. It was also proposed that there should be an entitlement to paternity leave for fathers – the Prime Minister, Mr Blair, was an early beneficiary.

## The role of women in the workplace

It is sometimes imagined that it was the loss of a large proportion of the male population into the armies of World War I that brought women into the workplace. This is a misconception: the war may have increased the number of women in employment and increased their skill base but women had formed an important part of the employment statistics long before 1914.

Long-established industries in the UK, such as coal mining and the cotton industry, had made considerable use of women and children, although public outcry led to the passing of a number of legislative measures throughout the 19th Century banning the use of women and children in coal mines, outlawing the use of children as chimney sweeps and eventually raising the age at which children could work. Whilst child labour is virtual unknown, except for pocket money activities, e.g. newspaper rounds, in the developed world, it has by no means been eradicated in less developed areas.

There is no logical reason for the reluctance of many organisations to promote women to higher positions. The concept of a glass ceiling inhibiting the progress of women has been postulated by a number of writers, e.g. Davidson and Cooper, *Shattering the Glass Ceiling* (1992); Morrison *et al.*, *Breaking the Glass Ceiling* (1994). The progress towards equality was painfully slow at times during the 20th Century, women in the UK not receiving the vote until some years after the end of World War I and equality of pay for similar tasks not being a statutory requirement until the Equal Pay Act of 1970.

One of the major developments of the late 20th Century was in the growth of part-time jobs and concepts such as job sharing. Originally developed in connection with lower paid work, even some of the most high-powered jobs can be undertaken in this manner and this provides an antidote to often quoted but erroneous ideas that child care may inhibit effective performance by female workers. Abercrombie & Warde (1992) have pointed out that the role and numbers of women in the workplace have been rising steadily (from 30% of the total workplace in 1911 up to 42% in 1981) and that the number of part-time workers rose from 47 000 males and 784 000 females in 1911 up to 361 625 males and over 3 million females in 1981. The growth in part-time work, taking into account the huge rise in the UK population over the period, has been dramatic and provides organisations with access to a much wider skills base.

In the developed world, little differentiation is now made between education and training by gender and it is in those areas that equality begins to have a marked and unalterable effect.

# The end of careers?

Writers like Handy (1989) in the UK and Tom Peters (1987) in the USA have postulated (and indeed been found to be correct) that the concept of a job for life is certainly dead, as is the idea of a working life in the same career. For many years up to and for some time beyond World War II, many individuals would expect to spend their entire working lives in the same career if not with the same organisation. By the 1990s such a concept was no longer tenable in the volatile employment market that had developed. Somebody entering work today can expect to change both organisations and roles and even careers a number of times in their working life. In an earlier age, the idea of a gold watch for long service was something that showed loyalty and those who moved around were frowned upon. Today a varied experience is a good point on a *curriculum vitae* (CV) provided that a reasonable time has been spent in each field. The ease of communications has made changes in organisation and careers more achievable, a factor that will be considered in the demographic section of this chapter.

# Education

The concept of universal education, like that of universal suffrage (to be covered in the next chapter), is a relatively recent one. In the UK the provision of state funded primary (5–11 years) education was not introduced until 1870 and state funded secondary (post 11 years) education not until 1902. As more and more skills have become required for even the most mundane jobs, an educated and skilled workforce has become more and more vital. Early objections to the provision of education for all centred on the fears that an educated population might question the status quo and that this might lead to revolution. Whilst there have been major upheavals in the social order through revolution, that in Russia in 1917 being a prime example, education has tended to engender change in an evolutionary rather than a revolutionary manner.

The increase in skills brought about by the Industrial Revolution led to the first stages in some form of further education and links with employers, with the development of 'Mechanics Institutes' offering after-work tuition in the UK and similar developments in the rest of Europe and the USA. Whilst the apprentice system had always involved employers in the development of skills for at least some employees, the links between employers and external providers of training were a 19th Century development. Up to the end of World War II, a university degree level education was still the preserve of the privileged few and was rarely vocational in nature, but since 1945 there has been a huge increase in university provision throughout the world. According to the UK National Statistical Office, in 1972 there was a total of 647 000 people in full- or part-time higher education in the UK, with 29 700 staff employed in university teaching or research. By 1997 these figures had risen to 1 194 600 full- or part-time students and 77 900 university teachers or researchers.

Throughout the world there have been programmes to widen access to further and higher education. According to EU statistics, in 1996 48% of EU citizens aged between 19 and 21 had undertaken some form of tertiary, i.e. post compulsory, schooling education, the figure for the UK being 41% and that for Belgium 61%. In 1980 11% of those in the UK had a first degree, the target for 2000 being 30% (Smithers, 1997). Such an increase has required a large investment in tertiary education, the complaint from academics being that resources have not met government expectations.

The higher the skills level of the potential workforce, the easier it is for an organisation to undertake the developments it wishes, and thus organisations are very much stakeholders in the sense that the word was introduced in Chapter 1. Organisations have a considerable vested interest in the education system.

In the USA, the concept of the community college has been developed. Such institutions provide a wide range of both vocational and academic programmes at various levels up to and including degrees that are relevant to the local community.

In the UK, the growth in tertiary education continued after World War II with the building of new universities, including Canterbury, Lancaster and Stirling, and the development of the polytechnics designed to provide more technical/vocational tertiary education. The Robbins Report, *The Demand for Places in Higher Education* (1964), predicted the growth in demand but interestingly underestimated the demand from girl school-leavers by a considerable degree, it being double that predicted by Robbins (Abercrombie & Warde, 1992), an example of the glass ceiling effect mentioned in the previous section. There was also a huge growth in local further education colleges offering qualifications below degree level. By the end of the 20th Century the polytechnics had become universities in their own right and many of the further education colleges were offering degree programmes, thus widening the local skills base.

Two other developments are worth mentioning. In the late 1960s the Open University (OU) was founded in the UK. Using open learning materials, home-based science kits, television, radio and summer schools, the OU gave an opportunity to complete a degree level course for those who had not attended university in their youth or who had failed or lacked the opportunity to acquire university entrance level qualifications. By the 1990s the OU was a major player in the UK university sector and had served as the model for a number of similar developments worldwide. The success of the OU showed that there were many people of an age beyond the traditional 18–21-year-olds, who formed the major university market, who wished to undertake higher level studies for either personal or, often, career reasons. Globally this has led to a debate centring on inclusion and widening access.

In 1999, the newly instituted Scottish Parliament appointed a Minister for Lifelong Learning, reflecting the fact that formal education is no longer deemed to finish at age 21 or so but may well be a continuing feature of a person's life. University and college courses increasingly attract a wider age range of students, especially on part-time programmes.

The second major development occurred in the North of Scotland with the development of the University of the Highlands and Islands (UHI). This is an example of how important it is for all of the factors in the SPECTACLES analysis to be covered. The UHI has social, political, cultural, economic and technological ramifications as well as providing a pointer to the way tertiary education and the links to business may well develop in the 21st Century. It is an excellent example of the convergence of a social demand with political will and the technological means to satisfy the demand, as the UHI relies heavily upon electronic communications and video conferencing facilities to work with students in the more remote areas of the Scottish Highlands and offshore areas.

The links between high-quality education and employment are easy to demonstrate. The opening of a university campus invariably draws in organisations keen to access research and skills. Training and development can be difficult for smaller organisations to provide on their own and thus the value of links between employers and educational institutions is very important. As stakeholders in the education system, organisations have a right to a say on the standards of education aspired to and to insist on a high level of basic education for those entering the workforce.

More and more organisations have been developing very close links with local and national colleges and universities, often large organisations assisting in the setting up of centres of excellence. There are mutually advantageous benefits. The organisation has access to the latest thinking and research and a head start over competitors in recruiting graduates. The institution receives not only funding but also practical business intelligence and experience.

# Leisure

In medieval Britain (as in the rest of Europe), only the richest could undertake long pilgrimages but the poor could use their Holy Day to visit the nearest religious centre and associated with the religious festivities would be a fair. Indeed towns vied for the charter to hold a fair, as this was a guaranteed source of civic income.

It is interesting to speculate on the difference in origin between the British word *holiday*, from Holy Day, and the North American *vacation*, from 'to leave'. Today they are synonymous but their roots are very different. By the time North America entered its period of rapid growth after the Civil War (1861–1865), the emphasis in Europe had shifted from holidays being a religious occasion to a time for recuperation from work, and the concept of 'going away for a break' was gaining ground. Modern political correctness in the USA has replaced Merry Christmas with Happy Holiday, a supposedly non-religious greeting. There is some irony in that this is derived from Holy Day!

Closely packed housing and pollution led to a near breakdown in public health in urban areas in both Europe and North America during the latter part of the 19th Century, and the concept that bracing sea or mountain air could act as a cure led to the concept of the holiday as we know it today. The upper and middle classes had long valued the benefits of sea and mountain air, although the journey to such areas could be long and tiresome as roads were only fit for slow-moving carriages. These classes were the first to use the railways for vacations in the true sense, to get away from the city. Weekends and the grouse shooting season saw massive (by the standards of the times) excursion trains leaving the London stations of Euston and King's Cross for Scotland or Waterloo and Victoria for the South Coast.

The owners of the mills and factories could afford to be benevolent given the profits they were making, and in any case soon came to realise that there was a limit to the length of day and indeed the number of consecutive days and weeks an employee could work. As covered in an earlier section of this chapter, in the UK various Acts of Parliament were passed protecting the workforce and the idea of time off for rest other than Sunday began to become a right, e.g. the Holiday Act (1938). There was also a need to maintain plant and machinery, and a concept developed in the northern mill towns of England of a complete cessation of much of the commercial activity for a week so that such maintenance and improvements could be carried out. Using an old term for a public holiday, these 'Wakes' weeks, where a whole town would effectively shut down except for essential services, became common and the population began to travel to the seaside. Each town had a different 'Wakes week' and resorts such as Blackpool in Lancashire developed as working-class holiday destinations. The railways were able to service the travel requirements and whilst the wealthy might go to Scotland, the mill and factory workers from the early 1900s onwards began to take a week's holiday by the sea, especially where this was a mere hour or so train journey away.

Blackpool, together with other northern English and southern Scottish resorts, developed quickly. Even if a full week away was unaffordable, the railway companies ran day excursions to the resorts, a practice that continued until well after World War II. Huge cities could not shut down completely and there different trades had different holiday periods.

Towns like Blackpool in the north-west of England developed a whole range of types of accommodation, ranging from extremely large hotels to the boarding houses set in the back streets. The stories of the typical boarding house landlady are legion but as a type of accommodation it developed into the guest house and B&B (bed and breakfast) of today.

Developments post World War II were incremental rather than revolutionary during the 1950s and early 1960s. Car ferries were in their infancy, the first major UK car ferry operation being that of Captain Townsend with the *Halladale* (converted from *HMS Halladale*, a River Class Frigate of World War II).

Flying was for the few but when, between 1933 and 1935, the Douglas Aircraft Corporation introduced the DC 1, 2 and 3 – the latter to become the Dakota in the UK and one of the most successful commercial aircraft ever, the world of air travel began to open up However it was not until the introduction of short- to medium-range jet transports at the end of the 1950s that there was an inexpensive means to fly holiday-makers to more distant destinations on a charter basis. Previous jets, the Comet, the Boeing 707 and the DC 8, were essentially long-haul aircraft. Increasing prosperity in the UK and other European countries, coupled to the opportunities offered by the introduction of jet airliners, led to a huge growth in affordable foreign package holidays.

The reduction in the working week and the ability to retire early (although the UK government announced in April 2000 that it was concerned at the numbers, especially in the public sector, retiring between 50 and 55) have all led to an increase in the time available for leisure. The importance of considering leisure activities as part of any organisational analysis can be demonstrated by the vast sums of money invested in providing for leisure activities and by the amounts spent on them. Garden centres have become big business, as has the provision of ancillary products such as gardening-related programmes on television. The UK alone supports a number of magazines entirely devoted to model railways. Fitness has become an important part of healthcare, and more and more people are using their leisure time in sport and fitness-related activities. The holiday industry has been showing spectacular growth since World War II, with a proper vacation becoming the norm for most workers in the developed world.

Much of people's leisure time in the developed world has, since World War II, revolved around television. The impact of this medium, with an ever-increasing number of both general and special interest channels, will be discussed in Chapter 7 but the point should be made here that television, as part of a leisure lifestyle, allows organisations entry into people's homes. Indeed, interactive television can give organisations a detailed profile of the viewer, and the more viewing that occurs, the more information can be gleaned.

# Health

A talk to anybody over the age of 65 will demonstrate the enormous strides made in healthcare since the end of World War II. Some diseases, e.g. smallpox and diphtheria, have been almost completely eradicated from the developed world. A smallpox outbreak anywhere in the world today would be headline news. In the 19th and even early 20th Centuries, the disease was endemic over a wide part of the globe.

Modern medicine and an interest in healthier lifestyles have helped to increase longevity rates. This in itself, as will be shown in the next section, can cause problems in that older people may require more resources from healthcare. Health issues are not always an opportunity for organisations. It would be better, perhaps, if nobody smoked, ate fatty foods or drank alcohol. However, there are organisations involved in supplying all these types of products and they would see any moves to reduce demand and consumption as a threat. For many years tobacco companies denied that there was any causal link between smoking and lung cancer, despite medical evidence and public opinion.

As the world entered the 21st Century there were signs that this attitude was changing, especially with court awards being made to those affected by passive smoking. In 1999 Carnival Cruises (who feature in Chapter 12) made their 70367 Gross Registered Tonnes (GRT) cruise liner *Paradise* totally non-smoking for all 2594 (maximum) passengers and 920 crew. Those transgressing at all, including on open decks, would be fined $250 and removed from the ship at the next port of call. Passengers had to agree to this, in writing, prior to embarkation.

Attitudes to smoking in public places have hardened in recent years, as have attitudes to alcohol. Many cities now operate alcohol-free zones on their streets, making public consumption of alcohol a punishable offence. Attitudes to drinking and driving have become very strict, with public humiliation, large fines and even vehicle confiscation for those caught over the limit.

In the 1990s and beyond, one of the biggest issues facing society, especially in the developed world, has been the increase in the consumption of hard drugs. Not only do these lead to serious health problems for the users but also they fuel an increase in robbery and prostitution as users seek cash to finance their habit. If the eradication of disease was a major aim of the 20th Century, perhaps the removal of the scourge of drugs will be an objective for the 21st.

Whilst it is true that modern medicine can do marvellous things, it is at a price. Many treatments are very expensive, drugs may have unfortunate side-effects and there are increasing pressures on governments to commit more and more spending to health from electors who also seem to want to pay less and less tax.

## Demographic trends and influences

The first formal studies on the sizes of population were published by Thomas Malthus (1766–1834). Malthus observed that, in nature, plants and animals produce far more offspring than can actually survive, and that humans, bound by exactly the same biological rules, are capable of overproducing unless external factors intervene. Malthus concluded that unless population growth and family size were regulated, man's misery of famine could become a global norm. Malthus' belief that poverty and famine were natural outcomes of population growth and food supply did not receive immediate acceptance among social reformers, who believed that, with proper social structures, all the problems of the human condition could be eradicated entirely. A similar view pertained when the British National Health Service (NHS) was launched after World War II. Leading politicians believed that the NHS would actually eradicate major illness and that a healthy population would consume less, not more, health resources – sadly this has not proved to be the case.

Darwin's work on evolution gave credit to Malthus for many of the insights that had inspired the author. Darwin demonstrated that producing more offspring than can survive establishes a competitive environment among siblings, and that the variation among siblings would produce some individuals with a slightly greater chance of survival.

Malthus, who was by profession a political economist, blamed the decline in the living conditions of the majority in 19th Century England on two main elements:

- The overproduction of young through the irresponsibility of the lower classes in producing large families
- The inability of resources to keep up with the rising population.

To combat this, Malthus suggested the family size of the lower class ought to be regulated such that poor families do not produce more children than they can support. Whilst such ideas sound very politically incorrect in the 21st Century, it is not many years ago that China implemented both reward and punitive measures for family size and India has undertaken massive campaigns to control its population growth.

No living population can grow indefinitely. As Morris (1969) has pointed out, stress and disease are likely to reduce numbers long before the available nutrients are all used up. Nature appears to be able to balance populations against the availability of resources. Only if a species is unable to cope at all with changed conditions does it become extinct (and as humankind alters the environment, this is happening all too frequently). The usual pattern is for populations to decline in lean times and then recover, build up past the optimum and then reduce to the optimum. The optimum population size for any territorial range varies with the species and its lifestyle. Only so many plants of a particular species and size can occupy a particular plot of land. Solitary animals need more space than social ones.

Humankind has, by adapting the environment, been able to maintain higher levels of population density than other animals. We are also nearly unique in our ability to inhabit much of the landmass of the earth. Few animals have a range of major population centres that stretch from Greenland in the north, through the equator, to the Falklands in the south.

According to statistics published on the Internet by the UK Office of National Statistics, the population of the UK increased from 56.5 million in 1984 to 59 million in 1997 (the increases were in England, Wales and Northern Ireland, Scotland's population remaining constant at 5.1 million).

Within those raw figures is some interesting information which is summarised below, the first figure relating to 1984 and the second to 1997 (K denotes 'thousands'):

- The number of live births dropped from 729.6K to 725.8K
- Deaths decreased from 644.9K to 632.5K
- The percentage of the population under 16 dropped from 21% to 20.5%
- The percentage of the population between 16 and retirement age (i.e. the working population) increased from 61% to 61.4%
- The percentage of the population over 60 for women and 65 for men increased from 17.9% to 18.1%
- The percentage of the population over 75 increased from 6.3% to 7.2%
- Net migration increased from 37.2K to 60K.

In addition to the above, the infant mortality rates dropped, as did the number of marriages, whilst life expectancy increased, as did the number of divorces and one-person households. Deaths from respiratory diseases rose massively, 65.9K to 103.1K, whilst those from road traffic accidents dropped in almost the same proportion.

---

*Conclusions*: Britons are living longer and there are more of them and thus the number of the population over 75 is likely to increase.

Such information is important for all organisations because it allows them to predict the potential size of markets. An ageing population may present threats to some organisations and opportunities for others. Older people may well consume more health care resources and pensions will need to be paid for longer. Conversely, pharmaceutical companies may find that the need to provide medicines to support an increasing number of older people is an opportunity. In the developed world, the disposable income available to those who have retired has been growing and this provides opportunities for those in the leisure and holiday industries.

Increasing population numbers mean an increased demand for health resources, education, housing and employment. These need to be provided and most importantly they need to be planned for in advance. For example, if a sector of business normally recruits female school-leavers as its main source of replacement labour, then a cut in the birth rate will eventually be manifested some time in the future through a paucity of new recruits. This is exactly what was predicted for the nursing sector in the UK towards the end of the 20th Century. Steps were taken, well in advance, in order to change attitudes by encouraging young males and older adults to consider the profession. An increase in the birth rate one year will lead to an increased demand for primary education five or six years hence, more secondary school places eleven years hence and increased capacity for further and higher education eighteen plus years into the future. If the increase is just a one-year blip it may not be cost-effective to put up new buildings, but if it is part of a trend then building plans need to be made well in advance in order that the facilities can meet the demand. This of course requires expenditure to be incurred in advance of the developed demand.

Broadly speaking, as countries prosper the birth rate goes down. It may seem paradoxical that poverty is manifested in higher birth rates but it is not only birth rate that is an important determinate of population. High birth rates tend to be equated to lower survival rates and lower average age of death. In societies where there is little or no welfare provision, older people may rely on their children to support them in their retirement. If survival rates are low it is necessary to have more than the 2.0 children each couple needs to replace themselves. As some people will not have children, the actual average family size needs to be a little higher to ensure a stable population. According to Foot & Stoffman (1999), average family size needs to be 2.1. It must be stressed that that is 2.1 children surviving until they can produce children. In many poorer economies, survival rates have increased but this perception has not been worked through into changed patterns of behaviour. Thus populations in such areas are growing as more and more children survive to have children of their own. As resources are finite, this can increase rather than alleviate poverty. David Foot and Daniel

Stoffman's book, *Boom, Bust and Echo 2000*, is recommended as further reading at the end of this chapter. The authors provide a large number of examples, mainly from Canada, that will assist you in understanding the complexities of demographics. It is also worth noting that the age at which women have their first child is increasing, and this means that they will have less of a timespan to have children, although recent medical advances have made childbearing somewhat safer for older women.

Certain factors can have quite dramatic effects upon demographic trends. During World War I, the birth rate among the combatant nations declined because so many men were away at war. Those children who were born had, as Foot & Stoffman (1999) point out, an advantage as they were members of a smaller cohort and thus there was less competition for jobs, life partners etc. in their later lives. The same rules of supply and demand apply to demographics as economics. A larger number of people chasing jobs will find it harder than a smaller number. After the war, birth rates went up, especially amongst the victors. Confidence is one factor that will lead those in developed countries to have children. Post 1945 led to the 'baby boom'. The world was fairly safe, business was booming and birth rates went up. In the developed world there were the resources to cope with this and the introduction of the welfare state in many European countries at least helped to alleviate if not eradicate poverty. In 1957 the US birth rate was 3.7 per family (Foot & Stoffman, 1999). There was then a drop but, in the 1980s, the majority of the baby boomers were themselves having children and there were a great many baby boomers. By 2000, this boom was over and the much smaller cohort that followed the baby boomers had reached peak childbearing age. As there are fewer of them, a downturn in population is the result.

Births are one way a country grows or contracts, war is another and yet a third is migration. Economic migrants will tend to move from weaker into stronger economies, thus increasing the population of the latter. There are times when this is encouraged if there is a lack of labour; at other times governments may intervene to control migration. The USA has seen waves of migration and a visit to Ellis Island in New York Harbour, the processing centre for immigrants in the latter 19th and early 20th Centuries, is recommended to anybody who wishes to understand the culture, history and demography of the USA.

More people can mean more customers but, unless the customers can pay for a product or service either directly or through taxation, such an increase benefits nobody. As Hackett *et al.* (1978) postulated in a 'future history' which predicted World War III in 1995 (which thank goodness remained a work of fiction), a poor economy with a large number of unemployed males in their late teens and early twenties might well resort to placing them in its army and then using that army to gain resources from its neighbours. A frightening prospect but one that is only too plausible given primate territorial behaviour.

Demographic trends tend to be revealed very slowly and it is important for organisations to examine those relevant to their future developments with care. Will there be enough employees or customers? Are there markets where the population is growing or ones where it is declining and, critically, what are the age and gender balances and how may these impact upon the organisation?

# Employment

Employment is a social, political and economic issue and as such will feature under those headings in this book in addition to this chapter. Employment, that is the giving of labour in return for a reward, is an important social issue. High levels of unemployment may be of short-term benefit for employers as wage demands will be minimised and the employer will have a greater choice of workers, but high unemployment also diminishes demand for products and services owing to a lack of means of payment.

Large numbers of unemployed workers, probably desperate to feed themselves and their families, can and, as history has shown, does lead to social unrest and even war. It is tempting for a country with a large unemployed male population to put at least some of them in its armed forces, and the further temptation is then to use those armed forces against perceived internal or external foes. Indeed a 'foreign bogy' has been used by more than one government in the past to divert attention from its own internal problems. The examples of the Soviet Union in the Cold War era and of the Argentinean invasion of the Falkland Islands in 1982 (Hastings & Jenkins, 1983) spring to mind.

Full employment can fuel inflation (see Chapter 5) according to some economists, because the demand for workers may exceed supply and the earning power of those in work may be such as to raise prices owing to the demand for products exceeding supply.

High unemployment is a social curse as it saps the morale of a country, and for this reason governments try to ensure as low an unemployment level as possible together with a welfare system to protect those who are out of work.

## The currency of demographic information

As the basic statistics relating to demography change over time, actual lists of demographic information have not been provided in this chapter; rather, readers are advised to log onto the following websites for up-to-date information:

http://www.europa.eu.int/en/comm/eurostat/facts/wwwroot/en/index.htm (European Union statistics)

http://www.statistics.gov.uk (UK Government Office of National Statistics)

## Concepts covered

- Motivation
- Social classification
- Changes in society
- Work patterns
- The role of women in the workplace

- Careers and their future
- Education
- Leisure
- Health
- Demography
- Employment

## Summary

Social trends are varied and complex. Human motivation can be understood by taking Maslow's hierarchy of needs as a starting point, where the importance of belonging is shown as a fairly basic human need. In any society, individuals tend to belong to certain groupings at any point in time and the UK version of these groupings was introduced. This chapter has considered the importance of social analysis and examined some of the trends related to lifestyle, education, leisure and health. The science of demographics was introduced and the importance of long-term demographic planning and its implications for organisations discussed.

## Analysis

In carrying out the *social* analysis in respect of an organisation, the following need to be considered:

1. What social groupings do the customers belong to?
2. What is the current educational level of the workforce?
3. What is the anticipated future educational level of the workforce likely to be?
4. Are there social issues that are likely to impact upon the organisation's plans?
5. What demographic trends are likely to impact on the customer base?
6. What demographic trends are likely to impact upon the organisation's staffing requirements?

QUESTIONS

1. Why is belonging such a basic need in human societies? Illustrate your answer with examples showing how this need fits into others within the Maslow hierarchy.
2. Take one area of social activity, health, education, leisure etc., and show the types of social change that have occurred over the past 50 years. Why is it important for organisations to predict such trends?
3. How can an organisation use a knowledge of demographics to aid its planning process?

# Further reading

You are recommended to read *Boom, Bust and Echo 2000* by David K. Foot and Daniel Stoffman (1999) for further information about demographics, and *Social Change in Contemporary Britain* by N. Abercrombie and A. Warde (1992) for a discussion on social change.

# ▼ 4 Political analysis

*The political process and structures – Lobbying – UK politics – The electoral system – Devolution – European Union – EU institutions – Social Charter – EMU – Monetary union – EU expansion – US politics*

Politics is the art and science of government. Whilst organisations may wish to claim that they are apolitical and act outside the political arena, no facet of life has a greater effect on individuals and organisations than the political process. From that process come the key legislative and economic determinants that form such an important part of this book.

Whilst organisations may claim that they are apolitical, whatever happens in many areas of the political arena is likely to happen to them. Although legal issues are covered in Chapter 10 of this book it must be borne in mind that although it is courts which dispense the law, it is politicians who make it. In the UK issues such as:

- The minimum wage
- Trade Union reforms
- Health and safety at work
- Consumer protection
- Environmental protection
- Transport and distribution
- Employment legislation

all arise as a result of political decisions and thus, as these can all have considerable impact on organisational developments, any planning process must consider likely political policy developments.

Political structures seem to form an integral part of human society, as discussed in the previous chapter. The word 'politics' seems to dominate much of the media. Terms such as office politics, organisational politics and 'politics with a small p' are in common use. Office and organisational politics form part of the internal SWOT analysis of any organisation, as described in Chapter 2. This chapter concentrates on the external political influences that affect the organisation and of which cognisance needs to be made when planning development.

Political systems exist on a continuum between totalitarian and democratic. Totalitarian systems are those in which a single party or indeed individual attempts to control their society with no opposition allowed, whereas democratic systems are those in which enfranchised citizens choose the government by a form of electoral process that allows opposition. The last qualification is important because there have been (and remain) totalitarian systems that operate an electoral process but there is only one candidate or, if there are multi-candidates, they all belong to the same party. A joke among politicians in the West is that there are some countries which have a one-person–one-vote system, but what this really means is that there is one person standing and that is who the population must vote for.

The Western democracies may claim to operate the fairest political system but democracy is by no means a universal system. Hackett *et al.* (1978) claimed that in the 1970s there were probably less than a third of the world's leaders who could go to bed completely secure in the knowledge that there would not have been a *coup d'état* by the morning. The number may have decreased slightly into the 21st Century but there are still a large number of inherently unstable political regimes around the world. Democracies tend to be less vulnerable to a *coup d'état* than totalitarian ones because of the fact that there is a means of changing the regime every four to seven years, but democratic regimes have been and still can be removed and replaced often by totalitarian ones.

Organisations need to understand the workings of the political process. All developments will eventually require to be placed in the political framework of the regime in which they occur. If an organisational development runs counter to the prevailing political philosophy it can, in the last resort, be banned by the government. Employment policies, fiscal policies, foreign policies (as they affect overseas investment and even exports and imports), environmental, transportation and educational policies may act as either drivers or constraints upon the organisation.

Governance and politics operate at a series of level. In the UK these are *local* through the local authorities (usually the council), *regional* through the devolved parliaments of Scotland and Wales and their executives and also through the independent legislatures in the Channel Islands and the Isle of Man, *national* through the government at Westminster and *supra-national* through the European Parliament and its institutions (see later).

Nationalist politicians in Wales and Scotland would balk at being referred to as a region of the UK and the term is used here purely to aid understanding. These parties seek independence for their areas, which are considered countries in their own right forming part of the United Kingdom and in no way subservient to the largest partner, England.

Governments are usually formed from political parties. In a democracy there will be two or more major parties vying for the popular vote. In a dictatorship there is usually only one party allowed, although subsidiary parties, often supported to a considerable degree by the ruling party and designed to give a semblance of democracy, may be tolerated. Nevertheless there is nearly always an underground opposition in even the most ruthless dictatorship. In dictatorships, opposition parties are often banned. In the UK, the second party in an election becomes His/Her Majesty's *Loyal* Opposition. Opposition is thus actually encouraged by the constitution and indeed is seen as an important counterbalance to the power of the party in government.

# Governance of the UK

The following section, which explains in simplified terms the political process, takes as its model that of the UK Westminster Parliament. The implications of UK devolution are covered later in this chapter.

The government of the UK is formed by the party with the most Members of Parliament (MPs) following a general election. The maximum term for a UK parliament between general elections is five years and this is how long an MP is elected for, unless the government is defeated on a no-confidence vote in the House of Commons during the course of a Parliament or the Prime Minister decides to go to the country early.

The UK is divided into 600+ constituencies, the number and boundaries of which are decided by the Boundary Commission at periodic intervals. One of the roles of the Commission is to ensure that constituencies do not become too large in terms of population and that the organisation of Parliament is reflective of the demographics of the whole country.

The UK Parliament, often referred to as the 'Mother of Parliaments', has its origins in medieval times and is currently divided into two houses, the directly elected House of Commons and the unelected House of Lords; the latter is due for major changes in the early years of the 21st Century with legislation being passed in 1999 to diminish and eventually abolish the power of the hereditary peers.

The main political parties supplying members to the House of Commons at the beginning of the 21st Century were the Labour Party (which formed the government since 1996), the Conservative Party (which had been the government since 1979, much of that time under the leadership of Margaret Thatcher), the Liberal Democrats (an amalgamation of the old Liberal Party and the newer Social Democrat Party) plus the two nationalist parties – Plaid Cymru (the Party of Wales) and the Scottish National Party (SNP) – and the various Northern Ireland parties. The importance of the two nationalist parties will be considered later in this chapter under devolution.

Each of the major parties has a constituency organisation in every constituency (or group of constituencies) they intend to contest. The Labour, Conservative and Liberal Democrat parties usually contest every seat in the mainland UK, whilst Plaid Cymru and the SNP field a candidate in every Welsh and Scottish seat respectively. Politics in Northern Ireland tends to be carried out on a more sectarian divide and there are separate Northern Ireland parties, with the Unionist grouping who wish the province to remain part of the UK at one end of the political spectrum and the Nationalists/Republicans whose aim is a united Ireland at the other.

Most democracies show a similar spectrum between parties of the left (usually equated to a socialist grouping) and those of the right (a conservative grouping). In the USA the two major parties are the Republicans and the Democrats, the former to the right and the latter to the left, although the polarisation between left and right is much less in the USA than in many other democracies. The political process in the USA is covered briefly later in this chapter.

Prior to an election, parties produce a manifesto setting out the policies they intend to put before the electorate. Whilst opposition parties may try to hold the winners of an election to these manifesto commitments, the nature of politics, especially within the UK, means that an incoming government may not have all the relevant facts about the economy etc. beforehand and thus may find that some manifesto commitments are unachievable.

## Lobbying

It is in the interests of organisations to ensure that their concerns (and wishes) reach the ears of those who will be deciding taxes, disbursing government funds, making laws etc.

In recent years, firstly in the USA but now throughout the developed world, systematic lobbying has developed. Specialist firms, often fronted by retired politicians, will put forward (for a price) the views of individual organisations or sectors of industry. In recent years there have been concerns over politicians being paid to represent organisational interests and in the UK there have been a number of high-profile 'sleaze' investigations. Whilst lobbying is likely to remain a fact of political life, its operation is now regulated in many countries. In the UK there are also limits on the amounts political parties can spend on elections, unlike the USA where there are huge donations from organisations to candidates and parties of their choice whom they believe may help further their interests.

## The UK electoral system

The UK electoral system underwent considerable changes at the end of the 20th Century. Prior to 1999, UK elections had invariably been based on a first past the post system. From 1922, when the franchise was extended to the whole adult population (save prisoners and those certified as mentally ill), a candidate won an election by being the one with the most votes. Whilst this system, it is claimed, leads to a clear result and stability, it is not necessarily fair especially to the third party in any national contest. A first past the post system can result in a party that has less than 50% of the popular vote gaining a massive majority, whilst a party gaining, say, 20% could receive few or even no members in Parliament.

European Union electoral procedures forced the adoption of a proportional system for the UK in respect of European elections. Similar procedures were adopted for elections in Northern Ireland in the late 1990s, as the importance of representation from all political and social groups within the Province was recognised.

The 1999 elections to select the first members of the Scottish Parliament (MSPs – Members of the Scottish Parliament) and the Welsh Assembly (AMs – Assembly Members) were also conducted on a proportional system. In Scotland, as will be seen later, this resulted in a Labour–Liberal Democrat coalition, as the

Labour Party did not win enough seats to achieve an outright majority. The Conservative Party, which held no Scottish Westminster seats since a disastrous showing in 1997, was able to benefit by gaining so-called list seats as a result of the proportional system before winning their first outright seat in the Scottish Parliament in a by-election in March 2000.

In 2000 there was speculation that changes to the governance of the UK might see an elected second chamber but with seats being held for 10–15 years and a system of proportional representation in local government elections.

One of the major roles of the party in government is to set tax levels. There are two major types of tax, *direct* and *indirect*. Direct taxation in the UK is that linked to pay, i.e. income tax, and the amount paid is proportional (within bands) to income. Levels of direct taxation began to fall from the 1980s with the balance being made up of indirect taxes, e.g. taxes on products etc.

The perceived wisdom among politicians seems to be that decreasing direct taxes is a vote winner, although this does mean a commensurate rise in indirect taxation.

# Devolution

The biggest change in recent years to the governance and political landscape of the UK has been in the granting of devolved powers. The Channel Islands, the Isle of Man and, until the latter part of the 20th Century, Northern Ireland have had a tradition of their own assemblies and parliaments; that on the Isle of Man, the Tynwald, being one of the world's oldest (Iceland has the oldest Parliament in the world).

The proposed political settlement in Northern Ireland included elections to and the setting-up of a Northern Ireland Assembly. Whilst this happened at the end of 1999, the Assembly was suspended in early 2000 after disagreements over the decommissioning of arms. Although the suspension was lifted after a few months following considerable negotiation, it remains a fragile piece of democracy whose survival depends on the goodwill and efforts of all involved in the province.

Prior to 1707, when England and Scotland were joined by the Act of Union under a common Monarch (James I of England/James VI of Scotland) and the annexation of Wales by England in the 1530s, both Wales to a lesser extent and Scotland had been independent countries.

Scotland had rebelled in 1745 under Bonnie Prince Charlie, and the fact that the country retained a separate legal and educational system to that south of the border has meant that Scotland has always felt different from England. Nationalist politics began to make headway after World War II, although it was not until the 1960s that the Scottish National Party won a by-election to Westminster. After the 1999 Scottish Parliamentary elections that followed the referendum on devolution and the passing of the Scotland Act setting up a devolved Parliament in Edinburgh, the SNP had gained sufficient ground to become the second party in the Parliament.

The Scottish Parliament has considerably more power than its Welsh counterpart (where the nationalist party, Plaid Cymru – The Party of Wales is also the second party). Prior to the Scotland Act, a referendum was held (as it was in Wales) in which Scots were asked firstly whether they approved of devolution and secondly as to whether the Scottish Executive should have the power to vary tax rates by up to 3p in the £ compared with the rest of the UK. The answer was 'yes' to both questions. At the time of writing the tax-varying powers have not been used.

The Scottish Parliament now has jurisdiction over large areas of Scottish life, although certain powers are still reserved to the Westminster Parliament including:

- Constitutional matters
- Foreign policy
- Defence and national security
- Protection of borders and immigration
- Criminal law in relation to drugs and firearms
- Stability of fiscal policy
- Consumer and competition legislation
- Postal services
- Telecommunications
- Employment legislation
- Social security policy
- Regulation of certain professions, e.g. health, veterinary surgeons, architects, auditors, estate agents
- Transport safety and regulation
- Nuclear safety
- Gambling and the National Lottery
- Genetic research.

The aim of the SNP is full independence for Scotland within the first one or two decades of the 21st Century albeit still with close cultural, economic and social ties to the country's neighbours.

From an organisational analysis viewpoint, devolution means that organisations operating in the UK may be dealing with different procedures in the devolved areas and thus will need to understand which powers are covered by which legislature.

# The European Union (EU)

Whilst today the nations of Western Europe appear very stable, many of them are fairly recent creations. Britain, Spain, France and Portugal have been sovereign states with fairly stable borders for centuries but others, including Germany, Italy, the Benelux countries and Ireland, are 19th or 20th Century creations. The European Union (the EU) is a direct consequence of World War II and a Western

Europe-wide desire never again to see such wholesale destruction of life, property and culture.

After 1945 the nations of Western Europe faced the perceived threat of Communism from the Soviet Union and its Warsaw Pact allies (allies in name only, as the countries under communist rule in Eastern Europe had little choice but to support the Soviet Union militarily, politically and economically).

The European situation in 1945 was roughly as shown in Figure 4.1.

Europe was divided into three main blocs. The Western Powers, i.e. those countries allied to the UK and the USA in World War I, the Soviet Bloc and the neutral countries. The first two faced each other across the inner German border as two military alliances formed in the late 1940s and early 1950s – NATO in the West and the Warsaw Pact in the East, the former including the USA, Canada and

| Political system | Countries | Notes |
| --- | --- | --- |
| Communist but technically independent | Soviet Union | Known as the USSR |
| | East Germany | Known as the DDR |
| | Czechoslovakia | |
| | Poland | |
| | Albania | Began to take an independent line |
| | Yugoslavia | Began to take an independent line |
| | Hungary | |
| | Bulgaria | |
| | Romania | Began to take an independent line |
| Communist and absorbed into the USSR | Latvia | |
| | Lithuania | |
| | Estonia | |
| Under USSR influence but became increasingly independent and neutral | Austria | Became neutral democracy |
| | Finland | Became neutral |
| Right-wing dictatorships but linked to Western Powers | Spain | |
| | Portugal | |
| Democracies allied to the Western Powers | UK | |
| | West Germany | |
| | France | |
| | Belgium | |
| | Holland | |
| | Luxembourg | |
| | Italy | |
| | Greece | |
| | Denmark | |
| | Norway | |
| | Iceland | Gained independence from Denmark in 1944 |
| Neutral | Monaco | |
| | Andorra | |
| | Liechtenstein | |
| | Ireland | Known as Eire |
| | Switzerland | |
| | Sweden | |

*Figure 4.1   Europe in 1945.*

Turkey and linked to a similar alliance in the Southern Hemisphere, and the latter dominated by the Soviet Union.

As World War II neared its conclusion, 44 countries met at the Bretton Woods conference in the USA in 1944 to discuss the financial implications of rebuilding a shattered world. From this conference came in 1947 the International Monetary Fund (IMF), the World Bank and the General Agreement on Tariffs and Trade (GATT) negotiated by 23 states. It was recognised that the post-war world would require greater co-operation between nations than had been the case previously. The European nations wanted much greater co-operation and in particular to ensure that France and Germany, whose enmity had been in part the cause of both world wars, could work together in peace and harmony. At the end of World War II, Germany was divided into two separate countries, West Germany and East Germany, the latter under considerable Soviet domination. Germany did not achieve reunification until October 1990 following the collapse of Communist domination of Eastern Europe.

The first moves towards the dream of greater European unity came in 1947 when the Netherlands (often referred to, erroneously as Holland in the UK – Holland is in fact just one of the provinces of the Netherlands), Belgium and Luxembourg agreed to form a customs union with common tariffs. Belgium and the Netherlands had been united politically for a brief period in the years after the Napoleonic Wars.

In April 1951, a treaty forming the European Coal and Steel Community (ECSC) was signed by Belgium, Luxembourg, the Netherlands, Italy, France and Germany. The driving force behind the formation of the ECSC was Robert Schuman, foreign minister of France between 1949 and 1953. The concept was that there would be a free market in the vital commodities of coal and steel between the partners. This economic aim was also overlaid by a political one, the first post-war West German Chancellor, Konrad Adenauer, making the point in 1950 that there were important political considerations, as a degree of sovereignty in national policy-making would need to be abnegated as a result of the ECSC's formation. By agreeing to co-ordinate the production of coal and steel and their associated products, the partners would be operating in a supra-national manner. The ECSC needed supra-national institutions to manage the partnership and these have evolved into the institutions of firstly the EEC (European Economic Community) and latterly the EU (European Union). It was recognised early on that there would be a need for a higher authority; indeed it was called just that, a court of justice to settle disputes between the partners, an assembly to provide a democratic input (members were not actually elected by the citizens of the partner countries but chosen by national parliaments) and a council of ministers representing the needs and aspirations of the partners.

The ECSC was instrumental not only in removing trade barriers in strategic materials between the partners but also in encouraging officials and politicians to work together.

The success of the ECSC was such that the partners agreed to extend its operation beyond that of the coal and steel industries and in 1957 they signed the two treaties of Rome. The first treaty established the European Economic Community (EEC) and the second Euratom, designed to expand ECSC operations into nuclear energy. Whilst the UK was originally interested in the proposal, initial membership was restricted to the six original members of ECSC. The UK, Austria (forbidden by the settlements arrangements following World War II to become involved with any form of political and economic union with West Germany), Denmark, Norway, Portugal, Sweden and Switzerland formed the European Free Trade Association (EFTA) in 1960 to act as a free-trading block outwith the EEC. EFTA was configured to give a greater emphasis on being a free-trading association without the political institutions being developed within the EEC. Nevertheless in 1961, the UK, Eire and Denmark applied to join the EEC. President Charles de Gaulle of France vetoed the entry of the UK and all three applications fell. De Gaulle's actions caused considerable anger in the UK as it had been the UK that had supported de Gaulle's Free French cause during the darkest days of World War II, and to many his actions seemed akin to betrayal especially when a Franco–West German Treaty of Friendship and Co-operation was signed in 1963, leaving the UK somewhat isolated on the fringes of Europe.

As the EEC grew in stature and its institutions (these will be covered in more detail) gained more supra-national authority and influence, a debate began that is still ongoing. Should the Community become wider and accept more members, or deeper and develop further towards political and economic union?

In respect of expansion, the 1961 application by the UK, Denmark and Eire has already been mentioned; there was an associate agreement between the EEC and Greece in 1961, the UK, Denmark and Eire re-applied for membership in 1967 together with Norway, although France still opposed UK membership. Special agreements were made with Spain in 1970, and in 1972 the UK, Denmark and Eire were finally admitted to the EEC. Norway's membership was agreed but the Norwegian population voted in a referendum not to become EEC members. A referendum on continuing membership was held in the UK in 1975, with a large majority voting in favour of remaining within the EEC.

There was further expansion in 1981 when Greece became a member and again in 1985 when Spain and Portugal joined. By 2000, Austria (relieved of an obligation not to enter any form of union with Germany), Finland and Sweden had also joined the Community (1995) and there were a large number of countries, mainly from the old communist Eastern Bloc but also Turkey, having made applications.

Figures 4.2 and 4.3 show the new countries that have been formed in Europe since 1945 together with the membership of the European Union, as the EEC became in 1991/92 following the Maastricht Treaty on European Union.

# Common agricultural/fisheries policies

Up to the end of the 18th Century, i.e. the dawn of the Industrial Revolution, agriculture was the major occupation throughout most of the world. By the end

| Country | Formed from | Notes |
| --- | --- | --- |
| Latvia | USSR | Independent prior to 1941 |
| Estonia | USSR | Independent prior to 1941 |
| Lithuania | USSR | Independent prior to 1941 |
| Belarus | USSR | Still linked politically with Russia |
| Russia | USSR | Capital – Moscow |
| Ukraine | USSR | Still retains close links with Russia |
| Czech Republic | Czechoslovakia | |
| Slovakia | Czechoslovakia | |
| Slovenia | Yugoslavia | |
| Bosnia | Yugoslavia | |
| Macedonia | Yugoslavia | |
| Croatia | Yugoslavia | |

*Figure 4.2   New European countries after the break-up of the Warsaw Pact.*

| Country | Joined EU | Notes |
| --- | --- | --- |
| Belgium | 1957 | |
| France | 1957 | |
| Germany | 1957 | Joined as West Germany, now reunified with East Germany |
| Italy | 1957 | |
| Luxembourg | 1957 | |
| Netherlands | 1957 | |
| Denmark | 1973 | |
| Ireland | 1973 | |
| United Kingdom | 1973 | |
| Greece | 1981 | |
| Portugal | 1986 | |
| Spain | 1986 | |
| Austria | 1995 | |
| Finland | 1995 | |
| Sweden | 1995 | |

*Figure 4.3   Composition of the EU on 1 January 2000.*

of the 20th Century, in the EU counties agriculture only accounted for a mere 2.4% of Gross Domestic Product (GDP) and 6.5% of employment (Nugent, 1995). Despite the decline in the economic importance of agriculture and its much lowered impact on employment it is still a very important sector of commerce within the EU. People have to eat and if food cannot be produced within the EU, it must be imported; also, from its inception the EEC, as the EU was formerly known, has subsidised agricultural production through a Common Agricultural Policy (CAP). Agriculture has also been responsible for many of the quarrels between the UK and its EU partners, particularly over lamb and beef exports from the UK to other EU members, and especially with France where the farming lobby is very powerful.

Agriculture is of political importance because price fluctuations on basic foodstuffs can have an immediate detrimental effect on the whole population. Large rises in the price of bread have led to political unrest, riots and the fall of governments in the past, so there is a political imperative in ensuring price stability within the foodstuff market. As Nugent (1995) has pointed out, agriculture may be only a small percentage of GDP but food purchases constitute over 20% of an individual EU citizen's domestic budget, a high percentage indeed.

The more food a country or linked group of countries can produce for domestic consumption, the less there is a dependency on other countries to supply. Food can be as potent a weapon as any other. On a number of occasions during the Cold War post 1945, the US and Canada sought political concessions from the Soviet Union as a *quid pro quo* for supplying surplus North American cereals to the Soviets following poor harvests in Eastern Europe.

Since the start of the Industrial Revolution at the end of the 18th and beginning of the 19th Centuries, the developed countries of the world have seen a drift in employment away from the countryside and into urban situations, as shown by the decline in those employed in agriculture, covered above. Increases in the efficiency of technology to support agriculture have greatly reduced the dependency on labour, although there are widespread differences in the agricultural employment levels within the EU. Whilst, as stated above, on average the percentage of EU citizens employed in agriculture is about 6.5%, in the UK it is just over 2% whilst in Greece it is around 25%. Member states which have a more labour-dependent agricultural sector are likely to be more favourably disposed towards a Common Agricultural Policy that supports their farming methods, even if these are less efficient.

The Common Agricultural Policy has remained relatively intact since its inception as part of the Treaty of Rome in 1957, the founding treaty of the EEC. Its main aims are, in simplified terms to:

(a) Increase productivity and maximise labour utilisation
(b) Ensure a fair standard of living for those working in the agricultural sector
(c) Stabilise markets
(d) Assure the availability of supplies
(e) Maintain reasonable price levels for consumers.

In order to achieve these aims, the CAP proposed a completely open market for agricultural products across the member states. Whilst this may be the situation in theory, British farmers in particular have been outraged to find that their products have been refused entry into France (even when only in transit to other member states) as a result of actions by French farmers worried about their standard of living. The French authorities have not always been quick to step in, leading to some acrimonious comments from UK farmers' leaders and politicians and legal action from the EU itself.

The CAP and the associated Common Fisheries Policy use subsidies to maintain prices for farmers. The complaint of the more efficient producers is that such a policy can actually encourage inefficiencies even if it does protect farmers from the vagaries of weather and price fluctuations. Basically the EU will intervene in the market if the price drops below a certain level. Whilst the CAP was reformed to some extent in the early 1990s it has not proved as popular in the UK as the EU might have wished. Mainstream UK agriculture is highly efficient and thus attracts fewer subsidies, and policies of setting land aside or growing huge crops of oil seed rape and linseed oil have promoted environmental concerns.

The existence of the CAP also means that EU prices are kept artificially high in comparison with the rest of the world, where food prices tend to be lower as prices to the farmer are not guaranteed. The EU has had to negotiate preferential deals with other countries to allow their products to enter the Union. This has been particularly important to the UK which had a large trade with many Commonwealth countries prior to EEC entry.

Supporters of the CAP argue (Nugent, 1995) that the system has produced some very important benefits in that:

- Efficiency of agricultural production throughout the EU has increased
- Agricultural incomes have kept pace with other occupations
- The EU agricultural market has attained stability
- The EU is much more (but not completely) self-sufficient in basic foodstuffs.

However it cannot be denied that whilst farmers may have gained, consumers have lost due to the exclusion of cheaper imports.

The fishery policy has also been politically problematic as not all of the EU members have a fishing industry or indeed even a coastline. The EU has a 200 mile zone around member state's coastlines that is reserved for EU fishing vessels, with the previous national 12 mile zones being for the fishing boats of the nation concerned. There are national quotas imposed as part of the measures to conserve fish stocks. These need to be not only numerical but also species related, as individual consumer preferences in member states mean that each nationality tends to eat different species. The UK has been hit by the fishery policy because most of the huge UK fishing fleet post the 1960s and 1970s fished the North Sea and Icelandic waters which were forbidden to them following the 'Cod Wars' with Iceland. Many UK fishing vessels are now owned by Spanish interests to whom UK operators have sold quotas.

## EU law

Community law, adopted by the Council, or by the Parliament, may take the following forms:

- **Regulations**: These are directly applied without the need for national measures to implement them
- **Directives**: Bind member states as to the objectives to be achieved while leaving the national authorities the power to choose the form and the means to be used
- **Decisions**: These are binding in all their aspects upon those to whom they are addressed. A decision may be addressed to any or all member states, to undertakings or to individuals
- **Recommendations and opinions**: These are not binding.

EU directives and decisions normally require national legislation to be enacted according to the procedures of the member states before becoming law. That legislation must ensure that the directive/decision is followed to the letter, although the wording etc. may differ between states according to national procedures.

Community legislation, as well as the Council's common positions transmitted to the European Parliament, is published in the *Official Journal* in all the official languages.


# Social Charter

For an organisation such as the EU to both function and to be accepted by all its citizens, it must ensure that there are no major disparities between those living in one part of the EU from those in others. As Pettinger (1998b) has pointed out, the harmonisation of social policy had been a long-term aim of the original six founders of what was the EEC. A format for such harmonisation was agreed in 1989 with the Social Charter (as it became known) being a separate part of the Maastricht Treaty which changed the name of the EEC into the EU. The reason for the separation was the refusal of the then Conservative government in the UK to adopt any form of social charter, thus the UK was provided with an opt-out clause. The Labour government elected in 1997 signed up for the Social Charter in November of that year. Despite the opt-out, the UK government put into law the Trade Union Reform and Employment Rights Acts in 1993, at the behest of the EU, in addition to minimum statutory maternity rights, secret ballots for trade union activities, protection for employees who were transferred between organisations and absolute rights regarding health and safety at work. As UK citizens would have been entitled to take any issues relating to these to the European Court (see Chapter 10), the government had to mirror EU legislation, hence the Social Charter entered the UK political scene via a back door.

The Social Charter deals with provisions in the following areas, many of which provide for a statutory obligation upon employers and are thus also covered in Chapter 10:

- Freedom of movement for workers within the EU
- Protection for employment and pay
- Improvements in living and working conditions
- Adequate social protection and social security
- Freedom to join trade unions etc. (and of course the right not to join)
- Adequate and continual vocational training
- Equality of treatment regardless of gender
- Information to all workers on workplace issues
- Health and safety at work protection
- Access to labour markets for the elderly
- Access to labour markets for the disabled
- Protection for children and young persons at work.

The last provision was the cause of much concern in the UK media, as it was feared that youngsters might be forbidden to undertake paper rounds – this has not proved to be the case but illustrates the 'Europhobia' that occasionally sweeps the UK!

A full explanation of the Social Charter and the implications for organisations can be found in *The European Social Charter* by Richard Pettinger (1998b).

# European Union institutions

The four main institutions of the European Union are the Commission located in Brussels, the Parliament in Strasbourg, the Council of Ministers and the European Court in Luxembourg (not to be confused with the International Court in The Hague).

The following sections summarise the structure and work of these institutions. Each member country of the EU also has its own institutions and these need to interface with those of the EU. There is an important precept that must be accepted by each member country in that European law is superior to national law.

## The Commission

The European Commission (often maligned in the UK during the 1990s) could be described as the engine room of the EU. Nugent (1995) makes the point that the commission is at the heart of all that the EU does and says. It is in someway similar to a national civil service although with much greater decision-making powers. The Commission is able to devote more of its time to policy because that implementation is usually a task for the civil services of the member states.

In 2000 there were 17 Commissioners (originally there were only 9), each heading up a department responsible for particular policy areas. France, Germany, Italy, Spain and the UK, as the largest members of the EU, nominate two of their nationals as Commissioners and the remaining, smaller members one each. In 1999, following pressure from the European Parliament, all of the Commissioners resigned although a number were then re-appointed.

The President of the Commission, in effect the President of the EU, is appointed by member states. The President and the Commissioners serve for a term of five years after which their appointment can be renewed. The appointments must be confirmed by the European Parliament, thus that body holds a veto.

It is not surprising, given the political nature of the EU, that Commissioners have usually been major political figures (often ministers) within their national political systems prior to appointment to the Commission.

As citizens of a member state, the Commissioners have to maintain a careful balancing act in that they will have natural national interests and yet they are appointed to serve the whole of the EU community; this can lead to criticism from all sides.

In 1993 the EU employed approximately 26 500 staff and of these over 18 000 worked directly for the EU Commission with two-thirds of these being administrators – 4000 holding 'A' grades and thus being directly involved in policy.

The Commission works through 24 Directorates General and a series of special units. The Directorates General are designated by Roman numerals, as detailed in Figure 4.4.

The EU Council and the European Parliament need a proposal from the Commission before they can pass legislation, and thus policy tends to be generated by the Commission which is a difference from national civil services. EU laws are mainly upheld by Commission action, laws that often refer to the integrity of the single market. Agricultural (CAP, see earlier) and regional development policies are sustained, managed and developed by the Commission as is development co-operation with external developing countries. Development programmes, vital for the future of Europe, are orchestrated by the Commission.

The Commission, working in close collaboration with the European Council, provides the impulse towards further integration of the EU. Decisive initiatives in recent years have included the launch of the strategy which culminated in the completion of the single market in 1993, the plans for economic and monetary union and the drive to strengthen economic and social cohesion between the regions of Europe, all strategic rather than tactical issues.

| DG | Function |
| --- | --- |
| I | External economic relations |
| IA | External political relations |
| II | Economic and financial affairs |
| III | Internal market and industrial affairs |
| IV | Competition |
| V | Employment, industrial relations and social affairs |
| VI | Agriculture |
| VII | Transport |
| VIII | Development |
| IX | Personnel and administration |
| X | Audiovisual, information, communications and culture |
| XI | Environment, nuclear safety and civil protection |
| XII | Science – research and development |
| XIII | Telecommunications and information technology |
| XIV | Fisheries |
| XV | Financial institutions and company law |
| XVI | Regional policy |
| XVII | Energy |
| XVIII | Credit and investment |
| XIX | Budgets |
| XX | Financial control |
| XXI | Customs and indirect taxation |
| XXII | Not in current use (2000) |
| XXIII | Enterprise, distribution and tourism |

*Figure 4.4   EU Directorates General.*

The members of the Commission provide political leadership and direction to the EU as an entity. Commissioners, as mentioned earlier, are obliged to be completely independent of their national governments and to act only in the interests of the European Union as a whole. Such impartiality and commitment, it is believed, enables the Commission to be an effective honest broker, mediating conflicts of interest between member states when needed.

The President of the Commission is chosen by the Heads of State or Government meeting in the European Council after consulting the European Parliament. Not surprisingly there is often a considerable amount of wheeling and dealing in this process. The other members of the Commission are nominated by the 15 member governments in consultation with the incoming President.

The Commission meets once a week to conduct its business, which may involve adopting proposals, finalising policy papers and discussing the evolution of its priority policies. Commissioners are expected to give full support to all policies, even when they are adopted by a majority decision, mirroring the concept of collective responsibility practised by the cabinets of democratic regimes.

The democratic accountability of the Commission to the citizens of Europe, i.e. the citizens of the member states, is controlled through parliamentary vetting of the President and his colleagues and debates in the European Parliament, plus the oversight of the Council of Ministers drawn from each of the member states. The full Commission has to be approved by the European Parliament before its members can take office. They can be required to resign en bloc by a parliamentary vote of censure – a power which has never yet been used but which the Commission pre-empted in 1999. Although a vote of censure failed in the Parliament, the whole Commission chose to resign following allegations of sleaze.

The Commission is not an all-powerful institution. Its proposals, actions and decisions are in various ways scrutinised, checked and judged by all of the other institutions, with the exception of the European Investment Bank. Nor does it take the main decisions on Union policies and priorities – this is the prerogative of the Council and, in some cases, of the European Parliament.

There are three distinct functions to the Commission's role, namely:

- Initiating proposals for legislation
- Guardian of the Treaties
- The manager and executor of European Union policies and of international trade relationships.

In fulfilling these functions, the Commission has as part of its brief the obligation to keep the needs of the ordinary citizen firmly in mind and to minimise red tape and bureaucratic regulations, although many EU regulations have been criticised in the media for being over-bureaucratic. The Commission also works very closely with the Court of Auditors to eliminate fraud in the demands made on the Union's budget, again an area of some adverse press comments, especially with respect to certain agricultural practices.

## The legislative role of the EU Commission

The legislative process begins with a Commission proposal, as EU law cannot be made without one. In devising its proposals, the Commission has three constant objectives: to identify the European interest, to consult as widely as is necessary and to respect the principle of subsidiarity.

The European interest means that a legislative proposal reflects the Commission's judgement of what is best for the EU and its citizens as a whole, rather than for sectoral interests or individual member states.

Consultation is essential to the preparation of a proposal. The Commission listens to governments, industry, trade unions, special interest groups and technical experts, including its own, before completing its final draft of any proposal.

Subsidiarity is an important concept enshrined in the Treaty on European Union and is applied by the Commission in such a way as to ensure that the EU only takes action when it will be more effective than if left to individual member states. The UK has been very keen to see subsidiarity applied to its maximum, i.e. the EU only takes action when absolutely necessary – other member states have taken a more relaxed view!

Once the Commission has formally sent a proposal for legislation to the Council and the Parliament, the EU's law-making process is very dependent on effective co-operation between the three institutions.

## Guardian of the treaties

It is the Commission's task to ensure that Union legislation is applied correctly by each member state. If they breach their Treaty obligation, they will face Commission action, including legal proceedings at the Court of Justice. As this book was being written, a complaint from the UK regarding the refusal of the French government to accept British beef into their marketplace despite a positive EU ruling on safety was being dealt with under the treaty. It was the Commission and not the UK that was taking action against France, as the EU had ruled that a breach of the treaty had occurred thus making the Commission responsible for taking the necessary action.

In certain circumstances, the Commission can fine individuals, firms and organisations for infringing Treaty law, subject to their right to appeal to the Court of Justice. Illegal price-fixing and market-rigging cartels have been a constant object of its attention and the subject of very large fines – in late 1994, one group of firms were fined a record 248 million ecu (EU figures). The Commission also maintains a close scrutiny over government subsidies to industry and certain kinds of state aid must, by Treaty, receive its assent. Subsidies to car manufacturers and airlines by national governments have been the subject of considerable scrutiny in recent years.

## Management of policies

The Commission manages the Union's annual budget, which is dominated by agricultural spending (through the CAP, see earlier) allocated by the European

Agricultural Guidance and Guarantee Fund and by the Structural Funds, designed to even out the economic disparities between the richer and poorer areas.

The Commission's executive responsibilities are wide: it has delegated powers to make rules which fill in the details of Council legislation; it can introduce preventive measures for a limited period to protect the Community market from the dumping of products by countries outwith the EU; it enforces the Treaty's competition rules and regulates mergers and acquisitions above a certain size.

The Union's effectiveness in the world is enhanced by the Commission's role as negotiator of trade and co-operation agreements with other countries, or groups of countries. More than 100 countries have such agreements with the EU.

## The European Parliament

The European Parliament meets in Strasbourg for monthly plenary sessions, Brussels for committee meetings and additional sessions with the General Secretariat being based in Luxembourg. The distances and travel costs involved have led to calls for a rationalisation of the Parliament.

The role of the Parliament is as the guardian of the European interest and the defender of the citizens' rights. Either individually, or as a group, European citizens have the right to petition the Parliament and can seek redress of their grievances on matters that fall within the European Union's sphere of responsibility. The Parliament has also appointed an ombudsman to investigate any allegations of maladministration within the EU, and ordinary citizens have the right of access to the ombudsman.

In order to operate effectively, the European Parliament maintains links with national parliaments through regular meetings between speakers and chairs and between parliamentary committees. These contacts have also been furthered by discussions of Union policies in major conclaves known as 'parliamentary assizes'.

The 626 MEPs (Members of the European Parliament) are elected every 5 years. In 1999, the disposition of numbers between the member states was as shown in Figure 4.5, with the number of MEPs being based upon the size of the national population.

The powers of the European Parliament fall into three categories:

- Legislative power
- Power over the EU budget
- Supervision of the executive.

## Legislative power

Under the original terms of the Treaty of Rome (1957) the European Parliament was given a purely consultative role, with the Commission proposing and the Council of Ministers (see later) deciding legislation. Subsequent Treaties have extended Parliament's power to amending and even adopting legislation so that

| Member state | Number of MEPs |
| --- | --- |
| Austria | 21 |
| Belgium | 25 |
| Denmark | 16 |
| Finland | 16 |
| France | 87 |
| Germany | 99 |
| Greece | 25 |
| Ireland | 15 |
| Italy | 87 |
| Luxembourg | 6 |
| Netherlands | 31 |
| Portugal | 25 |
| Spain | 64 |
| Sweden | 22 |
| United Kingdom | 87 |

*Figure 4.5 Composition of the European Parliament.*

the Parliament and Council now share the power of decision-making in a large number of areas.

The consultation procedures require an opinion from the Parliament before a legislative proposal from the Commission can be adopted by the Council.

The co-operation procedure allows Parliament to improve proposed legislation by amendment. It involves two readings in Parliament, giving members ample opportunity to review and amend the Commission's proposal and the Council's preliminary position on it.

In cases of conflict, a conciliation committee – made up of equal numbers of Members of Parliament and of the Council, with the Commission present – seeks a compromise on a text that the Council and Parliament can both subsequently endorse. If there is no agreement, Parliament can reject the proposal outright.

Parliament's assent is required for important international agreements such as the accession of new member states, association agreements with third countries, the organisation and objectives of the Structural and Cohesion Funds, and the tasks and powers of the European Central Bank.

## Budgetary powers

The European Parliament approves the Union's budget each year. The budgetary procedure allows Parliament to propose modifications and amendments to the Commission's initial proposals and to the position taken by the member states in the Council of Ministers. On agricultural spending and costs arising from international agreements the Council has the final say, but on other expenditure the Parliament decides in close co-operation with the Council.

The European Parliament has voted to reject the budget when its wishes have not been adequately respected. It is the President of the Parliament who signs the budget into law.

Monitoring of expenditure is the continuous work of the Parliament's Committee on Budgetary Control which seeks to make sure that money is spent for the purposes agreed and to improve the prevention and detection of fraud. Parliament makes an annual assessment of the Commission's management of the budget before approving the accounts and granting it a 'discharge' on the basis of the Annual Report of the European Union Court of Auditors.

## Supervision

The Parliament exercises overall political supervision of the way the Union's policies are conducted. Executive power in the Union is shared between the Commission and the Council of Ministers, and their representatives appear regularly before Parliament.

## Parliament and the European Union Commission

The European Parliament has an important role every five years in appointing the President and members of the Commission. It exercises detailed scrutiny through a close examination of the many monthly and annual reports that the Commission is obliged to submit to the Parliament. Members may also put written and oral questions to the Commission and they can, and do, interrogate Commissioners at Question Time during plenary sessions and at meetings of parliamentary committees.

The European Parliament can pass a motion of censure on the Commission and force it to resign, as very nearly happened in 1999 (see earlier).

## Parliament and Council

The President of the Council presents his or her programme at the beginning of a presidency and gives an account of it to Parliament at the end of that period. He or she also reports on the results of each European Council and on progress in the development of foreign and security policy.

Members attend plenary sessions and take part in Question Time and in important debates. They also carry out similar tasks to those of national and regional MPs in respect of constituents.

## Political organisation

All of the EU's major political currents are represented in the Parliament, ranging from far left to far right, and numbering close to 100 political parties. These are organised in a limited number of political groupings.

Overall management of the Parliament's activities is the responsibility of the Bureau which consists of the President and 14 Vice-Presidents. All of its Members are elected for terms of two and a half years.

The chairs of the political groups participate with the President of Parliament in the Conference of Presidents, which is responsible for organising the Parliament's work and drawing up the agenda for plenary sessions.

Much of the effective work of Parliament is conducted in its 20 committees covering all areas of the Union's activities, ranging from Agriculture to Common

Foreign and Security Policy, from Legal Affairs and Citizens' Rights to Overseas Co-operation and Development.

Parliament maintains friendly relations with elected assemblies all over the world, and European Parliamentarians meet regularly with representatives from other Parliaments in inter-parliamentary committees and delegations in a similar manner to the contacts between national parliaments.

## Elections

Elections to the European Parliament are held every 5 years, as simultaneously as possible throughout the member states. A system of proportional representation is used and it is up to the individual member state to divide up its own country into constituencies. In the UK, turnout for European Elections has been very low, despite the seats being contested by all of the major political parties.

All EU nationals over 18 are eligible to vote, even if they are living in another member state. They will vote for a candidate in the constituency (and country in which they are resident) and not in their country of origin unless that is their main abode.

## The Council of the European Union – The Council of Ministers

The all-important Council of Ministers is made up of ministers from the governments of the current 15 member states.

The Presidency of the Council rotates every six months in the following sequence: Spain, Italy, Ireland, the Netherlands, Luxembourg, the United Kingdom, Austria, Germany, Finland, Portugal, France, Sweden, Belgium, Spain, Denmark and Greece, and meets in Brussels, except in April, June and October when all Council meetings take place in Luxembourg.

The Council of the European Union (Council of Ministers) has no equivalent anywhere in the world. Within the Council, ministers legislate for the Union, set its political objectives, co-ordinate their national policies and resolve (or at least try to resolve) differences between themselves and with other institutions.

As the EU states, the Council is a body with the characteristics of both a supranational and inter-governmental organisation, deciding some matters by qualified majority voting (see later), and others by unanimity. In its procedures, its customs and practices, and even in its disputes, the Council depends on a degree of solidarity and trust which is unusual in relations between sovereign states.

## The Presidency

The Presidency of the Council rotates between the member states every six months: January until June, July until December. The Presidency's role has become increasingly important as the responsibilities of the Union have broadened and deepened. It must:

- Arrange and preside over all meetings
- Elaborate acceptable compromises and find pragmatic solutions to problems submitted to the Council
- Seek to secure consistency and continuity in decision-taking.

## Decision-making and Qualified Majority Voting (QMV)

The Maastricht Treaty on European Union based the Union's activities on three 'pillars' and established that decisions should be taken mainly either by qualified majority voting or by unanimity.

Pillar One covers a wide range of Community policies (such as agriculture, transport, environment, energy, research and development) designed and implemented according to a well-proven decision-making process that begins with a Commission proposal. Following a detailed examination by experts and at the political level, the Council can either adopt the Commission proposal, amend it or ignore it.

The Treaty on European Union increased the European Parliament's say through a co-decision procedure, which means that a wide range of legislation (such as internal market, consumer affairs, trans-European networks, education and health) is adopted both by the Parliament and the Council.

In the vast majority of cases (including agriculture, fisheries, internal market, environment and transport), the Council decides by a qualified majority vote, with member states carrying the following weightings based on the population of the member states:

| | |
|---|---|
| Germany, France, Italy and the United Kingdom | 10 votes |
| Spain | 8 votes |
| Belgium, Greece, the Netherlands and Portugal | 5 votes |
| Austria and Sweden | 4 votes |
| Ireland, Denmark and Finland | 3 votes |
| Luxembourg | 2 votes |
| Total | 87 votes |

When a Commission proposal is involved, at least 62 votes must be cast in favour. In other cases, the qualified majority is also 62 votes, but these must be cast by at least 10 member states. In practice, the Council tries to reach the widest possible consensus before taking a decision so that, for example, only about 14% of the legislation adopted by the Council in 1994 was the subject of negative votes and abstentions (EU figures).

Those policy areas in Pillar One which remain subject to unanimity include taxation, industry, culture, regional and social funds, and the framework programme for research and technology development. In these areas a veto can be applied by any member state.

For the other two pillars created by the Treaty on European Union – Common Foreign and Security Policy (Pillar Two) and co-operation in the fields of Justice and Home Affairs (Pillar Three) – the Council is the decision-maker as well as the promoter of initiatives. Unanimity is the rule in both pillars, except for the implementing of a joint action which can be decided by qualified majority.

The objectives of the Common Foreign and Security Policy are to define and implement an external policy covering all foreign and security aspects.

Co-operation in Justice and Home Affairs aims to:

- Achieve the free movement of persons inside the Union
- Promote measures of common interest in the fields of external border control, asylum policy and immigration policy
- Fight against terrorism, drug trafficking and other serious forms of international crime.

## European Council

Since 1974, Heads of State or Government meet at least twice a year in the form of the European Council or 'European Summit'. Its membership also includes the President of the Commission. The President of the European Parliament is invited to make a presentation at the opening session.

The European Council has become an increasingly important element of the Union, setting priorities, giving political direction, providing impetus for its development and resolving contentious issues that have proved too difficult for the Council of Ministers.

### Organisation

Each member state has a national delegation in Brussels known as the Permanent Representation. These delegations are headed by Permanent Representatives, who are normally very senior diplomats and whose committee, called 'Coreper', prepares ministerial sessions. Coreper meets weekly and its main task is to ensure that only the most difficult and sensitive issues are dealt with at ministerial level.

Coreper is also the destination of reports from the many Council working groups of national experts. These groups make detailed examinations of Commission proposals and indicate, among other things, areas of agreement and disagreement.

Member states use their holding of the Presidency to bring forward their own ideas. Early in 2000, Portugal assumed the Presidency with an agenda that sought greater harmonisation of tax powers etc., ideas not particularly acceptable to the UK.

## The European Court

The Court of Justice plays an essential role in the institutional system set up by the Treaties. In particular it is responsible for maintaining the balance between the respective powers of the Community institutions on one hand, and between the powers transferred to the Community and those retained by the member states on the other. In exercising its powers the Court is often called upon to settle questions of a constitutional nature or of major economic significance. The Court is also the ultimate forum for resolving differences between member states where those differences have an EU implication. If one member state feels that another member is acting contrary to EU law, it is the Court that will decide the issue.

Further details on the European Court are found in Chapter 10 on Legal analysis. It is important, however, to understand that European law is superior to the national laws of member states and that all members join the EU knowing that their national laws can be challenged and that if the challenge is upheld, national law must be amended.

# Banks and the euro

## The European Investment Bank (EIB)

The European Investment Bank (EIB), the financing institution of the European Union, was created by the Treaty of Rome. The members of the EIB are the member states of the European Union, which have all subscribed to the Bank's capital.

The EIB has its own legal personality and financial autonomy within the Community system. The EIB's mission is to further the objectives of the European Union by providing long-term finance for specific capital projects in keeping with strict banking practice.

The EIB grants loans mainly from the proceeds of its borrowings, which, together with 'own funds' (paid-in capital and reserves), constitute its 'own resources'. Outside the European Union, EIB financing operations are conducted principally from the Bank's own resources but also, under mandate, from Union or member states' budgetary resources.

## The European Central Bank (ECB)

It was in June 1988 that the Council of Ministers confirmed the objective of the progressive realisation of economic union and mandated a Committee chaired by the then President of the European Commission (Jacques Delors) to study and propose concrete stages leading to this union. The Committee was composed of the governors of the EC national central banks and specialist experts.

On the basis of the *Delors Report*, the European Council decided in June 1989 that the first stage of the realisation of economic and monetary union should begin on 1 July 1990 – the date on which, in principle, all restrictions on the movement of capital between member states were abolished.

In view of the relatively short time available and the complexity of the tasks involved, the preparatory work for the final stage of Economic and Monetary Union (EMU) was also initiated. The first step was to identify all the issues which should be examined at an early stage, establish a work programme until the end of 1993, and define accordingly the mandates of the existing sub-committees and working groups established for that purpose.

For the realisation of EMU it was necessary to revise the Treaty establishing the European Economic Community (the 'Treaty of Rome') to establish the required institutional structure. To this end an Intergovernmental Conference on EMU was convened, which was held in 1991 in parallel with the Intergovernmental Conference on political union. The negotiations resulted in the Treaty on European Union which was agreed in December 1991 and signed in Maastricht (Netherlands) on 7 February 1992. However, owing to delays in the ratification process, the Treaty (which became the Treaty establishing the European Union as opposed to the European Economic Union) did not come into force until 1 November 1993.

In December 1995 the European Council agreed to name the European currency unit to be introduced at the start of Stage Three the 'euro' and confirmed that Stage Three of EMU would start on 1 January 1999. A chronological sequence of events was announced for the changeover to the euro. Draft bank notes were produced and consultations on design undertaken.

On 2 May 1998 the Council of the European Union – in the composition of Heads of State or Government – unanimously decided that eleven Member States (Belgium, Germany, Spain, France, Ireland, Italy, Luxembourg, the Netherlands, Austria, Portugal and Finland) fulfilled the necessary conditions for the adoption of the single currency on 1 January 1999. These countries will therefore participate in the third stage of EMU and form the first tranche of countries adopting the euro.

The Heads of State or Government also reached a political understanding on the persons to be recommended for appointment as members of the Executive Board of the European Central Bank (ECB).

On 1 January 1999 the final stage of EMU commenced (in respect of participating members) with the irrevocable locking of the exchange rates of the currencies of the eleven member states participating in the euro area and with the conduct of a single monetary policy under the responsibility of the ECB.

# The UK and the euro

The UK is one of the major members of the EU but decided to remain outside the original euro zone. The Labour government post 1997 declared that the UK would join when the economic circumstances were right and the Conservative Party have become increasingly hostile to the idea of EMU.

One of the main reasons expressed for this hostility relates to national sovereignty. There are those who believe that monetary union is but a step on the road to full political union which will set up a United States of Europe, something many UK politicians are against. The argument is that as monetary union negates the influence a national government has on fiscal policy, the natural step is political union.

However whilst remaining outside the euro zone, the UK's fiscal policy cannot help but be influenced by the relationship of sterling to the euro. The high pound of the early months of 2000 and the UK's reluctance to embrace EMU is one of the reasons given by the board of BMW when it divested itself of its only recently acquired UK subsidiary, Rover, in March 2000. The UK government refuted these comments but nevertheless a number of global organisations have expressed a wish to see the UK within the euro zone and trading in the currency. Supporters of EMU argue that Britain will be marginalised by its major trading partners (other EU members) unless the country joins France, Germany etc. in adopting the euro.

Even if the UK does not adopt the euro for some time to come, organisations will often be dealing with suppliers and customers who are in member states which have adopted the common currency and thus they will need to be cognisant of the exchange rates etc. It may well be that the UK experiences 'creeping euroisation' as more and more organisations begin to quote using the euro.

## EU expansion

Within the EU, there have been two distinct views on the way the Union should develop. Firstly there are those who believe that the EU should enlarge, taking in more and more countries, whilst on the other hand there are those who would wish to deepen the Union so as to move closer and closer to a federal state. Whilst the views are not mutually exclusive, they might be difficult to achieve simultaneously.

The UK has traditionally favoured expansion and the principle of subsiduarity, whereby decisions etc. that are best taken at local, national level are so decided, and only pan-EU matters are dealt with by the institutions of the EU.

## The United States of America

The political system of the United States of America is important in organisational analysis because of the economic standing of that country and thus its effect on world affairs. The USA can, at times, be very protective of its own organisations and in a global economy it is important that any outside organisation seeking to do business within the USA is able to access information on the systems and procedures pertaining there. However, it is not the intention of this book to delve deeply into the complex world of US politics, and those wishing to know more can do no better than to consult *The American Political Process* by Alan Grant (1991) – see Bibliography at the end of this book.

The USA has a strong Constitution with amendments that have been made to cope with changing conditions. So important is the Constitution in American life that each morning school children face the US flag, place their hand over their heart and perform the act of allegiance: 'I swear allegiance to the flag of the United States of America and the Constitution for which it stands . . .'.

The United States of America comprises the 50 States of the Union plus a number of dependent territories, most important of which are the US Virgin Islands in the Caribbean purchased from Denmark in 1917 to protect the Atlantic end of the Panama Canal, and Puerto Rico. Only two of the States are not contiguous with continental USA, Hawaii in the Pacific and Alaska, which was purchased from Russia in the 19th Century.

US culture is a blend of British, French, Spanish (the original colonisers of the country), African as a result of slavery which existed until the end of the American Civil War in 1865, Eastern European, Italian and Irish as a result of immigration, and Chinese/Japanese as a consequence of the relationship between the Far East and the US West Coast. The author of this book has worked extensively in the USA and agrees with the distinguished writer Shelby Foote, as quoted in Ward, Burns and Burns (1990), that unless one understands the reasons for the US Civil War and its effect upon the development of that nation, then one's understanding will be flawed. The USA has been a recent melting pot of cultures and has developed its own unique brand of governance to meet its particular needs.

The USA does not have the separation between the Presidential/Monarchical and the Prime Ministerial roles seen in many other countries. The US President is both a political and a representative figure. The President and the Vice-President are elected for a period of 4 years, being allowed (since the end of World War II) to serve a maximum of two terms in office. The original concept of the founding fathers of the USA was that the Vice-President would be the losing candidate in the Presidential election, but this proved unworkable in practice.

Governance of the USA is clearly divided into the roles of the States and those of the Federal Government. The Civil War was only partially about slavery *per se*, the other immediate cause was the relationship between the States of the Union and the Federal Government, and the rights of the former to institute their own systems and procedures.

Each State has its own legislature and Governor and more elected officials than in the UK. Whereas the Crown Prosecution Service (CPS) officials are appointed in the UK, senior District Attorneys who carry out a similar task in the USA are elected.

The Federal Government consists of the Executive headed by the President, officials appointed by the President at the head of the Civil Service and then career civil servants. The Presidential appointees are expected to offer their resignation after each Presidential term and even if they believe they have been effective, the resignation may be accepted as Eddy *et al.* (1976) have shown in the case of a former head of the FAA.

The legislature consists of the House of Representatives (the Senate) and the Congress, which perform comparable tasks to the Houses of Commons and Lords in the UK, although there are many differences. The Constitution is guarded by the US Supreme Court.

The USA is effectively a two-party system with some independents. The vast majority of politicians are either members of the Republican or Democratic Parties, although the divisions are less blurred than in many other countries including the UK. There is a considerable degree of bi-partisan agreement on many issues. Often equated to right and left wing parties, they are actually both centrist with the Republicans slightly to the right of centre and the Democrats slightly to the left.

The President is also either a Republican or a Democrat, and the common sense of the US people often ensures that if the President is a Democrat either the Congress or the Senate will be Republican. Whilst this may restrict the President in some respects, it does provide certain checks and balances.

Organisations working in the US need to realise that the States still have considerable powers. The death penalty may be imposed in one State, e.g. Texas, and not in another, e.g. Massachusetts – even such a critical decision is left to the State to decide. All the Constitution states is that punishments must not be 'cruel or unusual'. Federal law and State law may be different but tend not to overlap. States may also set their own sales tax regimes etc.

Grant's book, cited early, should be consulted by all who have an interest in US politics and legislation.

## Summary

Politics is about the governance of people. Organisations need to be cognisant of the political process because it is politicians who make laws, decide priorities and set tax rates. Organisations in the UK need to consider regional governance, national politics, the European Union, whose role is becoming stronger and stronger (especially since the UK signed up for the EU Social Charter), and the USA as the world's major single economy.

## Analysis

In carrying out the *political* analysis in respect of an organisation, the following questions need to be considered:

1. What political systems are in place in those areas in which the organisation operates?
2. What political priorities in areas where the organisation operates are likely to impact on the organisation?
3. What relationships does the organisation have with politicians and political parties?
4. Will developments such as EMU impact directly upon the organisation?

## Concepts covered

- Political systems
- UK governance, electoral system and devolution
- Lobbying
- European Union (EU)
- EU Common Agriculture and Fisheries Policies
- EU legislation and courts
- EU Social Charter
- EU Commission
- EU Parliament
- EU budgetary powers

- EU Council of Ministers
- EU Presidency
- EU Qualified Majority Voting (QMV)
- European Council
- EU banking and the euro
- US political system

QUESTIONS

1. Why is an understanding of the European Union so important to organisations operating within member states of the EU?
2. Describe reasons why organisations need to take cognisance of the political processes within their areas of operation. Illustrate your answer with examples of political policies and developments that have directly impacted upon particular organisations.

# Further reading

You are recommended to read *The American Political Process* by Alan Grant (1991) for further information about US politics, and *The Government and Politics of the European Union* by Neill Nugent (1995) for details of the European Union. A full explanation of the Social Charter and the implications for organisations can be found in *The European Social Charter* by Richard Pettinger (1998b).

# omic analysis

*Closed ~~...~~ ns in respect of economic factors affecting organisations – Money – Sources of finance – Stock markets – Inflation – Interest rates – Local, regional, national and global economies – Employment – Supply and demand – The influence of politics on economics*

This chapter examines the economic aspects in the external environment that an organisation needs to take into consideration. There are a large number of texts on economics and its associated theories and it is not the intention to provide a potted economics course in this chapter. Rather the aim is to direct you to the key aspects that need to be taken into consideration with an appreciation of how the economic environment operates.

In these days of global marketplaces, economies are complex systems. Unless it is the example of a large organisation being the main component of the economy of a region or company, organisations are to a great extent at the mercy of the economies within which they operate. A study of economic trends can, however, assist organisational planners in forecasting possible economic movements and thus benefiting from upswings early and having good contingency plans in place to anticipate downturns.

It might be thought that economics is mainly concerned with money. Whilst there is some truth to that, economics is in reality a function of human behaviour. The operation of economic systems is as unpredictable as it is because human behaviour can be unpredictable. One of the most important words in economics is confidence – how much confidence do individuals and organisations have that their resources will be safe, will grow etc. When confidence is lost, economies suffer.

## Supply and demand

Perhaps the most important economic concept is that of supply and demand.

Assume that an organisation has a product (call it $X$) of which 1000 can be produced per month. The total cost of production including all overheads etc. for each unit of $X$ is £10. If the organisation sells all 1000 at £10 it will break even. At any price that is less than £10 the organisation will make a loss, and at any price that is greater than £10 it will make a profit. The organisation would like to make £3 profit on each unit, so needs to sell at £13.

However, once the product is on the market it appears that there is only a monthly demand for 900 units at £13, whereas the demand would be 1000 at £12, 1100 at £11, 1200 at £10 and 1300 at £9.

In this simplification, remember that the cost of production for each unit is £10, so sales at £9 are unacceptable unless the item is sold as a loss leader in order to stimulate sales of another product, a technique often used by retailers in order to attract customers. It may also be that the marginal cost (i.e. the cost of producing one additional unit) of each item of X over 1000 units (if production can be extended) is so small as to bring the overall cost of production of 1300 units down to less than £9.

If the above is not the case, and there are 1000 customers willing to pay £12 for the 1000 units produced, demand matches supply at an acceptable cost to the supplier.

# Closed and open systems

It is impossible for any organisation or indeed any country to ignore wider economic factors. Biologists conceived the concept of a 'closed system' in order to aid their studies, and this concept has also been adopted by economists as a starting point for understanding their subject.

Closed systems do not, in reality, exist. A closed system is one that has no connections whatsoever with the outside environment. Even the simplest living organism (bacteria fall into this category, but there is still debate as to whether the even simpler viruses are actually living organisms or not) interacts with its environment in that it must take in some form of nutrients and it expels waste. It also impacts on the environment either by the changes it causes to that environment or through the extra space it takes up through reproduction. As we know only too well when we suffer from the effects of a virus, even that simple piece of genetic material can have a profound effect on its environment – indeed it can destroy it.

If an organisation were a closed system it would be possible to study its workings without having to factor in any external influences and this book would be unnecessary. However, almost by definition, organisations exist in order to affect the external environment and must draw their resources from that environment.

A comparison between the workings of a biological organism and an organisation as discussed in this book shows in fact remarkable similarities. The Mintzberg configurations discussed in Chapter 1 could easily be adapted to represent the human body. Living organisms can be characterised by certain features:

- The need for external resources – nutrients
- The need to remove waste
- Growth
- Reproduction

- A life cycle
- A genetic coding.

Whilst one could not describe organisations as living, they do display some of the attributes listed above. Organisations need a constant supply of resources, money, power etc., to function, and they nearly all produce some form of waste products (if it be only paper) which need to be cleared out if the organisation is to continue functioning. The owners and managers of most organisations wish to grow (or at least stay the same during lean times) and many organisations reproduce as they grow, i.e. they set up new operations which are akin to their children.

In Chapter 1 the concept of an Organisational Life Cycle (Cartwright & Green, 1997) was introduced and that is based on the natural life cycle that operates throughout nature. For some organisms it may be very short, a matter of hours or days, for others it can be very long – certain trees live for centuries. For humans it is about 70 years. Like organisms, Cartwright & Green showed that organisations also follow similar life cycles.

It is the possession of deoxyribonucleic acid (DNA), the material that makes up the chromosomes found in every living organism, the complex structure of which carries the genetic code, that distinguishes the living from the non-living. Viruses possess only the related RNA (ribonucleic acid) and this is why there is a debate as to their status.

It is possible that there could be a closed economic system. Occasionally a tribe is found living in a remote part of a rain forest that has no contact with the outside world but, for the vast majority of the world, economic systems interact one with another on a constant basis and to do that some form of standardised exchange mechanism is necessary. It is also necessary to have some type of common rules and a common economic language. For the vast majority of economic systems, what happens in one has an effect on others; the old adage that when New York sneezes, London catches a cold is very true.

Whilst completely closed economic systems are virtually impossible in the current global economy, Hubbard (1997) makes the point that, because of the vast amount of domestic trade compared to only a small quantity of foreign transactions before World War II, the USA operated what was virtually a closed system before that war. In contrast, the UK economy, given Great Britain's early reliance on international trading, was a much more open system. This chapter continues with a consideration of what money, an essential resource for human enterprise, actually is.

## Money

Money forms an important factor in the lives of both organisations and individuals and yet there is often a misunderstanding as to what exactly is meant by the term money.

Goods are articles produced to be sold or exchanged (and thus the word can include services when used in a strict economic sense). There is a singular, a good, i.e. an article produced to be sold or exchanged.

Money is basically a mutually acceptable, standardised good used as a method of exchange. If organisation *A* sells an article to individual *B*, there is no theoretical reason why *B* should not pay in another article that *A* requires, say stationery supplies. Indeed this form of barter is still used in some parts of the world and even within specially set up exchange projects within small communities in the UK. These work on the 'I will bake you a cake if you will mow my lawn' basis. Barter, however, is just not sophisticated enough for anything other than a very small, closed economy. Once trade occurs with those outwith a barter system then a common denominator is required for payment, and humankind has developed the concept of money as that common denominator.

Money is a commodity that has an accepted value and can thus be used in exchange. Technically anything can be used as money but if, say, pebbles off the beach were used there are just too many of them for an individual one to have much worth. If you wanted more money, one would just go and collect some more pebbles and so could anybody else. Value comes with rarity and so from ancient times those commodities with rarity value have become accepted as forms of exchange. The precious metals, gold, silver etc. and precious stones diamonds, rubies, emeralds etc., were acceptable because of their rarity value. Although the Chinese invented paper money many centuries ago, a large number of countries and economies retained systems based on rare commodities until quite recent times. Even when notes were introduced, they were backed up by an amount of gold equal to their value held in the central bank. In medieval times, the UK exchequer used to carry the wealth of the country around with him. Gold has always been a key part of the economic system. Up to the 1930s, exchange rates between currencies were fixed using the gold standard. In theory this required economies to carry out the promise on their notes. On a UK bank note is the legend 'I promise to pay the bearer on demand (and then the sum)' and this is signed on behalf of the Governor of the Bank of England or the relevant Scottish bank. The note is really an IOU for £10 of gold although it is unlikely that the bank would actually give you that amount of gold. In the 1930s the US government suspended the right of the public to convert notes into actual gold, and now all that remains of the public's link to the gold standard is a line of print on a bank note.

Because gold, silver, diamonds etc. are rare, they tend to keep their value and in times of major crisis people try to convert their assets into these. One of the advantages of gold as an exchange medium is its chemical stability; it is a very non-reactive element and thus it is hard to adulterate or substitute with a fake having the appearance of gold. The hardness of diamonds makes them, like gold, difficult to fake. The dream of the alchemists of medieval times was to turn base, common metals into rare and pure gold. Gold is the value that it is because people have confidence in its ability to hold its value. Confidence, as stated at the beginning of this chapter, lies at the heart of economics.

If people have confidence in an economic system they are more likely to hold their assets in the intangible symbols of that economy, i.e. bank notes etc., whereas when confidence declines there is a likelihood that those who can will convert their assets into more tangible forms of exchange, for example gold. Had the alchemists succeeded, gold would have become useless as a medium of exchange as it would have been too freely available. Tom Clancy (1998), the best-selling American novelist, has produced an excellent albeit fictional account of how confidence in the economic system could be destroyed deliberately by exposing the fact that money actually has no intrinsic value, only the value that people, organisations and countries agree to place on it.

The use of tangible artefacts such as gold etc. is known as *commodity money*, whereas the money most people use throughout their daily lives, notes and coins, is known as *fiat money*.

Governments through their central banks usually issue money, although in the UK the three major Scottish banks also issue their own notes. As these are accepted by the UK central bank, the Bank of England, this causes no problems within Scotland. They may be refused in other parts of the UK, although stories about this tend to be more apocryphal than based in reality. Scottish notes are however rarely accepted abroad. By being the currency issuer, central banks are able to regulate the amount of money in the economy and thus aid government fiscal policies.

As the issuers, governments and their banks have always been concerned to ensure the 'purity' of money, hence the stringent penalties for adulteration in the days when coinage really was gold and silver, and forgery of notes (and occasionally coins) in modern times.

There are five basic criteria that any good must meet in order to be acceptable as a form of money. The world has developed a series of types of money, coins, notes, cheques, credit cards, banker's drafts etc., all of which meet the criteria for a good used as an exchange medium. These are:

- It must be acceptable to all the parties in a transaction
- It must be standardised, i.e. there should be no difference between two £10 notes issued by the same authority
- It should last for a reasonable amount of time so that its value does not diminish, i.e. it must be durable
- It must be transportable
- It must exist in different denominations.

Taking each of the criteria in turn:

## Acceptability

A simple anecdote can illustrate the importance of acceptability. You have just returned to your home in the UK from a holiday in Spain and have a wedge of peseta notes in your wallet. Will your local newsagent accept these in payment? The answer is probably 'no'. If you were a regular customer it is possible that as a one-off gesture of goodwill you might be allowed to tender them and they might be accepted, but that will incur extra work and possible bank charges for the shopkeeper. A shopkeeper in the UK would prefer payment in UK currency, i.e. the pound sterling. Scots, whose banks issue their own notes, often have trouble having Scottish currency accepted in other parts of the UK especially when patronising smaller retail outlets – it is a problem of acceptability. The common European currency, the euro, is acceptable alongside national currencies in those countries that have joined the euro system and the US dollar has a much greater acceptability throughout the world. In the research for their study of the cruise industry, Cartwright & Baird (1999) found that the dollar was becoming an almost universally accepted currency for tourists. Cruise ships, which can carry over 2000 passengers, probably spend only one or two days in any particular country and thus it is inconvenient for their customers to have to keep changing money. It is also expensive as the customer nearly always loses out when changing currencies because of the different rates offered for buying and selling foreign currencies. It is to the advantage of the traders in the various ports visited to accept a currency other than their own and, as the vast majority of the cruise passengers in the world are from the USA (in 1998, out of 6.5 million people taking a cruise holiday, 5 million were from the USA), it is the US dollar that has become the acceptable currency. The dollar has an added advantage that there is a small denomination note of US$1 which in January 2000 was roughly equivalent to £00.61 and at approximate parity with the euro. This makes it ideal for small purchases, tips etc. Often when a so-called hard currency (one that is acceptable for trading across a number of economies, e.g. the US dollar, the Canadian dollar, the Japanese yen, the pound sterling, the French franc, the Swiss franc, the Deutschmark etc.) is accepted by a retailer, change may well be given in local currency. It is usually only notes that are accepted and thus sterling, with its lowest denomination note being £5 followed by £10, £20 and £50 in common use, can be less flexible than the US dollar with $1, $2 (although they are rare), $5, $10, $20 and $50 bills, as notes are referred to in the USA. As a matter of interest, Scotland still produces £1 notes, as does the Channel Islands government. As part of the research for this book it was found that retailers in the following countries would happily accept dollars for payment: Barbados, St Lucia, Jamaica, Mexico, Brazil, The UK Virgin Islands, Russia, Ukraine, Romania, Bulgaria and Turkey. The government of the former USSR actually set up a chain of shops for tourists in which only hard currencies were acceptable, such shops refusing to accept their own currency, the rouble. Major commodities such as oil are routinely bought and sold using the dollar as a common currency for all.

## Standardisation

The currency we are all familiar with has evolved over time. One £10 note is of exactly the same value as another. In the days when currency was actually made out of precious metals this was not necessarily the case. Currency today is symbolic and with no intrinsic value *per se*. This was not always the case, as discussed earlier. In earlier times, some forms of currency were actually made out of precious metals and it was important that one gold piece was of identical weight and purity as another of the same equivalent value. This is not a problem today, as the coins and notes we use are purely symbolic.

## Durability

Anything that is used as a form of money needs a degree of durability. It would be useless if one person bought something from somebody, giving them a form of money that fell to pieces immediately. Money is only of use if the person receiving it can then use it at some time in the future. As is seen in archaeological excavations, coins can be remarkably resilient. Whilst coins cost more to produce than paper notes, they do have greater durability. It is interesting that the UK replaced the 10 shilling note with a coin followed by the £1 note (but not in Scotland and the Channel Islands, where they are still used but becoming rarer) and then introduced a £2 coin. As notes are still the only forms of currency accepted for exchange into foreign currency, they are likely to remain with us for some time especially as they are more easily transported (see next section).

Gold and similar precious materials tend to be highly durable. Sailors in previous eras used to convert their wages into gold which was then fashioned into earrings. This made their wages much more durable and also theft was made much more difficult!

## Transportability

In the cashless society where transactions are completed using credit cards and electronic transfer of funds (ETF), transportation of currency is less problematic than in the past. Nevertheless gold bars in central banks are still moved from one country's pile to that of another when necessary.

The heavier money is (and gold is a very heavy metal), the harder it is to carry around and thus to use for transactions. Paper is more convenient than coinage although, as discussed earlier, the former is more durable. Anecdotal evidence suggests that the sale of men's purses in the UK has increased as notes have been replaced by coins, the latter wearing out too many pockets!

## Denominations

Imagine paying for a purchase with a bar of gold. If the value of the purchase and the gold are the same, no problem. If they are not, you will require some change. An important facet of money is that, in order to be used in everyday transactions, it must be dividable into a series of denominations. The smallest such denomination, be it a US cent, a UK penny or a French centime, becomes the lowest price that can be charged for anything.

For many centuries this formed the basis of the currency systems. The development of computer systems, however, has led to the possibility of dealing with smaller amounts than the lowest currency denomination, a fact that can be important in commercial transactions. As money for commercial transactions is now nearly always transferred electronically instead of discrete notes and coins being transported, the small sub-denominational amounts can become important. The following example illustrates this.

A bank offers an interest rate of 6.25% on deposits. A person has £2503 on deposit. Simplified to a straightforward interest rate computation, the interest after one year will be:

£156.4375

As the lowest currency denomination in sterling is 1p, this means that the interest given must be £156.43 or £156.44, i.e. rounded up or rounded down. The sum would be rounded down leaving 0.0075p in the system. Not a great deal of money perhaps but, if the bank had 1 million customers all in this position, the 'free' amount of unallocated interest would be:

£7500

Over a banking day there may well be millions of transactions all leaving a very tiny non-allocable sum which can add up to a large amount indeed. There has been at least one recorded case (and probably many unrecorded cases) of fraud whereby a bank employee programmed a computer to collect these non-allocable amounts and place them in the fraudster's account. The logic is based on the fact that there are 50+ million people in the UK. If they all give you 1p, the majority will probably not miss it, indeed may not notice it. However you will be £500 000 better off! Banks are now well aware of this problem and are able to track even minute amounts of money in order to deter this type of fraud.

Hubbard (1997) gives an example of packets of Western cigarettes being used as currency by tourists in Eastern Europe during the collapse of the Communist system in the late 1980s and early 1990s. The author can verify this, having seen the practice in operation. A packet of cigarettes actually fulfilled all of the criteria above in that it was apparently acceptable to all the parties in the transaction, one packet was identical to another, the packets were durable provided the contents were not consumed, they were easily transportable and each packet could be broken down into twenty smaller units. There is a health danger in consuming this form of currency because of the dangers of smoking, but the author's experience in Romania in the early 1990s was that the cigarettes were rarely consumed but circulated throughout the country as an alternative form of money.

In the section on inflation later in the chapter, the point will be made that an economic system based on commodity money is much more inflation proof.

Inflation can occur when governments have the ability to print or coin extra currency that is not backed up by increased wealth. An increase in fiat money is not necessarily an increase in wealth; it is only so if the value of the fiat money actually increases.

## The money supply

Governments and economies are interested in how much money is actually in a particular economy. In accountancy, organisational assets are often prioritised using liquidity as a measure. Liquidity is an important component of measuring an organisation's ability to trade. A simple example can illustrate the importance of liquidity. You own your own house worth £90 000 including its contents. You have only £100 cash in your pocket and £500 in the bank. You will be paid your salary of £1800 after tax etc. at the end of the month. A builder requires you to pay £800 for work that has been completed. Despite the fact that your net worth at this moment in time is £90 600 you cannot in fact pay the bill as your liquid assets, i.e. those you can get your hands on immediately, are £200 short of what is required. The balance sheet for an organisation may show huge assets but the majority will not be 'liquid'. No organisation wishes to sell off its plant and buildings to meet debts, anymore than in the example above you would wish to sell your house to meet a small debt!

Such a test of how much of an organisation's assets are liquid is known as the 'acid test' and is basically a measure of how easily the organisation could meet all its commitments. Selling equipment or buildings takes time and thus such items are not included in the acid test.

A similar system is used when considering the supply of money within an economy:

- **M1** is the currency in circulation, including traveller's cheques and monies in banks which can be accessed on demand – normally money in current accounts giving zero or very low rates of interest
- **M2** is M1 plus savings deposits and money up to certain limits invested by individuals within the money markets
- **M3** is M1 plus M2 plus the monies invested by institutions in the money markets, examples of which include pension funds.

M1 is more liquid than M2, which in turn is more liquid than M3. There are also measurements designated M0, M4 and M5, details of which are included in economics' textbooks. M0, which is just the actual cash in circulation, replaced M1 as the main measure used by the government for regulating the money supply in 1983–84 (Browne, 1989).

Monetarist theory states that inflation (see later) is caused by too high a money supply. The basic equation is:

$$MV = PT \text{ or } PQ$$

where $M$ is the money supply, however measured, using M0 or M1 etc.

$V$ is the velocity of the money's circulation in the economy

*P* is the general level of prices

*T* is the number of transactions, or

*Q* is the quantity of goods and services produced.

Thus monetarists claim a direct link between money supply and the general level of prices; if the former is high, so will be the latter. Of course, if unemployment is high there is a justification for increasing the money supply, as this will stimulate demand for goods and services, which will in turn increase the demand for labour – provided the money is spent within the particular economy and not used to buy increased level of imports.

Both governments and organisations are interested in the money supply. Too much money freely available in the economy may fuel inflation and thus steps need to be taken to ensure that this is avoided. Money can be encouraged to be less freely available by encouraging saving, which can be accomplished by the government giving tax advantages to savers and by central banks increasing interest rates. As will be shown later in this chapter, whilst borrowers suffer when interest rates rise, savers benefit.

# Banks

To the average person in the street, banks are places where their money can be placed in a degree of safety. Banks act for the individual as a deposit, withdrawal, saving and loan service. In fact the major function of any commercial bank is to lend money. In order to have the funds available for loans, the banks have to attract monies in the form of deposits. Competition for these deposits has become very fierce.

There are three general types of banks within the UK:

- The central bank
- Commercial banks
- Merchant banks.

Included in the financial services market and operating in a similar manner to commercial banks are those building societies that have not converted into banks *per se*. Building societies, as their name implies, were a 20th Century device designed to facilitate home ownership. As they were not proper banks, they were originally limited to loans in connection with house purchases and associated savings. They were technically owned by the members of the society (the customers) and were often local in origin, although many grew to have a nation-wide branch network. From the 1970s onwards, the UK banks began to enter the mortgage market in a big way, providing additional competition to the building societies. Deregulation of the banking market under the Thatcher government post 1979 allowed building societies to convert into banks and offer a much wider range of services. The Abbey National and the Halifax, two of the biggest names in the UK building society sector, were quick to become banks and others have since followed, although the Nationwide Building Society resisted pressures in the late 1990s from a minority of members and remained a 'mutual' as the building societies are technically deemed. In terms of customer service, the building societies had one great advantage over the banks. The banks ceased Saturday morning opening in the 1960s and 1970s whilst the building societies continued to open on a Saturday morning, thus providing a service to customers who were out shopping. The 1990s have seen both the traditional and the new banks becoming much more competitive, with longer opening hours and the advent of home telephone and on-line banking.

In the USA, the building society role is carried out by Saving's and Loan Associations.

# The central bank

Every country has a central bank. In the UK this is the Bank of England (BoE), in Germany it is the Bundesbank and in the USA it is the Federal Reserve Bank.

One of the prime functions of a central bank is to issue currency. Thus the BoE is the main currency-issuer for the UK although, as noted earlier, banks in the Channel Islands, the Isle of Man and the Royal Bank of Scotland, the Bank of Scotland and the Clydesdale Bank also issue sterling currency. Such currency is, by agreement, accepted by the BoE as legal tender, although small retailers outwith the Channel Islands, the Isle of Man or Scotland may be reluctant to accept such currency and are, in fact, within their legal rights to refuse it.

The Bank of England was formed as a private concern as early as 1694, primarily with the purpose of raising money for the government. Until 1844 it was permissible for any bank to issue its own notes, but the Bank Charter Act of that year, whilst continuing to allow certain banks in Scotland, the Channel Islands and the Isle of Man to continue the issuing of their own notes, gave official currency-issuing powers to the BoE although other notes remained in circulation as late as 1921 (Browne, 1989).

The BoE is the government's bank and also the bank for the other commercial banks. The BoE also manages the national debt by trading in government stocks and bonds. A key function of the BoE is to issue the authorisation to operate to commercial banks, the BoE acting as the banking regulator, although there is also a banking ombudsman to deal with complaints from customers.

Until 1997 the level of the BoE's interest rate (MLR – Minimum Lending Rate) was set by the government through the Chancellor of the Exchequer. The limitation on the BoE in the setting of its own rates and thus in dependence on the government of the day was removed by Gordon Brown, the Labour government Chancellor of the Exchequer, and rates are now decided monthly by the Monetary Policy Committee of the BoE chaired by the Governor of the Bank. This committee takes advice from a wide variety of commercial and governmental sources before deciding any interest rate movements.

The BoE also acts as the lender of last resort to other banks and can intervene to assist an ailing bank. Whilst bank failures are fortunately few and far between,

BCCI and Barings in the UK and Penn Square and Franklin National in the USA being recent examples, the central banks have mechanisms in place to assist depositors in the unlikely event of a bank failure.

Internationally the BoE manages the UK's gold and currency reserves. Prior to 1979 when there were restrictions on the movement of sterling out of the UK, the BoE was responsible for enforcing these restrictions. As will be shown later when considering the implication of exchange rates on organisation decision-making, the BoE can and does intervene in the global currency markets to maintain (or attempt to maintain) the value of sterling against other currencies at a desirable level.

In the USA, the Federal Reserve carries out very similar functions to the Bank of England. The current Federal Reserve Bank was created in 1913 following the collapse of two earlier schemes. The issuing of currency in the USA is undertaken by the US Treasury Department, so that a unified currency system does not require a central bank. Like the BoE, the Fed, as it is known, manages the monetary policy of the USA. The system is more complex than that in the UK, comprising as it does twelve Federal Reserve districts each of which has a Federal Reserve Bank serving it. Those wishing to learn more about the operation of the US central banking system are recommended to consult Hubbard's (1997) excellent text which is listed in the recommended reading at the end of this chapter.

## Commercial banks

The commercial banks are those found on the vast majority of the high streets. In England and Wales, the major commercial banks are Barclays, Lloyds TSB, the Midland (part of the Hong Kong and Shanghai Group) and the National Westminster (acquired by the Royal Bank of Scotland in 2000). In Scotland, the Royal Bank of Scotland, the Bank of Scotland and the Clydesdale Bank (part of the same group as the Midland) are the major players.

Whilst Browne (1989) records that in 1987 there were over 350 listed banks in the UK, it is those listed above that have the vast majority of market share. The four major players in England (as listed above) are known as the London Clearing Banks because they administer the inter-bank clearing transactions.

The later 20th and early 21st Centuries saw the UK banks in England expanding into Scotland and those in Scotland moving into increased operations south of the border. The Royal Bank of Scotland had been involved in English banking through its involvement with various textile-related banks in the 1930s and finally brought Williams and Glyn's operation, headquartered in Manchester, under its own banner in the 1960s, becoming the first Scottish bank to operate an English branch network under its own name. In the late 1990s, Lloyds Bank acquired the Trustees Saving Bank which operated throughout the UK and the merged concern, Lloyds TSB, thus acquired a pan-UK network. In 2000 the Royal Bank of Scotland acquired National Westminster and with it a considerable share of the UK market.

The commercial banks take in deposits from individuals and corporate customers and lend to the same. Banks need to be regulated because of the huge quantities of their customers' assets that they hold, and the Bank of England undertakes this regulation. Banks also become involved with other projects such as insurance and even control of companies. They may also be involved in leasing agreements. Ships, aircraft and even jet engines may well be owned by a bank and leased back to the operator.

In the USA there are a large number of commercial banks (as there are in other developed countries) operating in the same way as those in the UK. Deregulation of banking in a number of countries has led to foreign banks acquiring interests in other domestic markets, a development that seems set to continue.

Commercial banks have become much more customer focused as competition has increased, and restrictive opening hours and officious attitudes are disappearing fast. The introduction of cash dispensers (ATMs – Automatic Teller Machines) allowed customers to withdraw cash at any time and now virtually every bank and building society throughout the developed world, both at their own facilities but also in supermarkets, shopping malls etc., offer this facility. This and other technological advances will be considered in Chapter 7. However there are other transactions that people need from their banks and, for those in work or in remote locations, contact with the bank during normal business hours can be difficult.

One method that the banks and building societies have used to solve this problem is the introduction of telephone call centres where information and certain transactions can be undertaken. Many such centres have extended access hours and indeed the trend is towards a 24-hour service. This provides the customer with greater time to contact their bank but at a further distance and with a less personal service.

The other method that is growing rapidly is the development of on-line banking, linking the customer's personal computer with the bank. The first UK bank to introduce such a service was the Bank of Scotland which offered its HOBS (Home and Office Banking Service) to selected customers from 1993 (Winder, 1999). This system required a special modem which, whilst quite revolutionary for the time, would seem very slow today. Working through the DOS system which was the standard operating system pre WINDOWS and the other more sophisticated systems which now sit on top of DOS, HOBS basically allowed customers to check their balances, a facility not available on the ATMs of the time, but commonplace today.

Modern on-line banking (Winder, above, lists eight UK on-line banking-providers in 1999 together with reviews of their services) allows, in most cases, for customers not only to check their balance but to print out statements, pay bills, transfer monies between accounts and to download data using other types of software, e.g. accounts packages. In 1999 in the UK, the Bank of Scotland and First Direct allowed the customer to apply for an overdraft on-line and there is no doubt that other providers are likely to follow suit. Charges in 2000 for home banking were zero or minimal, and competitive forces are likely to ensure that any fees remain relatively low given the convenience that such a system offers.

The advantages to the banks are self-evident. Branches cost money . terms of staff and premises; on-line banking costs far less. The custome. able to conduct the vast majority of day-to-day transactions at his or her convenience. The personal touch is, of course, lost and it remains problematic as to whether the branch network will completely disappear. The trend throughout the 1990s has been for mergers between banks, for building societies to convert to banks and for branch networks to be cut. Provided that there is a human available for those transactions that are not day-to-day but require discussion and negotiation, then the future of on-line banking seems set to grow.

Organisations usually have a very close relationship with their bank and modern technology allows this relationship to be even closer. Most organisations rely on their bank for loans at some time or other, indeed large organisations may well have senior members of their bank as board members, and there are times when the bank will insist on this.

Commercial banks lend not only to individuals and organisations but also to countries. There were major moves as the 20th Century became the 21st to wipe out the huge amounts of international third world debt. It was becoming apparent that many borrower countries were having trouble re-paying even the interest on their loans and that repayment of the capital would be an impossibility. The money for interest repayment was being taken from social spending and the argument of those advocating the wiping off of these debts centred around the need for social spending in these countries to increase in order to raise general prosperity. In accountancy terms, a debt actually remains as an asset to the lender even if not repaid and thus improves the balance sheet position. Wiping it off has a negative effect on the bank's balance sheet.

Large commercial loans will usually be underwritten by a consortium of banks, often international in composition. Thus when Douglas Aircraft experienced severe financial difficulties in 1966, there were a large number of US banks involved including Bank of America (San Francisco), Security First National Bank, First National City, Morgan Guaranty, Chase Manhattan, Mellon National and Continental Illinois. Thus it was a consortium of bankers that confronted the company management in October 1966 with demands that the company undertook urgent and immediate action (Eddy *et al.*, 1976). The result of their demands was the take-over of Douglas by McDonnell Aircraft to form the McDonnell Douglas Company early in 1967. To accomplish a rescue and thus secure the future of the monies they had invested, the banks also had to work with the US government whose Justice Department was concerned at the monopoly or near monopoly implications of such a merger. Thus are the close interrelationships between large organisations and their banks manifested.

The more money an organisation has borrowed from its bankers, the more say the bankers will have in the future direction of that company. As Eddy *et al.* (1976) point out, some of the banks involved with Douglas wanted to call in their loans immediately and force the company into bankruptcy if necessary. Others took the view that a rescue would allow for continued long-term business. As a matter

assenger aircraft manufacturing market became so competi-
that McDonnell Douglas eventually became part of Boeing, in
the success of Airbus Industrie, a European consortium. The
tween Boeing and Airbus has been well profiled by Lynn (1995),
gives a revealing insight into the world of global business and the
ncial institutions.

## Merchant banks

Before the development of the joint stock companies in the 17th Century, most
large commercial ventures were undertaken in a one-off mode. For instance, a
ship would be acquired, a crew taken on and then sent off to trade. On returning
from, say, the East with a cargo of silk, the crew would be paid off and the ship
sold. The profits would be disbursed among those who had financed the venture.
A series of banks grew up which had the funding of such ventures as their main
function. The merchant banks of today do not deal with public deposits but exist
to fund commercial enterprises.

## Economic indicators

The key economic indicators of immediate concern for organisations when
planning their development are:

- Interest rates
- Exchange rates
- Inflation
- Investment.

## Interest rates

The repayment of loans to both individuals and organisations comprises (with
the exception of certain strict Muslim economies where interest is against Islamic
law) the repayment of the capital sum borrowed and an additional amount
known as interest. Interest represents the earnings made by the lender and the
payment for the tying up of the capital.

The minimum level of interest charged is normally that of the base rate of
the relevant central bank. This rate is normally set by the central bank or the
government as part of the control of monetary policy.

The higher the interest rate, the less individuals and organisations will wish
to borrow and the more they will want to save. Thus money will effectively be
taken out of the economy and tied up in savings. It is not surprising that there
is always a wish to save at the highest possible interest rate and to borrow at
the lowest. In order for banks and other financial institutions to make a profit,

it is self-evident that they must lend at a higher rate than they pay to savers. In effect, banks take in money from savers on which they will pay interest and then lend it at a higher rate to somebody else, the bank receiving the difference.

Other bodies may well make short-term loans. Local authorities may have a surplus of cash from council tax collections available overnight and over the weekend, and this may well be lent on the international money markets. Whilst individuals may not need huge quantities of money for a short period, the method of payment used for large items of equipment such as aircraft or ships often necessitates a large short-term loan. Such loans normally receive a higher rate of interest than could be accrued by just leaving the money in the bank. In general terms, the higher the risk of non-repayment or the shorter the loan repayment period, the higher the interest that can be demanded. It costs far less, in interest rate terms, for a person to buy their house on a 25-year mortgage than it would to borrow the same amount over a series of shorter time periods. Even if repayment is not made, the fact that the collateral for the mortgage is the house itself means that this can always be re-possessed by the mortgage lender and sold to repay the capital. There were considerable problems in the UK in the 1980s and 1990s because some mortgage lenders had lent money to cover 100% of the value of the properties and were then faced with a falling house price market. This meant that borrowers had negative equity in their property. If a property on purchase was valued at £90 000 and the purchaser had borrowed £75 000, they would still have £15 000 of equity. If the house value increased over the years to £100 000, they would have £25 000 of positive equity. However, if the value dropped to £80 000 and they had in fact borrowed the full £90 000 and they could not repay the mortgage lender because they could no longer afford the repayments, there would be £10 000 of negative equity. In this case, even by selling the property the lender could not recoup the full amount of the loan.

In considering the interest rate at any point in time, cognisance must be given to the real as opposed to the nominal interest rate. The real interest rate is the stated (nominal rate) less the anticipated inflation. Lenders suffer from this, as the interest they receive will actually be worth less because of inflation. Fisher, as quoted in Hubbard (1997), believed that there was a direct linear relationship between nominal interest rates and inflation; they rise and fall point for point together. Whilst there does not, in practice, appear to be a one-for-one correlation, there is a general trend that supports this belief. The Bank of England uses interest rates as the main weapon in the UK's fight against inflation.

The effect of interest rates on exchange rates is discussed in the next section.

## Exchange rates

As stated earlier, no major economies operate in a closed system. It may be that simple closed economies operate deep within the world's rain forests, but in the main economies trade with each other.

It is obviously better for any single economy that it sells as much as possible outside the economy and thus money flows in rather than importing goods from outside which then have to be paid for. The relationship between the level of imports and that of exports is known as the *balance of payments*. The imbalance is critical. Too many imports and too few exports and the economy will have trouble earning its way. The other way around can lead to actions against the economy and tariff wars. Following World War II and its immediate aftermath, Japan became a major exporter of vehicles and fast-moving consumer goods (televisions, hi-fi equipment etc.) whilst placing considerable barriers on imports, often using quality standards as the mechanism. Japan's positive balance of trade led others to adopt strict controls on Japanese manufactured goods by introducing tariff barriers against them.

Large organisations may well be lenders to the international money markets and may well keep some of their assets in foreign holdings.

As more and more governments have relaxed exchange controls, it has been easier to buy and sell foreign currencies. Fortunes have been made (and lost) in trading on the foreign exchange markets and in trying to anticipate movements of one currency against another.

For many individuals, their main interface with the currency markets comes from foreign holidays. Even the most unobservant foreign traveller cannot fail to note that on a certain day one can receive $1.65 for £1.00 and on the next £1.61; exchange rates fluctuate.

Business needs to be very interested in the exchange rate. Even a country as apparently self-sufficient as the USA purchased 12% of all goods and services from foreign organisations in 1995 (Hubbard, 1997). Whenever a UK consumer buys a French product, two factors have to be taken into consideration. Firstly there is the price in francs of the item and secondly how many pounds sterling have had to be used to buy that number of francs. A currency appreciates when its value rises against another currency and depreciates when it falls. It is perfectly possible for the pound to appreciate against the Mark and depreciate against the dollar; it depends on the value of the dollar against the Mark. An appreciating pound against the dollar (a strong pound) means that goods and services produced in the UK will become more expensive in the USA, although it also means that foreign currency will be coming into the UK as foreigners buy sterling, so pushing its value up.

High interest rates in an economy attract foreign currency, as investors will wish to place their money where it can earn the most. If rates fall quickly, so the same people will wish to transfer their money into a higher interest rate regime. They are not interested in the financial well-being of an individual economy, only in having money where its earning power will be maximised. Statistics throughout the 1980s and 1990s suggested that whenever interest rates rise, the relative value of a currency does the same and vice versa.

In addition to investment there are those who speculate in the currency markets, buying a currency in anticipation of its value rising.

# Currency unions

In a global economy it is doubtful if any government and by definition its currency are truly sovereign and independent. The nations of the Eastern Caribbean share a common currency but its exchange rate is heavily pegged to that of the US dollar.

In Europe (see the previous chapter) there has been a gradual move towards a common European currency, the euro. Beginning with the concept of a European currency unit (ecu) for internal trading, the euro as a common currency running alongside national currencies but intended, eventually, to supplant them is now in operation in a number of member states, including France and Germany. Britain has adopted a wait-and-see philosophy before becoming part of the euro zone. Given that the value of a currency depends upon exchange and interest rates, it is important that countries entering a currency unit have economies that have converged. Part of the British argument has been that the sovereignty of Parliament to decide economic policy will be lost if Britain joins the eurozone. The adoption of the euro has necessitated the setting up of a European Central Bank to set interest rates for eurozone members, and thus this part of fiscal policy-making must be shared among the members. Part of the argument is also that currency union inevitably (according to its critics) leads to political union and a total loss of sovereignty.

# Inflation

According to the best-selling novelist Arthur Hailey (1975), the first recorded instance of inflation occurred in the 13th Century when the Mongol emperor, Kublai Khan, was unable to pay his troops in coin and therefore set up a printing system to produce 'military money'. Unfortunately, so much was produced that the currency quickly became worthless. Changes in the value of money affect its usefulness as a means of transaction. If the value of an economy's money falls, then individuals and organisations become increasingly reluctant to use it, preferring instead either a system of barter or to carry out transactions using a more stable form of money – for many, this is the US dollar. Inflation rates of over 50% are known as hyperinflation. In a case of hyperinflation, the value of money can decline dramatically over weeks or even days. In Germany, during the 1920s, the purchasing power of the Mark declined rapidly so that hundreds of thousands of Marks were required even for simple purchases such as bread etc. In 1989, Argentina suffered inflation running at 12000% per annum (Hubbard, 1997).

As mentioned in the previous section, there is a relationship between interest rates and inflation. In the UK, a 9% interest rate would be perceived as high but if inflation were 7%, the real interest rate would only be 2%, and quite acceptable.

Control of inflation and the price stability it brings are major political aims. Inflation not only has economic effects but it can lead to social unrest, especially when the price of basic necessities rises rapidly. This leads firstly to demands for increased wages and if these are met, the spiral is likely to cause a further rise in prices – spiralling inflation. Eventually this can cause public discontentment and in politically unstable environments the possible violent overthrow of the government.

## What causes inflation?

In the USA, a relatively stable economy, consumer prices rose from 1939 to 1995 by 950% (Hubbard, 1997). One is quite used to grandparents recounting tales of what they could buy for a pound sterling in their youth compared to what it costs for a similar item today. In 1970, UK petrol was approximately 30p per gallon, by 1999 a gallon (4.5 litres) cost on average £3.35. Part of the increase is due to the government's attempts to reduce vehicle emissions by use of the fuel price escalator, but the figures illustrate how the price has risen over time. Fortunately for those in the UK (and other developed countries), incomes have also risen. According to the UK National Office of Statistics, retail prices (with 1987 = 100) in the UK rose from 74.8 to 157.5, just over a doubling, whilst average annual earnings rose from £6500 to nearly £20 000, i.e. virtually tripling. This would suggest that those in the UK are becoming better off, because a tripling of income but only a doubling of prices provides additional disposable income.

For much of recorded history, prices remained relatively stable; major increases only became an economic problem leading to inflation when it became possible for economies to increase the money supply by printing more notes or producing more coins made from base metals and thus having less intrinsic value (see earlier). As markets become more global and commerce depends more and more on oil as a major resource, a sudden increase in the price of a raw material (especially oil) in one part of the world can lead to a price increase in another. Indeed the price of oil is also a political weapon, being used to manipulate the policies of governments in non-economic areas such as foreign relations.

Such increases would not of themselves lead to inflation which is a sustained upward rate of change in prices. Most economists attribute inflation to a sustained growth in the supply of money, a growth that is higher than any change in the velocity of money within the economy.

Socially and politically, in recent times people have wanted to improve their position. The social revolutions from the 18th Century onward were rooted in a belief that poverty need not be tolerated and that it was possible for people's aspirations to be met. The idea of the 'rich man in his castle and the poor man at his gate' as an unchanging law of society was still around in early 20th Century Britain.

As success in modern life is often measured by financial status, wage demands not only meet the need for the purchase of essentials but are also concerned with such issues as maintaining differentials. One of the ideals of the early Communists in the Soviet Union was that all workers would be paid equal amounts. In fact such concepts were socially and politically unacceptable.

As pointed out earlier, unless money is actually backed by some form of tangible wealth its value can be illusionary. If a 5% wage increase leads to a 5%

increase in prices through the increased costs of production following the wage increases, then nobody is actually any better off. Because of human nature, when inflation decreases the value of money the natural instinct is to acquire more money, whereas rationally the supply of money should be restricted. Restricting the money supply is however nearly always politically unwelcome.

Interest rates are the main method used by governments to control inflation. Increasing interest rates cuts spending. As more and more spending by individuals is financed through credit, then increasing the interest rate also makes the amount of interest to be paid undesirable. If consumption falls then so, economic theory suggests, will prices. Additionally, higher interest rates will encourage saving and increasing amounts of money tied up in savings will effectively reduce the supply of money circulating within the economy. Unfortunately, as stated earlier, higher interest rates also increase the strength of a currency in the international money markets, thus making imports cheaper and exports more expensive. As governments prefer to export rather than to import, as this leads to a decrease in the balance of payments, interest rate rises to control inflation can be a double-edged sword.

## Investment

A large number of private sector organisations, with the exception of small businesses and partnerships, are owned by groups of shareholders. There are some large organisations that are owned by just a small number of people, often from the same family, but the vast majority of organisations with plc (or Ltd), Inc, SA or GmbH after the company name, depending on whether they are British, American, French or German, are owned by groups of shareholders. These shareholders may be individuals or they may be other organisations including financial institutions.

Individuals and organisations invest in companies in order to have money working for them. If they invest, it is in the anticipation that they will receive a return over and above that which they could have received from the same money placed in normal saving's accounts.

In the UK (similar rules applying elsewhere) a publicly limited company (a plc) must exist within a strict legal framework. The company has an identity that is entirely separate from that of its owners (the shareholders), who have only a limited liability for any debts or malpractices of the company. The shareholders liability for debts is limited to the nominal value of their shares in the company. Whilst there are individuals who have an ownership interest in a particular company because of some form of special relationship with the company, the vast majority of shareholders hold a portfolio of shares, often managed by their stockbroker. Although the number of shareholders in the UK increased dramatically in the 1980s and 1990s as the government privatised the majority of public utilities, gas, electric, British Airways, British Telecom etc., with in most cases special allocations of shares for small investors, in fact a large number of Britons are shareholders even if they are unaware of the fact, because of the huge shareholdings of pension funds. Pension funds are only able to make the payments that they do because they invest the premiums collected in a constantly changing portfolio of companies. This practice has led to criticisms of short-termism. The pension fund is only interested in the return on its investment over the short-to-medium term and less in the long-term viability of the company; thus, if the company suffers a short-term reverse there is the danger that the fund will sell its existing shares and buy shares in another company.

Shares are used to measure the worth of a company. They represent the price somebody is prepared to pay to be a part owner of that company. If the share price in a particular company drops from £5 to £4, it is because ownership is seen as less attractive; similarly, a rise in the share price indicates that ownership has become more attractive. Thus when a lucrative take-over appears in prospect, investors may wish to buy in the hope that ownership will appear more attractive, the value of their holding will increase and they will be able to sell at a profit; in this case, demand is likely to exceed supply and the share price will rise. If a company appears to be in difficulties, current investors may wish to sell and minimise any losses. Supply will exceed demand and prices will fall.

Shares can fall (or rise) not only because of company-specific issues but also as a result of general confidence. If a particular sector looks set for a difficult time, shares in all companies in that sector may fall. If investors become concerned at the general direction of a country's economy, then a large number of companies operating in that economy may see their share price fall as investment is transferred to other, more attractive economies.

Shares were originally traded in coffee houses but today most capital cities operate a stock market system using sophisticated computer technology. The main shares traded form the 'popular' stock market measures such as the Dow–Jones in the USA, the Nikkei in Japan and the Footsie (the *Financial Times* Index) in the UK. The prices of the shares that make up the index are tracked and published and it is these results that indicate a general rise or fall in the markets. When it is announced that so many millions were wiped off the stock market, this does not mean that money has disappeared. It simply means that confidence in the shares making up the index for that market had dipped and that investors had switched either to other markets or into commodities, government bonds etc.

When take-overs are in process, companies under attack will normally wish their shares to be at a high value, as this will reflect the cost to the company seeking to acquire them, indeed it may put the predator off. Shares are likely to rise anyway in this situation, as many investors will wish to buy at one level in the hope that the offer will have to be increased and they can then sell at a profit.

Investors gain income from the stock market in two main ways. Firstly, they will hope to receive a dividend, which represents their share, as owners, of any profits made by the company. Secondly, they may wish to sell their shareholding at a profit to themselves. Dividends provide income; selling shares can provide a capital gain but is subject to tax.

Companies will wish to invest any profits paid after dividends etc. in other companies, and thus many are major buyers and sellers in the stock markets. The main players, however, remain financial institutions, especially pension funds who need to generate the money to pay out to those who have put their retirement funds into their care.

Governments and those responsible for the financial sector need to have regulations in place to control stock market activities. Insider trading, that is the use of knowledge gained as a result of knowledge of a company not available to outside investors in order to make personal gains, is a criminal offence in most jurisdictions. Following the partial deregulation of the markets in the 1990s, there have been a number of high-profile insider-dealing cases. These have often centred around somebody within a company or associated with it gaining advance knowledge of a development and then using that knowledge to buy (or sell) shares, hoping to either profit or to minimise a loss. As buying often stimulates buying from others, this can artificially inflate the value of a company in the short-term. The miscreant can then sell at a much higher price and pocket the difference. Not only is this considered a financial offence but unless such activities are checked, confidence in the stock market system can diminish, which has ramifications far beyond the original company or companies involved. There is usually a government department, in the UK it is the Department of Trade and Industry (DTI) and in the USA the Securities and Exchange Commission (SEC), who undertake this role when self-regulation fails.

For a fuller explanation of the share system you are advised to read the latest edition of *How the Stock Markets Work* by Colin Chapman, published by Century (2000).

## Summary

Economies have become increasing global and thus operate in a far more open environment than in previous eras. Fiscal policy is a government function, although there has been an increasing trend for central banks to be some-what independent of direct government control. Supply and demand is a key economic concept, having implications for matters as diverse as the price of goods in shops to the value of a particular currency against other currencies. Money is the major means of transactions but it needs to be remembered that money in itself, as used in the world, has no intrinsic value but only the value that users agree to place on it, including the importance of the money supply and the effects and causes of inflation. The chapter described what constitutes money in the sense that the word is in current use. The chapter continued by looking at the role of banks, exchange rates, interest rates and, briefly, the role of the stock markets.

## Analysis

In carrying out the *economic* analysis in respect of an organisation, the following need to be considered:

1. What is the financial position of the organisation in respect of assets, worth and liquidity?
2. What is the effect of exchange and interest rates changes on the organisation?
3. How does the organisation invest its excess monies?

## Concepts covered

- Supply and demand
- Closed and open systems
- Money
- Money supply
- Banking
- Economic indicators
- Interest rates
- Exchange rates
- Currency union
- Inflation
- Investment

QUESTIONS

1. Why is it important that all organisations take an interest in the exchange rates, even if they do not trade outwith their own economy?
2. Illustrate the link between interest rates, inflation and unemployment. How can these impact upon an individual organisation?
3. Explain what is meant by *money*. What characterises money and how is it used to facilitate transactions? Why is money more useful than more tangible commodities?

## Further reading

You are recommended to read *Money, the Financial System and the Economy* by R. G. Hubbard (1997), and *How the Stock Markets Work* (2000) by Colin Chapman, in order to further your knowledge of economics and the financial markets.

# ☒ 6 Cultural analysis

*What is culture? – Cultural transmission – Organisational cultures – Culture clashes – Cultural change – Cultural web – Regional and national cultures and their implications for business – Far Eastern culture*

## What is culture?

Although the word 'culture' is often used to mean different things, in organisational terms a simple definition is:

### The way things are done around here

From this definition, which is also useful for national cultures, it can be discerned that there may well be different ways of doing the same thing. It is important to note that in many cases a particular way is not better than that chosen by another organisation or even a national group – it is just different. Different does not imply a judgement, it is a pure statement of fact. In the USA, manslaughter often carries a twenty-year prison sentence; in the UK, this may be much less. No one has the right to say that the USA is right and the UK wrong or vice versa. They are different and have adopted different procedures and laws to suit their national cultures. The USA and the UK are often compared because in many instances the cultural roots are the same, and Britons and Americans think and act very similarly much of the time, although there are some major cultural differences.

Many of the world's problems stem from a misunderstanding by one culture of another and the belief that one's own culture is best.

Culture is something that develops over long periods of time and is transmitted from one generation to the next. In the context of national cultures this is done from parents to children and through the education system. Organisational culture is transmitted from longer-serving staff to new employees and via corporate events, publications etc. The *cultural web* developed by Johnson & Scholes (1993) and covered in a later section of this chapter is an important vehicle for the transmission of organisational culture.

This chapter is divided into a series of sections that consider organisational culture, building on the content of Chapter 2, national culture and its implications for organisations working on a supra-national basis, and the importance of popular culture.

# Cultural transmission

Whatever the type of culture, organisational, national, youth, popular etc., there needs to be a means of transmission. In researching ideas of culture for this book it has become clear that culture evolves in a similar manner to species evolution. The pattern for the young of a species is carried as genes attached to the chromosomes found in each cell. In asexual reproduction, each new organism is formed by a straightforward division of the cells of the parent and is thus a copy of that parent. This form of reproduction is used by many single-cell organisms (and also in cloning techniques) but does not allow for any differences other than those caused by accidental mutation. In sexual reproduction, the new individual receives half of its genetic code from one parent and half from the other. This combination of genes means that the new individual will be genetically unique (except in the case of identical twins, triplets etc.) and whilst it may have many of the characteristics of its parents, it will not be a 100% copy. Sexual reproduction encourages genetic variation and is the main method of reproduction for most living organisms. Over millions of years, the subtle changes to each generation may produce a completely new species. Darwin's concept of the 'survival of the fittest' was that those changes which confer a competitive advantage on a species (this may be connected with speed, vision, types of food eaten etc.) are likely to be perpetuated over successive generations, whilst those individuals possessing disadvantageous characteristics will be less successful and will eventually die out.

Could it be that similar systems are involved in organisational evolution? When organisations merge, it can be akin to a form of sexual reproduction. Cultural genetic material from the merging organisations is combined to form a new organisation. If one of the merging organisations is much bigger and stronger then the new organisation may be more in its image, but if the two organisations are of equal strength then the new organisation will hopefully have the best from each of them as part of its organisational genes. The human genome project is currently working on plotting the position and function of human genes on the chromosomes, and concepts from genetics may provide useful information on how organisations evolve, merge and grow.

# Organisational culture

Organisational culture is both an internal and an external factor and was thus considered first in Chapter 2 and is now re-introduced in this chapter. You should make sure that you are familiar with the concepts of the Role, Task, Existential and Power/Club cultures introduced in Chapter 2 in order to understand the importance of possible clashes between organisational cultures considered later.

As mentioned in Chapter 2, it is not difficult to imagine the frustration that a Role culture might experience if it becomes the customer of an Existential supplier; the former's rules may well be alien to the latter. One can look at the possibilities of a whole range of combinations.

# Culture clashes both within and between organisations

It is perfectly possible for there to be different cultures operating within the same organisation. The accounts department may resemble a Role culture whilst research and development may operate in a more Task-focused manner. Nevertheless, especially within the same organisation, it is important that the cultures 'get on with each other' and this requires a knowledge of organisational culture from staff. Those working within another cultural form within an organisation may have difficulty dealing with the bureaucracy of a Role culture, whilst those in a Role culture may tear their hair out at the lack of procedures in a part of the organisation with an Existentialist format. However, at least if they understand each other, they can make allowances for differences in behaviour.

It may well be that huge organisations actually have divisions or controlled subsidiaries that operate to different cultural norms and, here again, understanding is the key to effective co-operation.

Every organisation has to deal with those outwith its own boundaries, indeed it is these relationships which form the foundation of this book. Whilst the organisation may be able to control the cultural behaviour within itself to a degree, that of outside organisations may be completely beyond its control.

Again, knowledge and a willingness to work together to overcome any cultural differences for mutual benefit are required. It is a truism throughout humanity that however different we are, our similarities are normally much greater, and this is also true of organisations. A willingness by all concerned to bend a little works wonders.

# Cultural change

It was stated earlier that there is a generational aspect to culture. This being the case, cultural change is also often generational. It is easy for the senior management to announce that they wish the culture to change, much less easy to achieve it in anything other than the long-term. Values, attitudes and beliefs, be they personal, national or organisational, are deeply held – indeed wars are often fought over them and people may be willing to lay down their lives for them, so they can be changed only gradually, hence the concept of generational change.

# Cultural web

In their excellent study of strategy that is recommended reading at the end of this chapter, Johnson & Scholes (1993) developed the concept of the cultural web (Figure 6.1) to show the various 'ingredients' that served to define the culture of an organisation. Indeed the model can be extended into national culture as well.

We will consider each of the ingredients in turn.

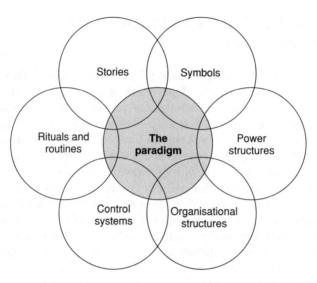

*Figure 6.1    The cultural web* (after Johnson & Scholes, 1993).

## Symbols

Symbols have always been very important to human behaviour. They may be tangible, such as trademarks (important assets to modern organisations), or they may form part of the Organisational Body Language (Cartwright & Green, 1997; Cartwright, 2000) to be covered in Chapter 8. Much money is spent on logos, designed to send out a positive message about an organisation. It may be that reality does not accord with desire. At least one organisation has put out a message about how all staff are considered equal and yet the uniforms worn by staff clearly acted as separators. Janitorial staff wore brown coats, manual staff blue, technical staff white, whilst managers and administrators wore their ordinary clothing. A glance in the organisation's canteen at lunchtime would show clearly grouped people in brown, blue, white or no coats. White coats were occasionally mixed in with the managers and administrators but elsewhere the canteen was remarkable for being monochromatic!

Shipping companies, airlines, rail franchises and even lorry companies are very concerned to ensure that their logo is displayed prominently. Aircraft tailfins are an ideal medium for this and there was a degree of outcry in the middle to late 1990s when British Airways abandoned their traditional corporate tailfin for designs produced to display the ethnic diversity of the countries and regions served by the company, Many Britons were upset at what they perceived as an affront to national pride. Modern ships do not need huge funnels but they are still designed with them as they provide a useful area on which to place the company logo.

As Cartwright & Baird (1999) have pointed out, from a marketing point of view, customers in the 1890s and early 1900s appear to have equated speed with the number of funnels. A German company of the time made great advertising play on the four funnels of their ships whilst the aftermost funnels of many vessels were actually dummies, being there for aesthetic reasons. In 1902 the Russians had a five-funnel cruiser, the *Askold*, which made a great impression on the inhabitants of the Persian Gulf. The Captain of *HMS Amphirite* actually rigged up two dummy canvas and wood funnels and had smoke fed to them in a feat of national one-upmanship (Trotter, 1975).

When the *Disney Magic* cruise ship was introduced in 1998 by the Disney Corporation, she was the first two-funnelled vessel since *France* (now *Norway*), and even her aftermost funnel was non-functional and indeed included public rooms. She also had a larger-than-life painting of Goofy overhanging her stern!

Funnels have always been an important design component of passenger ships. Originally there to take away the smoke caused by coal-burning boilers, they have survived into the present day with a slightly changed role. Many ships still use the funnel to carry away the diesel exhaust from the ship, and the height of the funnel means that fumes are carried well away from passengers. However, funnels are things we equate with ships (as a child's drawing often shows) and thus even when separate exhausts are provided, there is still a midship funnel carrying the corporate logo.

From the very early days of steam, as soon as heat-resistant paints (black was the best colour originally) were developed, ship owners have painted their ship's funnels in a distinctive house style. Red and black was often used – Cunard, French Line, United States Lines, Union Castle – whilst P&O funnels were always yellow. Nowadays funnels provide an ideal platform on which to place a company logo and in a 1970s development a lounge. The Viking Lounges of Norwegian Cruise Lines were distinctive trademarks as well as providing a unique viewing point for passengers. When ships were sold, the lounges were, in all but one case, removed, so distinctive of the company were they.

Organisations go to great lengths to protect their symbols, taking legal action if they believe that somebody has infringed their copyright. Even if a toy manufacturer wants to make a model of a railway engine, ship, aircraft or motor vehicle, permission to use a particular livery has to be agreed.

## Power structures

Different organisational cultures have very different power structures. An organisation may be very centralised or it may give considerable latitude to branches and subsidiaries. It can be difficult for an organisation which concentrates all power at the centre to deal effectively with one that empowers more junior parts of the organisation. Understanding the culture of those you are dealing with is again all-important.

Much knowledge can be gained by examining the structure charts of an organisation but the formal declarations of power may not always accord with reality. Hi-tech organisations may find that power, through technical expertise, can often reside much lower down in the organisation than might be deduced from an official structure chart.

## Organisational structure

Linked to the power structures above, much information about an organisation can be gained from a study of how it is organised.

The extent to which subsidiaries are allowed to develop their own identities and brands may give vital clues about the prevailing culture. If they are tightly controlled from the centre then it may well be that the majority of decisions are also made there.

Peters & Waterman (1982) described the concept of 'simultaneous loose–tight properties' where effective organisations kept certain operations, often financial decision-making, closely controlled at the centre whilst empowering other parts of the organisation to within corporate guidelines.

## Controls

In control terms, organisations may be described as operating somewhere along a blame–risk acceptance culture.

In a blame culture, managers often seem to spend much of their time trying to catch people out, whereas at the other end of the continuum they are looking to catch people in. Another method of describing the continuum is one that stretches from punishment centred to reward based. Employees in a blame culture are unlikely to take risks, as failure means punishment. Peters & Waterman, as cited earlier, believed that successful organisations should encourage a degree of controlled risk-taking, provided that the risks were not too great and that lessons were learnt from failure. It is only in such a culture that true, groundbreaking progress can be made.

## Rituals and routines

Anybody who has served in the armed forces or similar organisations will know the important cultural role of rituals. They are part of the symbolism discussed earlier.

Rituals such as the UK spectacle of Trooping the Colour were once important parts of military life in a time when recognising one's regimental flag might mean the difference between life and death. Modern armies operate on much different lines yet the ritual has been preserved. Such rituals can mean a great deal to those who are directly involved with them. Even if the original significance is only faintly understood, the ritual can serve as an important mechanism for strengthening the bonds between members of a culture.

Ritual is just as important in national cultures. Outsiders often fail to understand the important bonding nature of national rituals and may pour scorn on them. Every society has its own rituals and part of their importance is that they mean something to that society, in effect they serve to set it apart from other societies. Routines are less important rituals and, like the latter, they often persist far longer than the original need.

Any organisation working with another needs to recognise the importance of respecting the rituals and routines, however strange they may appear, as they form part of the cultural heritage of the organisation and any attack or disrespect on an aspect of cultural heritage usually meets with a very strong reaction.

## Stories

Studies of childhood and education plus those of societies without a written tradition have shown how important stories are to human development. Like rituals etc., stories can seek to bind together members of a particular culture. Cultures that have diverged, e.g. the UK and the USA, still have very similar fairy stories etc.

Jokes are a sub-set of stories. Many jokes have a cultural root and all too many are disparaging about another culture, with possible dire consequences, a point that will be returned to in the section on national culture.

Whether organisational stories are true or not does not matter. They often act as an easy-to-remember, anecdotal means of passing on the values of the organisation. Many organisations have a fund of stories about the founder, many with just the bare foundation of truth. Over time, stories become embellished to suit the teller. Davie (1986) and Gardiner & Van der Vat (1995) have listed some of the stories that came out of the *Titanic* disaster in 1912. Despite there being over 700 survivors, all of whom had a similar experience, at least one said that their ship had been in ice all day, others saw no ice, some said there was panic, others praised the sense of calm etc. Stories become changed and embellished by the teller each time a story is repeated, and also twisted by those who tell the story second and third hand. The 1990s Oscar winning film *Titanic* actually showed one officer committing suicide, to the distress of his descendants as no such incident was reported at the time – poetic licence in the telling perhaps, but distressing nevertheless.

The cultural web is an important concept as it allows organisations etc. to be examined from a different perspective from that of formal structure charts and documents, but to do so it is necessary to probe beneath the public face of the organisation and talk to those who are intimately involved with it.

It cannot be stressed too strongly that it is important to study the culture of any organisation one is dealing with, as it is the culture that will be a main determinate in how the organisation will behave in particular circumstances. Forearmed is forewarned, as the saying goes, and it makes good business sense to be able to make an accurate prediction of how another organisation, be it a stakeholder, a competitor or a customer, will behave.

## Popular culture

Popular culture is often those cultural trends that diverge from the prevailing culture, e.g. the so-called youth culture.

Whilst popular culture is an ever-changing phenomenon, it is becoming a degree more global with the increasing growth of ICT and television. The areas that organisations need to consider when analysing the impact, if any, of popular culture include:

- Language
- Music
- Literature
- Fashion
- Spirituality
- Leisure.

The language organisations use, the music played on the premises or in their advertisements etc. all form part of the concept of Organisational Body Language to be covered in Chapter 8. From a cultural point of view it is important that those aspects of popular culture adopted by customers are reflected in some way by the organisation. An old-fashioned organisation may not appeal to younger customers unless it goes some way towards appearing to recognise and respect their culture.

Popular culture may be transitory, as witnessed by the short life cycle of many fashions, but it is important to its adherents for as long at it lasts, and therefore needs to be part of the analysis of the external environment.

## National culture

When Fons Trompenaars published *Riding the Waves of Culture* in 1993 he produced, what in the opinion of this author, was one of the most influential texts of the late 20th Century. In 2000, R. D. Lewis published *When Cultures Collide*. Both texts are recommended reading to support this chapter.

As the world, especially the world of business, becomes smaller through improved communications, so paradoxically does the importance of understanding cultural diversity become more important. As covered earlier, cultural change is generational and responds at a much slower rate than technological change. Thus, whilst communications between different cultural groups are much quicker and much easier, the differences between those groups still remain. Only perhaps in the field of popular culture (see earlier) is there rapid global convergence.

It stands to reason, therefore, that as organisations undertake their operations on an increasingly global basis, the need for cultural understanding becomes greater and greater.

Trompenaars set out to explore the cultural diversity aspects of business and one can only recommend his work to the reader in the highest terms. This section seeks to summarise the work of Fons Trompenaars as a taster for those who wish to examine his findings in more detail.

Trompenaars considered cultural diversity in terms of a series of differing attitudes held by various national groups. It should be noted that such attitudes are always just a tendency – not all Britons will react in one way to a particular set of circumstances and all Danes in another, but his research did show a series of national tendencies.

The attitudes Trompenaars believed were most critical were:

- Attitude to time
- Universal v particular

- Individualism v collectivism
- Emotional v neutral
- Specific v diffuse
- Achievement v ascription
- Attitudes to nature.

To these this book also adds:

- Attitudes to age
- Attitudes to gender.

None of these concepts is absolute; national tendencies lie on a continuum between the two factors. In the following section, the factors are described and where appropriate the cultures lying at each end and in the middle are given. Trompenaars spent many hours researching this, often by asking multiple choice questions requiring a response to a certain set of circumstances, for example how much right does a friend have to expect you to lie for them in a certain set of circumstances? His replies were interesting, as in some cultures it is expected that friends will support each other, come what may (a particular response), whilst in others if a friend breaks the rules then those rules must apply whatever the circumstances (a universal response).

## Attitude to time

It might be thought that time is a universal constant, as an hour is an hour is an hour whether it be in London, New York or Shanghai. In looking at the cultural effect of time, however, it is not the absolute nature of time that is important but the attitudes towards it.

Eastern cultures often have a reverence for ancestors and historical precedent. The USA, according to the research, was less interested in the past and much more in the future. Even the importance of time is an issue. In many Western cultures, punctuality is, as many of us had to write as lines at school, 'a very desirable virtue'. In other cultures, punctuality is perhaps of less importance. This can immediately lead to a cultural clash. The author of this book spent some time working in an Eastern country where his belief in the importance of punctuality was constantly challenged. It should be noted that in that culture a delayed aircraft seemed to generate far less stress than it would have done in London or New York. What was noticeable was that the culture within which the author was working paid much more attention to good manners, and a casualness that might be acceptable in the UK was certainly frowned upon. Different cultures have different norms within their value systems.

Those working across cultures need to adapt their ideas to those they are working with, and they need to understand and adopt the prevailing attitudes to time in the culture within which they wish to do business. There will be times, of course, when it is necessary for delivery dates etc. to be met and here a sympathetic method of insisting is required, with the reasons being clearly stated and not just a blanket insistence made.

## Universal v particular

In some cultures, a set of rules or laws is universally applied (or so perceived wisdom tells us, despite the fact that there is sometimes one law for the rich and one for the poor, as the old adage goes). In others, rules and norms may be applied contingent upon the circumstances. Trompenaars points out that relationships such as friendship may confer special rights and obligations in a particular oriented culture which are less welcome in a universal one. In a universal culture, your friend has much less right to expect you to cover up for them than in a culture where particularism is the accepted norm. In general, the USA and Japan were very high on universalism when tested, whereas the former Yugoslavia and certain Far Eastern countries (excluding Japan) tended towards the particularism end of the continuum, although it must be stressed that the overall tendency was that there should be universal rules followed by everybody. The UK tended towards the universalism end but to a lesser degree than the USA. It is noticeable that members of the Royal family rarely lose their driving licences, even when caught at speeds well above the national limit!

In dealing with a culture at the particularism end of the spectrum, organisations need to know exactly which rules are being applied and to whom.

As Trompenaars points out in his excellent tips for doing business with different cultures, in a universalist culture there will be one way of doing things, whilst in the particularist there may be a number of alternatives.

## Individualism v collectivism

Basically, people regard themselves as a member of the group first and an individual second, or vice versa. Perhaps not surprisingly, the USA is an individualism-oriented culture whereas the Japanese came out, together with countries such as Nepal, East Germany under the Communist regime and other Far Eastern groupings, as tending towards a more collectivist approach. This should not be surprising, given the political and social creeds of many Eastern areas and of Communism. The UK was fairly individualist but again less so than the USA.

In conducting business it is important to realise that it may be the group as opposed to a key individual who need to be satisfied in a collectivist-oriented culture, and that the building of collective relationships will be of great importance.

## Emotional v neutral

To what degree is it culturally acceptable to show feelings, especially in business relationships? In the UK and Japan it may be frowned on, less so in Italy and France. Latin cultures tend to accept displays of emotion more readily than those designated as Anglo-Saxon. Emotion is a good psychological safety valve and maybe this, plus the use of olive oil instead of fat for cooking, may go part of the way to explain the apparent lower incidence of heart disease in Latin areas.

Whereas a display of emotion and even temper may be acceptable in Italy, it will certainly be less likely to produce effective results in the USA.

## Specific v diffuse

In many cultures there is expected to be a personal relationship between those involved, whereas in others the relationship is more organisation to organisation. In some cultures, work and home are closely related; in others, people are not expected to bring domestic issues into their workplace. The question then is: how is one supposed to leave a problem at home? It is the belief that the two should not mix and not the actual reality that is important here. Trompenaars quotes China as a very diffuse culture, using the example of how many respondents would refuse to help their boss paint his house. In China, 72% would help, whereas in the much more specific culture of the UK only 8% would agree to give up their own time this way (the US figure was 11%). Similarly, in China 89% of employees believed that the organisation had a responsibility to help house its employees, compared to 55% of Japanese; but only 18% of those in the UK and 15% of USA respondents. There has been a change here in the UK since, during the late 19th and early 20th Centuries, organisations often provided housing for staff.

An organisation in a specific culture may appear to those also adopting that culture to be much more focused on its objectives, whereas in a diffuse culture, time may be spent talking about non-organisational-related issues. Neither is right or wrong, as both suit their cultures. It is again a matter of knowing, understanding and reacting in a culturally acceptable manner.

## Achievement v ascription

An achievement-oriented culture ascribes status dependence on what people have done, whereas ascription is about position, connections and even birth. The USA is the most achievement-oriented culture studied, where it is believed that with hard work and education anybody can rise to the top as the careers of many early emigrants and their immediate descendants showed. As Trompenaars points out, achievement societies ask what somebody has studied, whereas ascription ones may be more concerned with where the studies occurred. To that extent even the USA, with its Ivy League of Universities (Harvard, Yale etc.), is not a wholly achievement culture and nor is the UK. India, where the author of this book worked for some time, was characterised to him by the degree of detail about his education (including the names of colleges and universities attended) that seminar audiences required before any work was undertaken.

Titles and qualifications are much more important in ascription-oriented cultures and great offence can be caused by omitting them or quoting them incorrectly.

Trompenaars listed attitudes to age and gender in this category but for the purposes of this book they are being treated a separate factors.

## Attitudes to nature

To what extent does a culture believe that it is right and proper for humans to try to control nature. The developments in genetic engineering in the USA and the UK suggest that these cultures believe that this is acceptable. Trompenaars claimed a score of 35% in the UK and 38% in the USA who believed that it is worth trying to control nature, compared with only 10% in Japan. His highest score was Brazil with 53%; perhaps this will decrease as Brazilians realise the importance of the rain forest and the global effects of too few trees.

As will be shown in Chapter 11, environmental issues are now very important and people are beginning to realise that one cannot trifle with nature as global warming etc. have shown.

There is also a related issue as to how much people feel they are the masters or mistresses of their own destiny. In the developed world they believe this far more than those in Communist regimes did. Controlling one's own destiny and controlling nature are closely linked, as is the concept of individualism v collectivism. Fate, so important in many Eastern cultures, plays a much lesser role in the cultural psychology of the West.

## Attitudes to age and gender

Different cultures have very different attitudes to these issues. Age is revered in many Eastern cultures, whereas it may be difficult for an over-40 to find employment in the West. This is despite results from the UK Do It Yourself chain, which found that employing over-50s brought immense benefits in productivity, timekeeping, punctuality etc.

Similarly the position of women, covered in Chapter 3, differs from one culture to another. Sending a young man or woman to negotiate on behalf of the organisation may be good practice in certain cultures but frowned on in others, especially if they are ones that denigrate the position of women or revere age. Sensitivity is required with these issues.

As was stated in Chapter 3, organisations that discriminate against people on the grounds of age, gender or even race do themselves a grave disservice, as well as breaking the law of many developed jurisdictions. Sex and race discrimination are illegal in the UK and to these are added age in the USA.

## Far Eastern culture

The Far East has already been mentioned a number of times. Throughout much of the second half of the 20th Century there was a belief that the West could learn much from management styles of the East and especially Japan, which had produced a revolution in quality manufacturing after World War II, albeit encouraged and led by the USA.

Whole books were written about Japanese management, *The Art of Japanese Management* by Pascale & Athos (1981) being a good example that compared US and Japanese management styles.

For a while it was believed that only the Japanese themselves could work a system that involved a fair degree of formality and considerable loyalty to one's employers, but recent developments where Japanese manufacturing plants have operated successfully in the West using indigenous staff have proved that the

Japanese concepts of quality are transmittable to other cultures. At the same time, the 'meltdown' in many Asian economies in the late 1990s has led to an end to the job-for-life concept in those areas, with a lessening of loyalty to the organisation.

Japanese management became known in the West as theory Z, a concept that stressed the importance of group dynamics in the workplace. As these ideas have been accepted in the West, so both quality and output have risen to approach Japanese levels. Weihrich & Koontz (1993) have provided some interesting examples of cultural issues in their excellent text *Management – a Global Perspective*.

Modern communications make cultures less isolated, and ideas can pass more quickly between them. Just as Japan was adept at adopting the ideas of US quality gurus post 1945, so the West has learnt Japanese techniques fairly quickly after the near decimation of the car and electronic manufacturing bases in the 1960s and 1970s. It is clear that, as more and more organisations become truly global in operations, then an understanding of the different national cultures operating as components of the global organisation will become of increasing importance.

## Summary

Culture, the way we do things around here, operates at a national, organisational and even a popular level. Organisations need to recognise, understand and react to the culture of whomever they are dealing with if they wish to operate successfully.

In a global economy, such understanding is vital to success and cannot be underestimated.

## Concepts covered

- What is culture?
- Cultural transmission
- Organisational culture
- Cultural clashes
- Cultural change
- Cultural web
- Popular culture
- National cultures
- Far Eastern culture

## Analysis

In carrying out the *cultural* analysis in respect of an organisation, the following need to be considered:

1. What is the organisational culture of the organisation?
2. What organisational cultures are found in stakeholders?
3. What clashes might there be between the culture of the organisation and that of stakeholders?
4. What national cultures does the organisation operate within?
5. How might the 'home' national culture of the organisation clash with that in other areas in which it operates?

QUESTIONS

1. Why is an understanding of both organisational and national culture vital to the success of an organisation and what cultural factors (and why) must an organisation take into account in its dealings with others?
2. 'Cultures can never be right or wrong only different.' Discuss this statement with reference to possible clashes between cultures on issues they might fundamentally disagree about.

# Further reading

You are strongly recommended to read *Exploring Corporate Strategy* by G. Johnson and K. Scholes (1993), *Riding the Waves of Culture* by Fons Trompenaars (1993) and *When Cultures Collide* by R. D. Lewis (2000).

# ☑ 7 Technological analysis

*Major technological changes affecting all organisations – Understanding the technological needs of a business – PIN numbers – Communications (telephones etc.) – The implications of electronics and computers – Ecommerce – Home shopping – The Internet – Call centres – Manufacturing – GM foods*

Technological advances are often not linear but synergical. Synergy is the phenomenon that occurs when two or more things come together with the result that the whole is actually greater than the sum of the parts. The linking of telephone technology to computer technology and to copying has produced advantages beyond those which could have been predicted at the time. Computers have been linked using relatively unsophisticated telephone technology to increase their power many times. In turn, the use of computers has increased the functions of the telephone system. The Internet is a result of synergy more than anything else: two technologies combining to form a third that is far more powerful than the originals.

To give examples of just how rapid change has been: up to 1815, the fastest that a normal person could send a message to somebody else was about 15 mph – the speed of a horse. By 1829, the locomotives of the Liverpool and Manchester Railway could achieve double that, and by 1904 the Great Western Railway locomotive *City of Truro* had achieved 100 mph (Casserley, 1980). The development of railways produced a need to communicate for signalling purposes and this led to the development of firstly the electric telegraph, then the telephone and later wireless (radio) communications. These operated at the speed of light, so thus, in a few short years, communication speeds increased from a few miles per hour to many thousands of miles per second.

Incidentally, the increase in speed brought about by the development of railways led to the introduction of a standard time throughout the UK. When people only moved at the speed of a horse, the time differences caused by using local time, i.e. setting noon as the time when the Sun was directly overhead at each individual location, caused no problems. As the speed of transport increased, it became necessary to keep the same time at both ends of a railway line for obvious reason and so 'Railway Time' was adopted, where noon was defined as the time the Sun was overhead at the Greenwich meridian, this soon becoming known as Greenwich Mean Time – GMT.

The railway revolution really was a revolution not only in transport terms but also in sociological ones. Railways brought towns and cities closer together in time and the tramways that sprang up in nearly every UK city and town in the late

19th Century aided the geographical expansion of those towns. No longer did workers need to live within walking distance of their employment and, in cities and towns across the UK, new housing sprang up along the railways and the tramways in a manner that became known as 'ribbon development'.

The ability to travel brought with it an increase in consumer choice. If something could not be found in Stockport, then Manchester was just a short train or tram ride away, and if the branch had not got the item in stock then the ever-increasing rail network meant that it could be delivered from a warehouse within a very short period of time. Advertising changed as well; newspapers could be distributed on a national basis, as could letters – W. H. Auden's evocative poem *The Night Mail* conveying something of the excitement and importance of a national, cheap mail service. If there was not yet a global consumer economy as we know it today, there was a rapidly developing national one. Soon the high street chains began to develop and a new era in consumerism had dawned, one in which customers were no longer dependent on a local supplier but could cast their nets much wider afield.

Cartwright (2000) has used the development of the facsimile (fax) machine to illustrate the rapid advances in technology in the latter half of the 20th Century. Up to the middle of the 1980s, very few people had actually sent or received a fax. Even large organisations possessed only a limited number (sometimes only one) of facsimile machines. By the middle of the 1990s, the fax machine was in everyday commercial use and the product was also being marketed for domestic use. Indeed, more and more people were finding that a combined telephone and fax machine was useful at home. By the end of 1999, the growth in email, both at work and through home computers equipped with modems and scanners, was beginning to supersede the fax machine to some extent. Whilst there is always likely to be a market for the fax machine in the foreseeable future, the product life cycle may not be all that long.

It is also worth remembering that yesterday's amazing technological advance is today's normality and may be tomorrow's obsolescence. The first flight of the Wright Brothers in 1906 confounded the many sceptics who had declared that manned flight was an impossibility. It should be noted that their first flight was actually less than the length of a Boeing 747 'Jumbo Jet'. By 1969, manned flight had advanced to the stage that not only was it common for people to use aircraft to reach their holiday destination and think nothing of the experience, but certainly there was less sense of awe and wonder after the first humans had walked on the moon; many people can name the first and second humans to walk on the moon, but how many can name the third? It has all become commonplace.

Many economists now believe that there is a direct link between technological advance and economic growth. They call this the S curve, in which waves of technological advance bring about ever-greater increases in productivity, thus raising the speed of economic growth. Available labour can be deployed more effectively and increased global competition acts so as to reduce prices to the consumer. As with all economic theory, there are those who are sceptical as factors such as fuel price and raw material price increases can nullify any technological gains.

In respect of a technological analysis, technology can be divided into a number of types, although there is considerable overlap between them:

- Technology that makes the operation safer for both the organisation and its customers
- Technology that provides the customer with something completely new
- Technology that allows the organisation to deliver something different, be it product or service
- Technology that provides the customer with a more convenient service
- Technology that provides the customer with a quicker service
- Technology that provides the supplier with more information about the customer and other stakeholders.

Whilst many of the current technological advances are concerned with electronics and the use of computers, there are other technological changes that have major implications for a great many organisations. The controversies regarding genetic engineering impact on both food producers and retailers. New manufacturing processes may make the impossible more likely. As an example, new metal-bonding technologies and propulsion methods allowed the de Havilland Comet of 1952 to halve the effective size of the world (Donald, 1999). However, as the world moved into the 21st Century, it was apparent that the computer was destined to play a major role in the lives of all humans and thus much of this chapter relates to technologies that have some form of electronics embedded within them.

## PIN numbers

Much of the technology that will be discussed in this chapter has at its heart some form of computerised operation. In order for any computerised system to be effective, it has to recognise the customer who is making the query, transaction, complaint etc. Surname and forename are not enough as there is every likelihood that these may be held by somebody else. How many John Smiths or Alan McDonalds are there in the UK – very many. Name, address and post (zip in the USA) code are more unique, but there could well be two people with the same name at an address. The only completely unique method of identifying a customer so that they are not confused with somebody else is to give them a Personal Identification Number (PIN). With ten digits (0–9) to choose from and the ability to repeat numbers, there are literally millions of possible combinations, thus allowing each customer to have their own unique number which can be encoded on to the magnetic strip on a card. The ability of computers to recognise PIN numbers and read information off cards has been one of the truly remarkable technological discoveries of the modern age. A large number of PIN numbers consist of just 4 digits that must also be linked to either a name or a coded piece of information on a card. Take the case of an ATM card. Most of these use a 4-digit code. To obtain money, the card must be inserted in the ATM which then reads the information on the card. The cardholder has then to, in effect, confirm the information on the card by inputting the PIN number. Only if the inputted digits match those encoded on the card will cash be dispensed. The chances of a matching PIN number being put in by chance are infinitesimally small.

It should go without saying that PIN numbers should not be kept next to items to which they relate nor given to anybody else at all. If the PIN number is revealed then the security of any system will be compromised. It will not be long before other identifiers are brought into common use. The idea of reading palm prints or eyeball patterns may seem far-fetched and from the world of science fiction, but the former is precisely how the INPASS card, covered later, identifies the user.

# Telephones

Any review of the implications of technology on customer relations needs to start with a consideration of the telephone, invented by Alexander Graham Bell at the end of the 19th Century and today a standard feature in nearly every home in the developed world and every business worldwide: a piece of equipment often taken for granted and yet at the heart of the communications and computer revolution.

Even in the 1950s most telephone calls in the UK were made either from business premises or from a public call box. The domestic telephone, although gaining in popularity, was not installed in the majority of homes. By the year 2000 the telephone had become a fixture in nearly every house in the developed world, with many people owning two or three landline telephones plus a mobile telephone. The telephone is possibly one of the great icons of the later 20th Century and when, from the 1980s onwards, it became possible to link computers using telephone lines, whole new possibilities of communication and business were opened up. The ATM machines covered later rely on a telephone link to a central computer to carry out the transaction with the customer; without the telephone this would be impossible.

The basic workings of a telephone system are relatively simple. A number of instruments that can both transmit and receive the human voice are connected either by wires or radio to a central switching point where the message is routed to the desired other receiver/transmitter. Originally the switching of calls was a manual task with switchboard operators plugging wires into the relevant sockets.

The author can remember that in the 1950s, until the introduction in the UK of STD (Subscriber Trunk Dialling), any calls other than local ones (that could be handled at a semi automatic telephone exchange) required the intervention of the operator who would connect the call. International calls needed to be booked in advance. As electronics improved, so it became possible to dial anywhere directly from home. In the UK, until the 1980s, telephony was a government monopoly, subscribers not buying but having to rent a telephone. (Like Henry Ford's famous Model T, you could have your telephone in any colour you liked as long as it was black!)

Without wishing to delve into the technology, an average UK domestic telephone set (or sets, as there are likely to be at least two in most homes) enables the customer to:

- Choose a telephone provider of his or her choice, not necessarily British Telecom
- Have separate lines – most new properties are constructed with at least two telephone line connections
- Place extension sets throughout the house
- See who is calling
- Receive answerphone messages
- Redial the last number automatically
- See who was the last person to call
- Set up call waiting
- Divert calls
- Set up three-way calls
- Send and receive faxes
- Access the Internet and email using a modem and even using mobile telephones.

The number of services increases almost monthly.

The first telegraphic connection between Europe and North America was laid by the giant (for the time) steamship *Great Eastern* in the late 1960s and the development of telephone services was limited by wires until well after World War II. The 'space race', which led to the first moon landing in 1969, produced as a by-product the telecommunications satellite and freed the telephone from a total dependency on wires and thus made it possible to use many more channels.

The introduction of ISDN (Integrated Services Digital Network) in the 1990s has led to an explosion of telephone-related services. Digital messages, unlike those sent by analogue means, allow the signal to be broken up into discrete packages. Thus a single wire can carry more than one 'conversation'. This allows computers (which use digital codes) to communicate very quickly as well as permitting much more complicated signals. Digital communications have made video conferencing much more accessible as well as improving the quality of the vision and sound. ISDN is rapidly gaining ground not only for business communications, where vast amounts of data need to be transmitted, but also in the home, where a modem linked to an ISDN line can handle data much more quickly than a traditional analogue telephone system.

As the number of home computers has grown, so has the requirement to access the Internet and email from home as well as at work, leading to the development of faster and faster modems and ISDN, as covered above.


# 'Plastic'

There can be few places in the world that do not recognise and in the vast majority of cases accept plastic cards with the words *MASTERCARD* or *VISA* on them. These are two of the major credit card organisations in the world and many millions of people own and use their product.

Credit cards are not the only form of 'plastic' in common use but they are possibly the most important from the standpoint of customer relations. The technological developments that will be covered in this chapter would be of little use unless complemented by an internationally recognised method of payment by customers to suppliers that is secure, quick and easy.

There are a number of types of 'plastic' in current use, which include:

- Credit cards
- Debit cards
- ATM cards
- Store cards
- Telephone cards
- Loyalty cards
- Identification cards.

Indeed, our wallets often seem to contain more plastic cards than cash!

## Facsimile machines

Introduced as a result of developments in World War II, the facsimile machine matches telephone and photocopier technologies to allow documents to be sent over telephone lines. Whilst it may well be superseded by a scanner + PC + email, many businesses rely on 'fax' to send messages quickly and conveniently. It is especially useful when complex instructions or diagrams need to be seen by somebody many, many miles away.

## Email

Email (short for electronic mail) is one of the major manifestations of the synergy gained by linking computer and telephone technology. Virtually unknown in the UK before the 1980s, email has become a normal method of business communications and has spread rapidly into the domestic market. With its ability to send document files, pictures and greetings cards to anybody in the world with an Internet connection, email has meant that time and distance have been truly overcome. A message typed in London can be in the inbox of somebody in New York in seconds and at the cost of a local telephone call.

Colleagues, family and friends who are on-line can be readily contacted and, as there is no telephone bell to ring and disturb people, the problem of time zones is eliminated. Email, despite its protocols, lacks the personal touch but for instant messages and indeed communications it is hard to beat.

As a simple example of how email and associated technology can aid customer relations, the author renewed a subscription to a US magazine over the telephone using a credit card. For some reason no magazines were received. The home office of the publisher is in Kansas, causing a time zone problem when wishing to get in touch. However, one short email explaining the problem produced not only a very quick reply but also expedited delivery of the missing copies – no fuss and the matter was settled using local telephone charges.

Just examining an email address can provide a number of clues, for example **.ac** near the end of an address indicates that the address is at an academic institution, **.gov** indicates a government body, **.co** is used for companies etc. and **.com** is used by communication-providers with other organisations using **.org**. US addresses have nothing at the end but **.uk** represents Britain (the United Kingdom), **.ca** being Canada etc. Thus **amazon.co.uk**, the UK part of the bookseller Amazon, to be considered later in this chapter, becomes self-explanatory.

# The Internet

Whole books have been written about the development and use of the Internet. The combination of telephone and computer technology through a gateway provided by one of the many ISPs (Internet Service Providers) allows people owning a computer with a modem to gain access to millions of web pages covering every possible subject.

In March 2000 the UK Prime Minister, Tony Blair, announced that he wanted to see universal access to the Internet in the UK by 2005. At the time, Finland topped the Internet access league with every school and library and 85% of those in small, medium and large businesses linked to the net. Britain was at the time 8th, with around 23% of the population having Internet access compared with a figure of 45% for the USA. The rapid growth in Internet-connected mobile phones in the year 2000 together with the growth in Web TV systems was seen as a major means of increasing UK connectivity.

There are two major implications of the Internet for customer relations, namely:

- Information for customers
- Ecommerce.

## Information for customers

Nearly every major organisation, from retailers to governments and charities, and an increasing number of smaller concerns have set up easily accessible web pages where customers and potential customers can find information about the organisation. Whether the customer is searching for a new motor car, wishes to know about a piece of legislation, train times in the Netherlands or wants details of a book, the chances are it can be accessed through a simple Internet search. Some searches require the use of passwords but most commercial and public service are open to anybody wherever they are in the world. All that is required is either the URL (Unique Reference Location) of the organisation in question or the use of the search engines provided by the Internet SERVICE PROVIDERS. Most addresses begin as **http:///www** etc. Like email addresses, to which they are related, they may appear complex but follow a logical pattern. The growth in the use of the WWW (World Wide Web) has been nothing short of explosive and many individuals as well as organisations now have their own personal web pages where they provide details about themselves.

As more and more people have become 'connected', there has been a massive growth in an area of business known as electronic commerce or ecommerce for short.

## Ecommerce

In September 1999, UK television news services reported that the UK Prime Minister, Tony Blair, was to appoint an 'E-envoy' to promote the effective use of commercial activities carried out using the Internet. The reports quoted the fact that in 1999 there were 500 000 companies actually conducting business on the Internet, a figure that was expected to grow to a staggering 8 million by 2002 with revenue exceeding £5 billion by 2003. In the UK alone it was predicted that by the end of 2000 no fewer than 9 million Britons would have access to an Internet connection (source: ITV Teletext service, 12 September 1999).

Companies using the Internet for business in 1999 ranged from the major holiday companies, airlines, travel agents, book suppliers and antique houses down to a small bakery in Whitby in the north-east of England.

In early 2000 there was a great deal of stock market speculation in the so-called 'dot com' companies, i.e. those companies set up to conduct their operations over the Internet. Whilst the share value of many such companies rose rapidly, there was a serious fall in share values in April 2000 leading many commentators to believe that the growth had been too rapid. There had been complaints that the UK government was neglecting traditional industries such as shipbuilding etc. and placing too much reliance on ecommerce for the future prosperity of the country.

Aldrich (1999) has postulated that future success will go to those managers and businesses that can function effectively and creatively in the emerging digital economy, with those who fail to grasp the opportunities being left behind. He makes the point that power now belongs to customers who demand products that deliver new dimensions of value both in terms of time and content, in addition to the more traditional price and quality values. By removing geographic constraints, ecommerce can achieve just that. As a simple example, somebody living in the Highlands of Scotland may be 70–80 miles away from their nearest bookshop and yet can obtain the volumes that they require through one of the on-line bookshops (see later) within 48 hours, with no fares etc. and without using up precious time. Whilst ecommerce will never replace the social aspects of shopping it can, and does, free up time considerably and thus adds value. *The Daily Telegraph Electronic Business Manual* by D. Bowen (1999) provides useful additional information.

## Home shopping

There is nothing new about the concept of home shopping. As the settlers poured across Middle America in the 19th Century, companies such as Sears realised that the massive distances involved in reaching the nearest department store created a market for mail order shopping. Such companies produced mammoth catalogues containing items as diverse as clothes and farm implements. Even today many people still use a home-shopping catalogue for mail order and this is a thriving sector of the retail industry. No longer do orders have to be placed by mail and an agent used to collect payment. Modern mail order uses the telephone and facsimile technology coupled to credit card payments for those who wish a quicker and more convenient service.

US television stations pioneered the introduction of shopping channels devoted entirely to promoting products and taking orders over the telephone, a development that is now gaining ground in the UK with the introduction of cable, satellite and digital television, which allow more channels to be accessed from home.

Ecommerce is a natural extension of home shopping, recent developments allowing those without a computer but with a digital television to become part of the marketplace.

Given such diversity it would be impossible to mention every type of business operating on the Internet as new companies and sectors are being added continually. In 1999, one of the latest applications of ecommerce was the conducting of antique auctions by the major antique houses. No longer did a buyer need to fly from New York to London to bid for a piece or employ an agent. They could see the piece on their personal computer at home, examine its provenance and then bid electronically and, if successful, pay using a credit card.

This section will examine three ecommerce operations, on-line banking, book sales and airline ticket purchases as examples of what ecommerce can do for both the organisation and the customer.

# On-line banking

An individual's relationship with their bank used to be a very personal one, with the bank manager knowing the vast majority of the branch's customers by name. For many years after World War II, banks were open six days per week, offering a Saturday morning service, although they tended to open later and shut earlier than the vast majority of retailers and other businesses. When the banks decided to stop Saturday opening, business was lost to the building societies that were open on Saturdays, a time when many people wished to withdraw cash for shopping. The introduction of ATMs (as said in Chapter 5, but repeated here for completeness) allowed customers to withdraw cash at any time and now virtually every bank and building society offer this facility. However there are other transactions that people need from their banks and, for those in work or in remote locations, contact with the bank during normal business hours can be difficult.

One method the banks and building societies have used to solve this problem is the introduction of call centres (see later) where information and certain transactions can be undertaken. Many such centres have extended access hours and indeed the trend is towards a 24-hour service. This provides the customer with greater time to contact their bank but at a further distance and with a less personal service.

The other method that is growing rapidly is the development of on-line banking linking the customer's personal computer with the bank. The first UK bank to introduce such a service was the Bank of Scotland which offered its HOBS (Home and Office Banking Service) to selected customers from 1993 (Winder, 1999). This system required a special modem which, whilst quite revolutionary for the time, would seem very slow today. Working through the DOS system, HOBS basically allowed customers to check their balances, a facility not available on the ATMs of the time, but commonplace today.

Modern on-line banking (Winder, above lists eight UK on-line banking-providers in 1999, together with reviews of their services) allows, in most cases, for customers not only to check their balance but to print out statements, pay bills, transfer monies between accounts and to download data with other types of software, e.g. accounts packages. In 1999, only the Bank of Scotland and First Direct allowed the customer to apply for an overdraft on-line but the other providers are likely to follow suit. Charges in 1999 were zero or minimal and competitive forces are likely to ensure that any fees remain relatively low given the convenience that such a system offers.

The advantages to the banks are self-evident. Branches cost money both in terms of staff and premises; on-line banking costs far less. The customer is able to conduct the vast majority of day-to-day transactions at his or her convenience. The personal touch is, of course, lost and it remains problematic as to whether the branch network will completely disappear. The trend throughout the 1990s has been for mergers between banks, building societies to convert to banks and for branch networks to be cut. Provided that there is a human being available for those transactions that are not day-to-day but require discussion and negotiation, then the future of on-line banking seems set to grow.

The challenge for the banks and building societies is to find a method of making the customer feel personally valued. Many of the banks and building societies, recognising this need, have introduced the concept of a 'personal banker' whom the customer can contact in the event of problems. Most transactions can be carried out quickly and conveniently on-line or on the telephone to any member of the bank's staff, but the 'personal banker' is available to discuss and rectify any problems. A leading UK bank came in for considerable criticism when, in the Spring of 2000, it announced a cut in its branch network because of changing customer behaviour. It appeared that attractive as electronic banking was, the personal touch was still important.

## Book sales

One of the earliest ecommerce success stories was that of **amazon.com** and its UK operation **amazon.co.uk**. The first Internet bookshop, **amazon.com**, was founded in the USA by Jeff Bezos in 1995 (de Jonge, 1999). de Jonge had spotted a crucial niche in the book selling market. Traditional methods of buying books had required a visit to a book shop or using one of the many book clubs that offered cut price editions via their membership magazines. Unfortunately the titles on offer from the latter tend to be restricted and, whilst browsing through a book shop is pleasurable, there are many people who know exactly which book they require and just want to acquire that volume with the minimum of fuss.

The concept of an Internet bookshop was an idea whose time had come. Book buyers could browse using the amazon website; this may not be as satisfying as actually holding the volume and browsing the shelves, but many of the books people require are not stocked even by the largest book shop and thus must be ordered unseen anyway. The concept of an on-line bookshop has certainly proved successful, with imitators entering the market, the expansion of amazon to the UK and, by 1999, no fewer than 6.2 million customers and a 1999 Wall Street valuation of $30 billion (de Jonge, 1999).

Using the amazon and similar services is simplicity itself. Just type in their URL (see earlier) and follow the instructions on the web pages. Enter name, address, preferred password and credit card details over a secure link and the customer can start shopping. Browsing from title to synopsis is done using an HTML (Hyper Text Markup Language) link and required items can be placed in a shopping basket; amazon confirms the order by email and it is delivered by the mail service within the time stipulated by the company. Items in stock are usually received within 2 to 3 days; those that have to be ordered take slightly longer.

For those who live some distance from a major bookshop, such as this author, companies like amazon provide a very convenient service. The company have been expanding, CDs and videos etc. being a similar market and well suited to ecommerce, and Bezos has recently started 'Shop the Web' which offers on-line links to other retailers.

There is no doubt that this is the true successor to the Sear's type catalogues mentioned earlier and provides a convenient method of purchasing those items for which there is little need to browse. Supermarkets are already experimenting with similar services, which will be a boon to the housebound etc.

# Travel

If you need to book a plane ticket between Denver and Los Angeles and you live in Manchester (UK), you can do it over the Internet. Many specialist flight-booking companies have facilities for searching for the best deals and then making a booking over the Internet. Hotels and even guesthouses can be booked directly from your own computer.

The UK budget airline, easyJet, commenced operations by only accepting telephone bookings paid for by credit card, and in the late 1990s began an Internet booking service with one in three bookings being made over the Internet by May 1999. Internet bookings even receive a discount. In May 1999 there were over 1 million visits to the company's website which provides flight details etc. as well as a booking facility.

Not only are flight details readily available on the Internet but so are virtual tours of cruise ship facilities and railway timetables for many parts of the world.

The Internet has made the acquisition of travel information far more convenient for potential customers who can make their plans in the comfort of their own home or office.

There is a downside in that facilitating such tasks by computer can lead to job losses among high street travel agents etc., in effect the Internet brings the same facilities into the home as have been enjoyed by the travel trade for some time. It is too early to see how this will affect traditional trade.

## Call centres

It makes economic sense, as customers become more and more distant geographically, to provide them with a central point of telephone contact. Given the benefits of the technology, this does not have to be in the same country, although the cost of telephone calls needs to be kept in mind, as more remote customers should not be disadvantaged. Fortunately it is possible to set up either freephone telephone calls or local rate calls to ease the burden on customers.

Airlines, especially British Airways, have used their telecommunications network to obviate time differences. A call for information on the London to Glasgow shuttle made at 2000 (GMT) may well be answered in New York, where it is the middle of the day and thus the maximum number of staff are on duty.

Many of the financial and large retail institutions have set up centralised call centres where customer enquiries can be dealt with, often on a 24-hour basis. The computer systems have access to the customer's details and routine matters can normally be dealt with efficiently and effectively, with supervisors on hand to deal with the more difficult queries.

In the UK, a number of such centres are located in the central belt of Scotland, as it is believed that the Scottish accent is particularly appreciated over the telephone. Banks that only operate in England and Wales have been known to set up their call centres in the Glasgow area, despite having no (or only a few) branches in Scotland.

Ticketing for flights etc. can be performed in India just as easily as in London, as data travels at the speed of light and so distance is no problem.

Call centres provide a point of contact with a human being and that is still of vital importance to the majority of customers, no matter how good the technology is.

## Teleconferencing

It may well not be long before there are also teleconference links to call centres. Domestic videoconferencing software and cameras are now freely available at relatively low cost and their use may make service that little bit more personal, although body language clues (see the next chapter) are hard to spot on a small screen that may not have the best picture resolution possible. One cannot say how this will develop, save that it will become better and cheaper!

## EPOS and bar codes

There is another link between computers and telephones, this time in relation to bar codes and EPOS (Electronic Point of Sale).

Virtually every product we buy has a computerised bar code. By reading this code at the till point, not only can customer preferences be assessed but data messages sent back to warehouses etc. to ensure that the customer has what they want when they want it, i.e. there is no excuse for accidentally running out of stock. Managers can see the stock situation in more or less real time and ensure that shelves are restocked and new items ordered in a very efficient manner.

# Manufacturing

Manufacturing processes have received considerable aid from technological advances, especially those linked to computer aided design (CAD) and electronic control mechanisms. The application of these techniques has enabled manufacturers to work to much tighter tolerances and to avoid 'interference': the problems caused when two parts try to occupy the same position in space. Sabbach (1995) and P&O (1995) have shown how this has aided both the speed and quality of production in aircraft design and construction and shipbuilding respectively. Such techniques, coupled with laser tools for highly accurate cutting, have brought undreamed of levels of quality to the manufacturing process.

# Genetic engineering

One of the most revolutionary technological changes of the late 20th and early 21st Centuries has been the ability of scientists to genetically engineer living matter. Whether it be the cloning of sheep and pigs (the latter in an attempt to find a viable source of organs suitable for human transplant surgery) or bigger tomatoes or disease-resistant crops, GM (genetically modified) developments have run into a fair degree of consumer resistance. The resistance has been so great that many UK supermarkets, food retailers and restaurants have forgone any advantages of GM produce in order to assure customers that no GM products are deliberately offered to them. Indeed, the consumer trend has been more towards organic foods. Even the UK government, which originally backed GM developments, began to back-pedal in early 2000 as a result of public concerns that rogue genetic material could escape into the natural gene pool for a species.

Mankind has always wished to control nature in producing the most efficient yields at lowest costs possible since agriculture and husbandry began. GM foods differ, in that science is now able to introduce genetic material across species, something nature normally does not allow. This has raised fears of diseases also crossing the species barrier, fears realised in the late 1990s with the BSE/CJD crisis in the beef industry, where CJD (the human version of BSE) appeared to have come from eating BSE-infected cattle.

GM foods have produced what might be called by the industry 21st Century 'luddites'. The Luddites were a movement in the late 18th and early 19th Centuries which campaigned actively and sometimes violently against the introduction of new technology, mainly because of fears that technological advances would affect the employment of those in traditional trades. Despite constant reassurance from scientists, the GM companies themselves and even governments, there appears to be a growing public resistance to purchasing such products. Given that early warnings about the effects of feeding cattle on sheep tissue went unheeded by many in the farming industry, thus leading to the BSE crisis, it may well be that the reluctant public are proved right.

## Summary

Technology is changing all the time and advances will benefit different organisations in different ways. The linking of telephones and computers through ICT has brought about a revolution leading to the Internet and ecommerce. Geographic constraints to commerce are being removed all the time.

Manufacturing has also benefited from improvements in machine tools and the ability to work to much more exacting tolerances.

The resistance to the introduction of genetically modified (GM) food crops has shown that the public do not always accept technological changes as beneficial and there may still be resistance to such advances.

## Concepts covered

- Speed of technological change
- Technological implications
- PIN numbers
- Telephones
- Plastic cards
- Computers
- Internet
- Ecommerce
- Home shopping/banking
- Call centres
- Tele/video conferencing
- Bar codes
- Manufacturing
- Genetic engineering

# Analysis

In carrying out the *technological* analysis in respect of an organisation, the following need to be considered:

1. What current technological advances are likely to benefit the organisation?
2. What costs will the organisation incur in putting the latest technology in place?
3. Is the organisation able to benefit from ecommerce?
4. Will staff need major re-training to use new technologies effectively?
5. Is there any danger of customer resistance to new technologies?

QUESTIONS

1. How can organisations benefit from the use of ICT and ecommerce, and how can they gain some form of competitive advantage?
2. Describe reasons why consumers may be resistant to technological advances. You should illustrate your answer with examples of advances that have been resisted and analyse the reasons for this.
3. 'Ecommerce is the latest trend in making the world smaller.' Discuss this statement with reference to other technological advances that have served to shrink the world, e.g. transport, telephones etc.

# Further reading

You are recommended to read *The Daily Telegraph Electronic Business Manual* by David Bowen (1999) and *Mastering the Digital Marketplace* by Douglas F. Aldrich (1999) for information about ecommerce.

# ▼ 8 Aesthetic analysis

*Communications – A model of communication – Noise – Means of communication – Promotion – AIDA – Image – Fashion – Organisational Body Language (OBL) – Public relations*

In its true sense (according to the *Oxford Dictionary*, 1990), *aesthetics* is concerned with beauty. In the context of this book, the word is used in relationship to image, the image an organisation presents to its outside environment. This includes the image that the organisation wants to project and the image that it actually does project – sometimes these can be radically different.

The chapter considers the main areas: communications, promotion and image, the concept of Organisational Body Language (OBL) and public relations.

## Communications

Given that this book is about the relationships an organisation has with its external environment, it stands to reason that communications form a key component in that relationship. All organisations need to communicate with their suppliers, customers, stakeholders and even, at times, competitors. The effectiveness of the communications process can play a key role in aiding overall organisational success. The right message communicated inappropriately can be as damaging as sending out the wrong message, indeed it may be perceived as just that.

### A model of communication

What follows is a simplified model of the communication process.

For the sake of simplicity it is assumed that there are two people, *A* and *B*, and that *B* wishes to communicate a fact about his or her organisation in response to a question from *A* who is part of the external environment (perhaps a customer or a supplier).

*A* and *B* possess a multi-function transmitter, a mouth and a hand, and a multi-function receiver, eyes and ears analogous to a microphone, a pointer, a screen and a speaker.

The process is as follows. *A* asks a question about *B*'s organisation; obviously at this point *A* is unaware of the exact answer, although there may be a perception of what the answer is likely to be. *A*'s brain, through a series of neural signals, formulates the question. At this moment in time, the signal is in the form of a neural signal so it needs to be coded into something that *B* can understand. (If humans ever develop telepathy, this coding stage will become redundant.) *A*'s brain codes the signal into *words*, which are the commonest form of communication for business purposes (Figure 8.1).

An important thing about any code is that the transmitter and the receiver need copies of it in order for the latter to be able to decode the message properly. In this example, *A* and *B* are using English. Were *A* using English and *B* spoke only French, then extra coding and decoding steps, perhaps using a phrasebook or a translator, would be required.

All messages need a medium of conduction. Speech uses sound waves that create a disturbance in the molecules of the air (this is why there is no sound in the vacuum of outer space).

*A*'s question is conducted through the air to *B*, who can also see *A* and may gain extra clues through *A*'s body language. The message reaches *B*'s receivers, the ears for the sound and the eyes for the visual image (Figure 8.2).

*Figure 8.1 Communications step 1.*

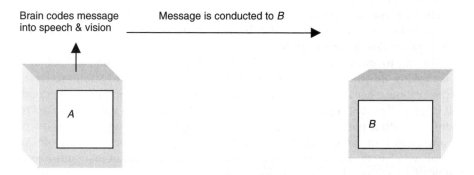

*Figure 8.2 Communications step 2.*

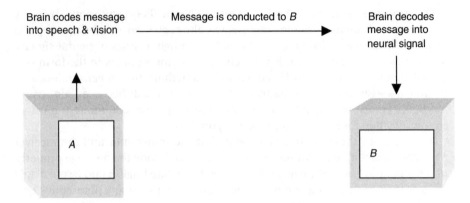

Brain codes message into speech & vision

Message is conducted to *B* ⟶

Brain decodes message into neural signal

*A*

*B*

*Figure 8.3    Communications step 3.*

The sound waves that hit *B*'s ears and the light that enters *B*'s eyes are decoded from speech and vision into a set of neural impulses and are sent to *B*'s brain (Figure 8.3).

Complex things will happen in *B*'s brain, as it questions:

- Do I understand the code?
- What am I being asked?
- Have I ever been asked this kind of thing before?
- Where is *A* in terms of space?

The latter may sound a trite question but sound waves etc. are quite directional and need to be accurately 'pointed' in the right direction. Assuming that *B* understands the message from *A*, the process can be repeated, this time with *B* giving the required answer (Figure 8.4).

*B*'s reply to *A* should provide an indication that *B* has correctly understood the message that *A* sent. As Cartwright (2000), from whom this section is derived, has pointed out, history is full of examples where one person *thought* that they understood a message when in fact they hadn't. The 'Charge of the Light Brigade' during the Crimean War is a classic example of somebody acting on what they thought they had been told, when in fact they had been told something completely different.

The message does not have to be verbal nor does there have to be line-of-sight between the parties. Telephones may be used or the message may be written. The same principles, however, apply.

The way to ensure that a message has been understood is to request feedback. Just asking 'do you understand?' is a very closed question and often receives a 'yes' response because the recipient believes that they have in fact understood. It is often illuminating to ask 'in your own words, what have you been asked to do?' It is often possible to gauge understanding by analysing the subsequent conversation to see if both the supplier and the customer are actually on the same wavelength. The acquisition of feedback is very important to organisations that wish to know that their products and services are acceptable and that the messages they are sending are the ones they wish the outside environment to

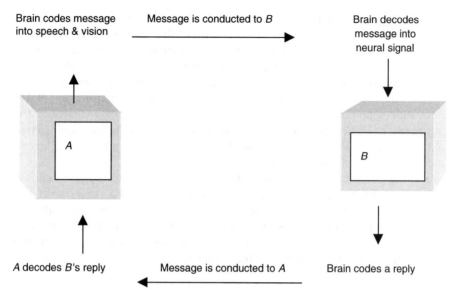

Figure 8.4   Communications step 4.

receive. Internal feedback, although outwith the scope of this book, is of equal importance.

## Noise

Communications both within and outwith organisations are often mis-understood because something interferes with the process. Anything that interferes with communications is called *noise*. It may be actual physical noise that distorts the message or it may be bad handwriting or conflicting meanings: e.g. the old chestnut about the two builders, 'I'll hold the nail and when I nod my head hit it with the hammer!'; hit what? – the nail or the person's head? (Cartwright, 2000). Noise can be the use of dialect that only one of the people understands or it could be the differences between an apparently common language; British English ascribes different words and meanings from American English to certain things. Anything that distorts the message or prevents reception or disrupts decoding is noise. In any communication with a customer it is important to ensure that noise is kept to a minimum or eliminated altogether. This involves checking that the receiver can actually follow and understand the message. The use of acronyms and jargons are typical examples of noise. Professional people and high-tech suppliers can often be accused of using 'in' terms that they understand but the customer doesn't.

Fortunately people can often gain a sense of the meaning of unfamiliar terms and phrases by using the preceding and following phrases to set the term in some form of context. Human nature being what it is, people are often very reluctant to show their ignorance and ask what the term means, and thus misunderstandings can and do occur. Anything that makes the receiver look foolish should be avoided, especially if the receiver is a customer, as a foolish looking customer soon becomes an ex-customer. Plain English with jargon-free terms is the best way to build up relationships. Governments, both local and national, have gained a reputation for writing documents in a manner that makes them indecipherable to the average person, and organisations such as the Campaign for Plain English have waged battle on behalf of the man and woman in the street in order to have official documents in a more readable and understandable style and format.

As Trudgill (1975) has pointed out when referring to the work of Bernstein, we all speak a number of languages, even if we claim not to speak a foreign language. We have a language type (or register) that we use at home, one for work, one when with our friends etc. It is important that a supplier can use the language register of the customer rather than relying on the customer to learn and understand the language register of the supplier.

## Means of communication

As the previous chapter showed, modern technology has greatly increased the speed and methods by which both internal and external communications can be accomplished. The advent of email has meant that distance is no barrier to communication and, thanks to the computer and the facsimile machine, time zone differences have been made of little account. Whatever means of communication are used however, firstly the medium must suit both the transmitter and the receiver, and secondly relationships are developed between people. Whatever the communications technology used, social skills are often actually more important than technological ones.

## Promotion and image

The vast majority of organisations wish to promote not only their products and services but also the organisation itself. Much promotion is accomplished through advertising. Advertising is normally arranged through specialist agencies.

Modern advertising is expensive and is thus carefully targeted. Advertising fits into the AIDA (Attention, Interest, Desire and Action) model whereby a four-stage process is used.

Firstly the *attention* of the proposed recipient must be attracted. This may be through a bold or even controversial message, the latter having been used with some success in the United Colours of Benetton campaigns, some of which have actually caused public outrage. By using devices such as clever story lines, brash colours, romance, evocative music and images, and even warnings etc. the advertiser seeks to attract the attention of a potential customer.

Once attention has been gained, the message must contain substance if it is to actually *interest* the recipient. This is where a knowledge of the recipient and their needs and wants is so important. Gaining attention which does not lead to interest is money wasted. If the recipient is to be interested then the message must have some personal appeal.

Interest should lead to *desire* which means concentrating on benefits. One of the problems of advertising 'grudge purchases' such as insurance, security or healthcare is that it is easy to gain attention and interest but less easy to stimulate desire from somebody who would probably rather not think about the issues in the first place.

If desire is achieved then pricing and delivery considerations, properly targeted should lead to *action*. This can be a positive purchase, or in health campaigns etc. may lead to the recipient not doing something – smoking is a good example.

> Attention is *attracted*, interest *gained*, desire is *stimulated* and action is *encouraged*: AIDA underlies all that advertising is about.

There is a further consideration of AIDA in the next chapter.

In addition to gaining new customers, the organisation will wish to use its advertising monies to remind existing customers of its products and services. These are people whose attention and interest are already there; it is the desire to repeat the purchase or experience with the actions to accomplish this that is the aim of the advertisers.

There are legal requirements in most jurisdictions (see Chapter 10) relating to the truthfulness of advertising, the UK Trades Descriptions Act being an example. From a customer relations point of view, it is important that advertising does not have a negative effect on the customer. A famous cigarette advert that showed a cigarette smoking man alone on a bridge late at night with the caption 'You're never alone with a Strand (the brand name)' failed because consumers associated the cigarette with being lonely and who wants to admit that!

A further danger is that promoting a brand also promotes the generic product. A successful coffee advertisement will stimulate sales for that brand but it may also stimulate the whole coffee market and thus provide increased sales for the competition.

It is important that advertisements do not mislead. Regardless of the legal consequences, disappointed customers are likely to become ex-customers.

People have become cynical about advertising – they know that they are only seeing the view of the product or service that the supplier wishes them to. Nevertheless, advertisements can still be powerful forces in commerce, as can overall image.

# Image

Image ranges from the appearance of a building to the packaging for a product or the promotional material for a service. Packaging may actually cost more to produce than the product itself. Perfumes and chocolates are often elaborately packaged in an attempt to promote a particular image. Human behaviour often works on the principle that 'if it looks good – it probably is good'. An example of this occurred during World War II when the De Havilland Company proposed a fast, unarmed bomber made mainly of wood. Dismissed by the UK military in the first instance, the wooden wonder, as the Mosquito became known, was eventually ordered into production (with guns and not unarmed) on a massive scale, over 2000 being built between 1942 and the final examples in 1948. The general comment on the aircraft was that it looked so right that it was bound to fly right, a perception that was proved to be the case.

The image presented by buildings etc. will be considered in the next section on Organisational Body Language (OBL), which is one of the most important concepts in organisational success as it relates to the actual image an organisation displays as opposed to the image it purports to espouse. This is shown through small things, such as the quality of stationery through to the design of buildings.

## Fashion

Fashion could be described as the image that is in vogue at a particular point in time. Fashions can be very transitory, often lasting just a few weeks. It is important that the image that an organisation displays does not appear to be as transitory as a fashion. When considering such items as design of materials, corporate dress styles etc., organisations need to ensure that these fit in with the views of their stakeholders and that they match middle-of-the-road fashions, i.e. ones that are usually long-lasting.

Whilst it might be appropriate for a clothes store dealing mainly with young people to dress up its staff in the latest fashion, this would present the wrong image in a bank or building society where a degree of conservatism might be more appreciated by the customer. The fashions adopted by any organisation should balance the wishes of both the organisation and the external environment within which it operates.

## Organisational Body Language

As part of the work for their book *In Charge of Customer Satisfaction*, Cartwright & Green (1997) introduced the term Organisational Body Language (OBL). Cartwright (2000) then expanded upon this concept, looking at it in terms of enhanced customer relations. Whilst individual body language has long been recognised as an important part of the communication's process, OBL shows that it is not only individuals who signal their true feelings through body language. Organisations also exhibit a form of body language that sends out messages about the organisation.

OBL relates to the whole atmosphere that an organisation creates. There are organisations that clearly welcome the customer with open arms and there are those that may claim to but in fact the message the customer actually receives is one that seems to state that the customer is rather a nuisance who has to be tolerated! Equally there are organisations that send out clear messages regarding their relationship with the external environment and ones that try to keep this hidden.

It might seem strange that there would be any organisation that does not positively welcome its customers but they abound. This is shown in an example from the companion volume to this, *Mastering Customer Relations* (Cartwright, 2000) – an organisation that has arranged its car park in such a manner that customers park at the end furthest from reception. The parking spaces next to the reception area are 'reserved for company vehicles'. A company mission statement claiming that customers come first will be of little consequence to a customer who has just walked from their car to reception in the pouring rain and passes the company parking spaces right next to the reception area.

An organisation that had thought about OBL would have put the customer first, customer parking being for the convenience of the customer and not the organisation.

When Cartwright & Green were developing the OBL concept they found many examples of the following, all messages that send out negative OBL signals to those outwith the organisation, and give the impression that the organisation thinks about itself first and the outside world, including its customers, second:

- There is no car parking space reserved for a customer who is expected
- The customer arrives to find a locked door and no explanation (the door may need to be locked for security reasons but the means of entry should be made clear to the customer)
- There is nobody in reception
- There is somebody there but they have their back to the customer
- There is somebody there but they walk off as the customer approaches
- There are people there but they are interested in each other, not the customer
- There is a large queue and only one person is serving while others are walking about doing other things
- There is loud music blaring
- There is someone at reception but nowhere to sit and wait
- Reception have never heard of the customer even though he or she has an appointment
- No-one answers the telephone
- The customer leaves a message on an answering machine and no-one calls back
- No-one answers the customer's letters
- The customer arrives in reception and no-one has ever heard of the person the customer has arranged to see!

- Those with a legitimate need for organisational details have difficulty in receiving them
- The organisation plays little or no part in the local community.

Outstanding organisations will pay close attention to Organisational Body Language and ensure that the customers and others are not only told that they are important but that their experience will bear this out. It is a known fact that a good initial feeling leads to a 'halo' effect, whereby subsequent events are judged from a positive point of view. A bad start to an organisational relationship can lead to a 'horns' dilemma. For example, if the first few transactions between an organisation and a customer are good and there is then a less-than-satisfactory transaction, the customer is most likely to put the bad experience down to a temporary aberration – they have put a 'halo' around the organisation. If the first couple of transactions are less than satisfactory then, provided that the customer has not gone elsewhere, a subsequent good transaction may be thought of in terms of 'well they managed to get it right that time but will it last?' The customer is on the horns of the dilemma as to which transactions really represent the organisation and should they defect anyway in case subsequent transactions follow the initial pattern.

Organisations have a perennial problem that one bad event can wipe out many good ones in an instant!

Another very important aspect of Organisational Body Language is communicating very negatively. This is often manifested in the extremely negative notices that organisations display, for example:

- Don't lean on the counter
- No credit; no cheques; no refunds
- Broken counts as sold
- Do not touch
- No push-chairs
- No food to be consumed on these premises
- No children
- No dogs
- No cameras
- Keep off
- No change telephones
- No bags beyond this point.

There may be very valid reasons for the above strictures but it is the manner in which they are communicated that sets the tone that the outside world perceives. Every one of the above would send a more positive message if the word 'please' was included. The message would appear much more positive if some form of explanation was given, for example:

- For security reasons please leave your bags with the attendant
- Newly sown grass, please keep off
- Dangerous area, please keep children away etc.

As Cartwright & Green (1997) have pointed out, customers who meet a barrage of prohibition notices are likely to interpret this as 'Go away, you're too much trouble' and this is a very foolish message for any organisation to send to customers and potential customers.

Organisation Body Language can even include the sense of smell. It is possible to purchase essences to place in air-conditioning systems so that the smell of roasting coffee or baking bread can waft through a supermarket and trigger an autonomic reaction in the customers. Having a pot of coffee sending its aroma through a property is a well-known ploy of those trying to sell their house!

Organisational Body Language determines what an organisation actually thinks about those it interacts with as opposed to what it says its policy is. There is no point in an organisation claiming to be family-friendly if there are no facilities to change or feed babies and if the seats and counters are too high for children. The British Airports Authority (BAA) is among a growing number of organisations that provide baby facilities in the male as well as the female toilets. Many organisations that claim to be family-friendly do not provide lowered urinals and toilets for children, a minor detail perhaps but one that goes a long way to showing how much the organisation has thought about its customer base, as Cartwright (2000) has pointed out.

## The major aspects to Organisational Body Language

In considering the impact of OBL on customers, organisations need to consider a series of factors, namely:

- Location/buildings
- Security
- Convenience
- Communications
- Ambience.

Each of these aspects has its own OBL implications which the organisation needs to consider not just in respect of the external stakeholders but also of internal customers and suppliers who form part of the value chain.

### Location/buildings

In most cases there is little that can be done in the short-term to change the location and the basic structure of the organisation's premises. They may have been in that location for some considerable time and, whilst 'modern' when built, may now be anachronistic and often unsuited to changing business conditions and systems. There are however actions that can be taken relatively easily and cheaply to improve the 'look' of the location and buildings.

The actual visual image of an organisation is one of the things that sets the all-important first impressions. Basic items an outsider may consider are:

- Do the organisation's premises appear in good repair?
- Are the premises, internally and externally, clean?
- Has the organisation considered the surrounding environment, e.g. are there flower beds, trees etc. and are they well tended?

Given that human beings are highly visual in nature, the visual image of premises is very important. Buildings that incorporate curves may be more pleasing to the eye than purely rectangular ones. Modern architects are well aware of the need not only to consider the functional aspects of buildings but also the aesthetic ones; function and aesthetic design are not separate but part of the image presented to the outside world.

## Security

Staff and people visiting organisations need to feel safe. Many a business has lost trade not because its own premises were unattractive but because they were located in an environment that made the customer feel nervous.

There may be little that the organisation can do about its immediate environment other than lobby the authorities for improved street lighting etc., but the organisation needs to bear in mind the importance of security as a motivator, as discussed earlier when the work of Maslow was considered.

Whether it is an office block or a shopping centre, those using it, or even near to it, need to feel that their security has been considered. Proper lighting, security staff where appropriate, CCTV (Closed Circuit Television) cameras, secure car parking, all send out a message that the organisation cares about the security of people as well as property.

## Convenience

How much has the organisation thought about the convenience of its facilities to those using it? Earlier in this section the example of an organisation that gave precedent to staff parking over the needs of customers was given. Many of the convenience factors that are put in place for customers will also benefit staff and suppliers.

Is there proper access for the disabled? 'Proper access' means not requiring wheelchair users to enter via a back door or via ramps that have never been checked for ease of use by a wheelchair. It may seem strange that nobody would actually check that ramps are suitable but during research for this book, two such examples were found. Are the doors arranged in such a manner that a wheelchair user can open them? There are now regulations relating to new buildings that ensure adequate access for the disabled.

Do lifts (elevators) have controls that can be reached by a wheelchair user? There is nothing that shows a lack of OBL knowledge more than seeing a wheelchair user having to use a stick to operate the lift buttons because they are situated too high. Modern lifts should also have Braille indicators and possibly voice systems that tell the visually impaired which floor has been reached.

Are the door arrangements easily operated by people carrying shopping or briefcases? Again a little thought can show that the organisation really does care. Organisations that neglect these simple ideas are actually telling many potential customers that they don't want them. Just because a person has a disability does not mean that they are not a potential customer or a potential valuable supplier or shareholder (or voter in respect of public sector organisations), and there are very few members of any of these groups that any organisation would want to disadvantage deliberately.

The public sector has been at the forefront of providing access and in recent years many commercial operations, especially in the retail and leisure sectors, have made themselves much more accessible.

Convenience also includes toilet facilities. Are these easy to find and, as mentioned above, are they suitable for children? How well are toilet facilities equipped and how 'comfortable' does the customer feel in using them? Whilst there has been a great improvement in such facilities in the UK in recent years, one really has to consider the 'restrooms' of the USA to see the standard to which such facilities can be provided.

Another important comfort feature is the provision of seating areas for customers. A recent trend in large stores (the Marks and Spencer store at Handforth Dean near Manchester Airport being an excellent example) is the provision of a waiting area near changing rooms. No longer should a person have to stand whilst his or her partner tries on clothes. Many motor vehicle franchises now provide a relaxing area with coffee and magazines where owners can wait whilst their vehicle is serviced, and there have been major improvements in doctors', dentists' and hospital waiting areas.

Airports have incorporated increasing numbers of food and retail outlets in a mutually beneficial manner; the customer has something to occupy them whilst awaiting their flight, and valuable income can be earned. These developments now extend to many mainline railway stations, again providing a distraction for the customer and income for the retailers and the station operator.

The final feature of convenience is a consideration of opening and closing times. There is no doubt that the decision of UK building societies to remain open on Saturday mornings after the high street banks discontinued the practice led to an increase in custom. There is no point in being open at times when customers cannot avail themselves of a product or service, and it is foolish to be closed when they can. The opening of 7–11 stores in the UK following the successful US model has led many other retail outlets to change their hours of opening. Twenty four-hour shopping is already an electronic reality and is becoming an actual reality in major towns and cities, a development being led with 24-hour opening of many major supermarkets.

# Communications

'If in doubt – ask' is no doubt a good maxim but one which many visitors to organisations do not follow. Asking may make the person appear foolish and thus it is not unusual to see people wandering about and trying to find what they want without having to ask staff. It is therefore very important that signs are visitor-friendly.

The use of internationally recognised signs for common facilities makes it easier to find facilities in a foreign airport, ferry port or railway station without speaking the language, and this needs to be extended (as it is being) to all organisations. Many facilities, from toilets to food outlets, from car hire to ATMs (Automatic Teller Machines – cash dispensers) have an international symbol and are thus easier to find.

The layout of reception or help desk areas is important. They should be welcoming, not threatening. They should be immediately visible upon entry and manned all the time. There is nothing more off-putting than a vacant reception or help desk. Ideally reception desks should be separate from switchboards. This is not always practical but where they are together, the receptionist (if there is only one, as is often the case) has to decide between dealing with the visitor or answering the telephone. Whatever he or she does, one person is going to feel either unwelcome or that their call is not being answered.

Reception areas should always have somewhere for a visitor to sit and, if possible, a collection of up-to-date magazines and the day's newspapers. Many organisations use the reception area as a shop window for their products and services; tastefully displayed, these provide useful advertising. Reception areas often have signs welcoming people, but the visitor needs to feel welcome, not just be told that they are and then have nowhere to sit!

## Non-face-to-face communications

Another aspect of OBL is the way an organisation manages its verbal and written non-face-to-face communications. Is there a policy of answering the telephone within a certain number of rings? There is only a finite amount of time a person will wait for the telephone to be answered. If answerphones and voicemail are used, how quickly does the company promise a reply? How are out-of-hours calls handled and responded to? As shown in the previous chapter, modern communications can greatly enhance the relationship between supplier and customer, but only if used sensibly.

How quickly are letters answered and does the use of standard replies make the recipient feel less of an individual? The written communications of an organisation help set the all-important image of that organisation. Much money is spent designing logos but it is important that the written word below the letter heading meets the customer's needs and answers his or her queries.

## Ambience

*Ambience* is a word that relates to the overall impression gained by the customer. The ambience of an organisation is built up from all the above OBL factors. If a person feels that he or she is important and that their comfort has been thought about in the way the organisation designs its operations, then they will be better disposed to the organisation. If they feel that they are of lower priority than the staff of the organisation, then if they are customers or potential customers they are likely to take their custom elsewhere. Organisational Body Language is a very important aspect of customer relations, and more and more organisations are carrying out OBL audits to discover exactly how a customer is likely to perceive the organisation – a view that is sometimes at dissonance with the view of senior management.

## Public relations

Three terms that are often confused are *public relations, publicity* and *advertising*.

*Publicity* is the result of actions by or to the organisation and is managed through the *public relations* process. Publicity can be active, where there is a deliberate attempt to put over a message or image about products, services and developments of the organisation, or passive, where something happens that is outwith the control of the organisation but an organisational response is required. It is easier to deal with things over which the organisation can have some proactive control rather than those where it must react and thus be at least one step behind the game.

*Advertising* can be defined as a type of active publicity, although it is usually considered as a separate subject as it is normally handled by specialist external agencies rather than through the public relations process.

The Institute of Public Relations, quoted in Brassington & Pettitt (1997), defines public relations as:

'The deliberate, planned and sustained effort to institute and maintain mutual understanding between an organisation and its publics.'

The use of the plural form for publics is important. Marston (1979) states that:

'a public is any group, with some common characteristic, with which an organisation needs to communicate.'

There are, therefore, a number of publics with whom any organisation needs to communicate including:

- Customers
- Suppliers

- Shareholders in the private sector
- The electorate for the public sector
- Local and national government
- Competitors (where there are matters of mutual concern)
- The media
- Its own employees
- Pressure groups
- Professional and trade bodies.

These often equate to the stakeholders mentioned earlier in this book.

Each of these groups will require different information to be used for different purposes. The Institute of Public Relations definition is rather wide and could be deemed to include advertising and related activities. It is proposed therefore to use the following definition of public relations (first used in *Mastering Customer Relations*) as it relates to this book:

> **Whereas advertising is related to the raising of interest in products or services, public relations is concerned with presenting a positive image of the organisation to its various publics in response to the needs of those publics.** (Cartwright, 2000)

Public relations is also not publicity (Jefkins, 1980). Publicity is the result of something that has happened, public relations is the response to that publicity, which may in turn generate more publicity. Public relations is concerned with minimising the damage caused by bad publicity or maximising the gain through publicity that is beneficial. The term 'spin-doctors' came into common usage in the late 1990s. One of the jobs of a spin-doctor is to transform bad publicity into good by placing a positive spin on it.

## The needs of the various publics

Each group that has a relationship with the organisation will have different needs, as discussed below. A key component of an effective public relations strategy is to cover as many of the groups as possible and to avoid providing conflicting messages to different groups.

### Customers

The individual nature of dealing with customers is very important but there will be times when the organisation needs to communicate to its whole customer base. One such occasion is when there needs to be a product recall due to a deficiency (normally related to safety in a product). It is obviously especially important to make urgent contact with customers when a fault has been found in a product, which requires immediate rectification. If the organisation has a list of purchasers then they can be contacted directly, but it must be remembered that the purchaser is not always the end-user of a product so that additional steps also need to be taken. Notices can be placed in the various outlets that stock the product, and notices can be placed in the appropriate media, e.g. newspapers, magazines and trade journals. Such notices need to do two things. They must provide clear and concise details of how the fault is to be rectified and they must give information on the nature of the fault. If the item must not be used, then this must be clearly stated. It is also possible to use such a notice to reassure the customer. Statements such as 'in a small number of instances' etc. will help achieve reassurance. As product liability has become very important, organisations are tending to veer to the side of caution in issuing recalls, as the legal/financial consequences of being complacent can be severe. Any recall, however, is likely to generate bad publicity but the 'spin' is that, by dealing with the fault quickly and being proactive with a recall, the organisation is actually looking after its customers – something that generates good publicity. It is important that the need for a recall should, ideally, come from the organisation and not the media. There have been a number of cases where faults have been highlighted by consumer organisations and television programmes, forcing the manufacturer to issue a recall. Good public relations should be proactive rather than in this case reactive.

Organisations can use technology to keep comprehensive databases of customers and these can be used for publicity as well as advertising. The organisation can write to its customers on a regular basis, not only about new products but to provide news regarding community initiatives and even organisational 'gossip'.

## Suppliers

The relationship between suppliers and an organisation is both delicate and dynamic. Suppliers will operate to their own values and culture but if the organisation they are supplying is a large one, then that organisation may be able to insist on its values being applied within the supplier, as discussed earlier in this book. There may well be issues, especially those of product liability, that concern a number of members of the value chain. Eddy *et al.* (1976) have shown how, in the case of the 1972 Paris DC10 air disaster, the public relations exercise involved not only Douglas, as the main builder of the aircraft, but also Convair, who built the fuselage and the defectively designed rear door (to the specification, it must be said, laid down by Douglas) and Turkish Airlines, the operator of the aircraft. Indeed, had the engines been considered to be a contributory factor in the crash, then General Electric would also have been involved. In this case the public relations exercise was not conducted well, with members of the value chain actually suing other members. The case does serve to illustrate the dependency on mutually supporting public relations for the various members of the value chain.

## Shareholders in the private sector/the electorate for the public sector

These have a financial stake in the organisation. In the private sector, obviously the shareholders; in the public sector, the whole of the electorate will have an interest in the image of the organisation as this may have financial implications for them.

In the 1980s and 1990s, the UK Conservative government began a series of privatisation exercises, taking a large number of publicly owned enterprises into the private sector. The aim was to produce a shareholding democracy, with those sections of the public who had never previously owned shares buying into these enterprises. British Airways, British Gas, the electricity generators and British Telecom were among the larger enterprises privatised.

These new private sector organisations had very large numbers of shareholders indeed, ranging from financial institutions down to individuals holding just a hundred shares.

Private sector organisations need to communicate to their shareholders. They are compelled to produce an annual balance sheet showing the financial position of the enterprise, and it has proved a good public relations exercise to provide easy-to-read summaries of the yearly accounts for those who had never previously had to read a balance sheet. The early annual general meetings of such organisations occasionally went into uproar as small shareholders attempted to make points. As time has gone on, the senior managements of these companies have demonstrated a growing awareness that small shareholders have different needs from those who have traditionally held large numbers of shares. In the case of many of the privatised enterprises, shareholders are also customers and this can provide an interesting view of the Porter Model, to be introduced in Chapter 12 with regard to bargaining power. As a customer, one wants the lowest price possible; as a shareholder, higher prices may well mean higher dividends!

In the public sector there has been a greater emphasis on public relations in recent years. State schools have been compelled to produce an annual report and hold an annual meeting for parents since 1986, hospitals are required to produce reports on their work and local councils have become much more adept at providing information to council tax payers. Demands for council tax now come with an explanation of how the money is allocated and many councils hold public meetings on planning and budgetary issues to ensure that the electorate can gain information if they so wish. As regards the payment of council tax, the electorate cannot legally withhold money, but they can 'spend' their vote (Cartwright, 2000).

A phenomenon that has been seen regularly since World War II has been the public relations aspect extended to armed conflicts – armies, navies and air forces are organisations as well. In 1939 the British Prime Minister, Neville Chamberlain, actually wanted to close down BBC Radio for the duration of the conflict. Today, news is broadcast directly from the front line and governments employ spokespersons to brief the press and through them the general public. Even as late as 1992 the UK government was criticised for the handling of the Falkland's conflict with Argentina in respect of the way it dealt with the public relations aspects of the conflict, especially in connection with operational matters and the tragic loss of personnel, ships and aircraft; the manner in which the sinking of the destroyer *HMS Sheffield* was handled was considered particularly inept (Hastings & Jenkins, 1983).

As more and more democracies enact Freedom of Information legislation, the role of the public relations staff in those organisations will become increasingly important and challenging. It might, of course, be argued that every election campaign is in fact a major exercise in public relations, although given the low turnout in some recent UK elections it may well be that the parties have not really succeeded in putting their messages across.

## Local and national government

The previous section considered the need for local and national government to undertake public relations for themselves. However, a whole range of organisations considers that one of their publics (as defined earlier) is the local, regional, national or even supra-national (e.g. the European Union) government. Individual organisations, trade bodies and professional associations lobby politicians and employ specialist public relations consultants (known as lobbyists) to put forward their views. Many sponsor politicians and in the UK it is a requirement for politicians to register any such interests. Smaller organisations that cannot afford to employ lobbyists may be able to lobby through trade bodies, and such bodies are often invited to provide the trade or sector viewpoint to legislative procedures.

## Competitors

Within any sector of business there will be matters of mutual concern. For instance, if the government is bringing forward legislation on a matter that has implications for all the players in a particular market, there may be an advantage in a common approach. In these cases, a trade body may handle the public relations aspects in order that there is a co-ordinated response. Whilst many organisations may be fiercely competitive, they may also work collaboratively on matters of safety. This is only common sense, as a lack of confidence in one player in a market may cause a lack of confidence in that sector of the marketplace in general.

There is also the issue of deliberate mis-information. An organisation may want a competitor to misread a situation to gain competitive advantage. Whilst lying can never be condoned, bending of the truth or putting a different spin on it can and does occur.

## Employees

Employees have a vital, if often informal, role in public relations. It is vital that any organisation makes sure that employees know what is happening in order that they will give out the required messages. To that extent they become the recipients of internal public relations. Brassington & Pettitt (1997) stress the importance of such internal PR.

## Pressure groups

The final half of the 20th Century saw a growth in the number of what became known as *single issue pressure groups*. This was not a new phenomenon, the anti-slavery movement of the 19th Century and the suffragettes of the first two decades of the 20th Century are good examples. Such pressure groups can be very focused and may be local, national or even international. They normally campaign on a single issue that allows them to put over a very simple message: NO BYPASS, BAN HUNTING WITH HOUNDS are examples, as are those that seek redress or justice for a particular individual.

Such groups are often very effective in their own public relations but are sometimes reluctant to listen to the message put out by other organisations. Any issue always has at least two sides and there is very often a public relations 'war' going on alongside the real issue as each party attempts to rally public support to its point of view. An acronym introduced by Cartwright & Green (1997) was LICAL, representing the five easiest ways to lose a customer: Lying, Ignorance, Complacency, Arrogance and Lethagy. Organisations should never lie and one can be sure that a single issue pressure group will uncover any untruths and then use the fact against the offending organisation. Such single issue groups are usually very tenacious and highly committed, and will probe any and all messages put out by their opponents.

## Professional and trade bodies

In terms of public relations, professional and trade bodies often act as a clearing house and co-ordinating centre for their members. By their very nature they are able to speak with a greater degree of authority than individuals or small organisations. They are also able to co-ordinate a response to any issue across a range of organisations. To do this, of course, they rely on receiving accurate, up-to-date information from their members. Membership of such a body brings many benefits to an organisation but, if the organisation is consistently at fault, there is the possibility of it being expelled and it is likely that the professional/trade body will be able to use public relations more effectively than the organisation. The organisation will have to explain its expulsion, whilst the professional/trade body can use it to show how concerned they are about maintaining standards.

## The media

The media have been left until last, not because they are not important but because they encompass much of what has gone before. The power of the press (the Fourth Estate), the television and radio companies, and increasingly the Internet cannot be over-estimated.

Much of the information people receive comes via the media and however pure that information was, it is in some way transformed. The media have their own agendas and deal with stories accordingly.

Public relations and the media may be either proactive or reactive; it is proactive if the organisation initiates the story, it is reactive when the media initiate and then approach the organisation.

## Newspapers and journals

Just as there are typologies of organisations, there are also typologies of newspapers and journals.

Newspapers fall into the following categories:

- Broadsheet nationals – daily, e.g. *The Times*
- Tabloid nationals – daily, e.g. *Daily Mirror*
- Broadsheet – Sunday, e.g. *The Observer*
- Tabloid – Sunday, e.g. *News of the World*
- Regional dailies, e.g. *Manchester Evening News*
- Regional weeklies or bi-weeklies, e.g. *Perth Advertiser*
- Local weeklies, e.g. *Strathearn Herald*
- Specialist dailies, e.g. *Financial Times/Racing Post*
- Specialist weeklies, e.g. *New Musical Express.*

Each type of newspaper has a particular type of reader with their own values, needs and wants. Suppliers of goods and services are normally fairly adept at knowing which newspapers are likely to be read by a particular target audience. Many of the questionnaires on lifestyles or even at the end of package holidays ask which newspapers the respondent reads. This is so that advertising, which is very expensive, can be properly targeted. It is unlikely that an expensive Mercedes car will be advertised in the *Daily Mirror* but it may well feature in *The Times*.

Whilst all of the daily newspapers may carry the same story, the manner with which it will be treated varies according to the readership and the views of the newspaper. Newspapers often espouse a particular political viewpoint or may take up a campaigning stance on an issue, especially if that is likely to increase sales. The newspaper industry is an example of where the customer accumulator introduced in Chapter 9 is especially relevant; a reader gained is normally a reader lost to the main competitor.

Regional and local newspapers tend to concentrate on a narrower front but, like the nationals, they may well take up particular issues. There are also specialist newspapers covering a range of subjects from finance to music.

The essential difference between newspapers and magazines lies in the word 'news'. Newspapers deal with the more ephemeral issues; a story that is on page one today may be on page three tomorrow and forgotten by the end of the week. The articles in magazines usually have a longer shelf life. All newspapers employ a considerable number of journalists and researchers. If they believe that there is a story then they will approach the organisation concerned, normally through the press officer or the public relations department. Dealing with the press is a specialised skill and best left to the experts. A throwaway line by a member of staff could be a banner headline in a national paper.

Magazines tend to fall into two groups:

- Special interest
- General interest.

Special interest magazines, e.g. *Autocar* and *Railway Modeller*, are targeted at particular interest groups, whilst the general interest publications, e.g. *Woman*, *Esquire* etc., are designed to appeal to a wide range of readership, often gender specific.


## Television and radio

It is salutary to consider that mass ownership of televisions did not commence until after World War II and that since then there has been such growth that few homes in developed countries are without at least one television set and many have additional sets. Radio was developed earlier, in the 1920s, and by 1939 there was a mass market for radio sets. Television and radio are able to react much more quickly to news items than newspapers, as the latter have to await the printing of the next edition, whereas television and radio can break into a programme. Where newspapers have an advantage is in the depth of analysis they can provide and, as with all written material, there is the ability to scan pages and return to items of interest. Television can now accommodate teletext and there are large numbers of text pages available to the viewer.

Radio does not have this advantage but is able to produce analytical programmes related to the news, with interviews of relevant personalities. Up to the 1970s, an advantage that radio had over television was the ease of outside broadcasting, with radio just needing a car as against the outside broadcast van required for television. The development of video cameras of increasing sophistication has led to the introduction of Electronic News Gathering (ENG) using lightweight cameras, allowing television crews to gather news in more remote areas and to broadcast it back to base. Jefkins (1980) considers that radio has four special characteristics that should guarantee its survival alongside television:

- The attractiveness of the human voice, regardless of the appearance of the presenter who is, of course, not seen
- The speed with which material can be produced and the immediacy of interactive programmes such as 'phone ins
- The low cost of personal radios
- The ability to broadcast in many different languages, thus allowing ethnic groups access to news etc. in their own language

and to the four above should be added a fifth:

- The ability to listen to the radio whilst driving.

Television has become an important part of people's lives. There has been a growth in consumer-related programmes where organisations have had their products and services put under the public spotlight, often unfavourably. In the late 1990s, organisations began to fight back. The holiday industry has complained that such programmes are actively seeking complainants and are thus a magnet for attention seekers who may have no real complaint but just wish to appear on television. It cannot be doubted however that programmes such as *That's Life* and *Watchdog* etc. have put companies on their mettle as regards the treatment of their customers.

## Accuracy

Contrary to popular belief, reporters are very concerned about the accuracy of their stories, and for good reason. The most reliable defence against a libel charge is that the story is the truth!

Inaccuracies should always be pointed out to the publisher of the story. Court action is rare because, even if the publisher has printed in error, few organisations wish for the publicity of a court case which will keep the issue in the public domain for some considerable time. Minor inaccuracies are normally corrected by a statement in the newspaper, magazine or by the television/radio company. It must be said, however, that the corrections usually appear in smaller print than the original story.

## Bias

Organisations and groups often complain about media bias. In many cases this is just because the media have not presented the organisation's view in the manner that the organisation would prefer. In recent years the BBC has been accused of bias against nearly every political party. If all the parties are complaining, then perhaps the Corporation's claim that it is neutral is perfectly logical.

In a democracy there is theoretically freedom of the press. In practice, all governments reserve the right to suppress stories on the grounds of national interest and security. Such powers are normally used sparingly by democratic regimes. Non-democratic regimes control the media to a much higher degree.

The Press Complaints and the Broadcasting Standards Council are able to adjudicate on complaints made against the media, although they are only able to make reports. Further action is left to the complainant.

## Marketing and corporate PR

It is possible to make a distinction between marketing public relations and corporate public relations. The former normally constitutes part of the wider promotion of the organisation and its products/services and is akin to advertising. As such it is a form of active public relations in that it will be generated internally. Corporate public relations is more concerned with the image of the organisation as a whole and may well be a defensive reaction to an externally generated issue.

Marketing public relations is capable of being planned well in advance and may well form part of an advertising campaign. Sponsorship can be considered a form of marketing PR. Whilst corporate PR can be planned, as in the case of a major development, it also needs to contain contingency plans to cope with the unexpected. 'Be prepared' is not only a suitable motto for the Scout movement, it applies as much to PR. There is nothing more damaging to an organisation than a spokesperson who has been poorly briefed giving out wrong or misleading information.

## Summary

The image that an organisation actually displays may be at variance with the one it actually wants the outside world to see. Organisational Body Language is a way of describing the actual messages that an organisation sends out to the external environment. All organisations need to communicate clearly with their various stakeholders in the external environment and to reduce 'noise' to a minimum to ensure that a clear message is put over. Public relations and advertising form important parts of this communications process.

## Concepts covered

- Communications
- Noise
- Promotion and image
- AIDA
- Fashion
- Organisational Body Language (OBL)
- Ambience
- Public relations
- LICAL

## Analysis

In carrying out the *aesthetic* analysis in respect of an organisation, the following components of OBL (taken from *Mastering Customer Relations*, Cartwright, 2000, with permission) need to be considered.

For the part of the organisation under consideration, or the whole organisation if required, consider the following points and rate them as either Excellent (E), Satisfactory (S) or Not satisfactory (N). For excellent ratings, comment on why that particular facet of OBL is so good. For Satisfactory or Not satisfactory ratings, suggest how improvements could be made.

| Facet | E | S | N | Comment |
|---|---|---|---|---|
| LOCATION/BUILDINGS | | | | |
| Easy to find | | | | |
| Attractive | | | | |
| Gardens etc. | | | | |
| Maintenance | | | | |
| Cleanliness | | | | |
| SECURITY | | | | |
| Well lit | | | | |
| Security of access | | | | |
| Internal security | | | | |
| CONVENIENCE | | | | |
| Car parking | | | | |
| Toilets | | | | |
| Children's facilities | | | | |
| Disabled facilities | | | | |
| COMMUNICATIONS | | | | |
| Signs | | | | |
| General information | | | | |
| Correspondence | | | | |
| Telephone techniques | | | | |
| AMBIENCE | | | | |
| Reception | | | | |
| Waiting areas | | | | |
| Drinks etc. | | | | |
| Staff attitudes | | | | |

QUESTIONS

1. Explain, using examples, the importance of reducing noise in the organisational communications process. Ensure that your answer covers not only external but also internal communications.
2. Show how AIDA (Attention, Interest, Desire and Action) can be used to explain how products and services can be promoted effectively.
3. Using good and bad examples, describe how organisations should use and develop public relations to improve their image within the external environment.
4. How can an organisation use OBL as a proactive tool to improve its relationships with its external environment and present a more positive, actual image to that environment?

# Further reading

You are recommended to read *Mastering Customer Relations* by Roger Cartwright (2000) for a more detailed description of OBL.

# ⚇ 9  Customer analysis

*The growth of consumerism – The importance of analysing the customer base – Customer needs and wants – Customer care – Anticipating future customer requirements and the product life cycle – Customer behaviour*

A consideration of the customer base, both existing and potential, as part of an external analysis is important for the simple reason that – no customers equals no work, equals no income, and eventually no jobs and no organisation.

It is necessary in order to understand the customer section of these analyses to explore the relationships between customers and suppliers (that is, the organisation).

It was John Wannamaker, a Philadelphia department store-owner, who coined the well-known phrase 'The customer is always right' in the late 1860s. Since then there has been a growth in the field of customer relations as organisations have realised that in a competitive environment the customer may not always be right but they do pay the wages and therefore require considerable care and attention. The field of customer relations is more than just providing excellent service and care at the point of a transaction. Relationships, by the very meaning of the word, have a temporal span; they have a beginning, a middle and unfortunately an end over a span of time. They also need organisational effort in establishing and maintaining them.

## Consumerism

As stated earlier, it was John Wannamaker, a Philadelphia department store-owner, who coined the immortal phrase 'the customer is always right'. (Popular belief in the UK ascribes the remarks to both Sainsbury and Selfridge. Perhaps, as Cartwright (2000) comments, there is nothing wrong with different groups claiming ownership in this instance!) The retail trade, dependent as it was and remains on good face-to-face, continuing relationships with customers, was far quicker to pick up on customer care concepts. By the early 1900s, the steamship companies taking immigrants from Europe to North America had upgraded their immigrant or 'steerage' accommodation considerably. As Davie (1986) has pointed out, this was less as a result of official rules on the transportation of immigrants (which had recently been put into place) and more to do with a realisation that there was profit to be made in attracting the immigrant trade and that those who went out steerage might, having done well in the New World, make visits home using second or even first class. If they were impressed by the steerage accommodation, they might well book themselves and their families in higher priced cabins for visits to their ancestral homes.

As competition increases, so the suppliers of goods and services have had to work at retaining their customers. The ability to travel, brought about firstly by the railways and then by the motor car and the aeroplane, has increased the radius that a customer is able to go in order to fulfil their requirements. Village and even city centre shops have found it difficult to compete with supermarkets situated on the outskirts of town, especially when those supermarkets provide good parking facilities, buses in some cases for those without cars and even petrol pumps.

Customers have become increasingly used to expanded choice and higher quality standards. The modern customer challenges and wants to know the why and not just the how. The medical and legal professions, local and national government, newly privatised industries and education have all been required to become more responsive to the needs of their customers.

As shown in Chapter 1, the late 19th and the 20th Centuries saw the development of huge organisations. Prior to the Industrial Revolution of the 19th Century, organisations were small, limited as they were by the lack of effective means of transport. Small organisations find it much easier to remain close to their customer base; this is much more difficult for a larger organisation.

The development of improved communication systems after World War II, in particular the telephone and the television, helped bring about a consumer revolution. It became much easier for consumers to exchange information and the development of commercial broadcasting, firstly in the USA and then in the UK, meant that viewers were exposed to increasing amounts of advertising. Customers were becoming much more aware of the choices open to them. These developments have been furthered by the massive increase in the use of home computers linked to the Internet which has brought global retailing into a large number of homes. Books, music, holidays and even motor cars can be brought on-line with a few clicks of a mouse.

The growing power of the consumer has been recognised in the growing numbers of volumes advising organisations how to manage customer relations. In 1982, Tom Peters & Bob Waterman published *In Search of Excellence*, their study of successful US companies, and made the point that closeness to the customer and active listening to customers were key attributes for successful companies (Peters & Waterman, 1982). A similar study in the UK by Clutterbuck & Goldsmith drew remarkably similar conclusions – *The Winning Streak* (as they entitled it) and *The Winning Streak Mark II* for the successful UK company were closely related to the care given to effective customer relations (Clutterbuck & Goldsmith, 1984/97).

The social revolution of the 1960s, which saw young people become much more challenging of authority than in the past, led to a much more questioning customer base. Doctors and lawyers began to find that their customers asked more questions and demanded excellent and in many cases a more personal service – questioning a doctor used to be unheard of. Dissatisfied customers are much more likely to resort to litigation if their problems cannot be resolved and the major television channels have espoused the cause of the consumer. In the UK, the BBC consumer affairs programme *Watchdog* and the ITV series *We can work it out* continue to attract excellent viewing figures and have provided embarrassing moments for those companies that have failed to respond to legitimate customer complaints.

Whilst the consumer revolution may have started in the USA, the introduction of cheap flights across the Atlantic from the 1980s onwards enabled the British and other Europeans to see at first hand how the US retail, hospitality and entertainment industries treated their customers, and that has led to a revolution in service standards in the UK and the rest of Europe. The USA has had a tremendous influence on British customer relations. Not every US company gets it right first time, every time, but there has been a greater awareness of the need to delight the customer and as the British have experienced the US standards of service, so they have returned demanding the same standards at home.

Market share is one of the aspects of an organisation's performance given considerable weight by investors. This is obviously only a factor with private, for-profit organisations, but it is an important one as the effect of a drop in market share on investor confidence can be quite dramatic, the importance of such confidence having been stressed in Chapter 5 dealing with economic analysis.

The effect of a loss of customers to a rival is not an arithmetic progression, it follows what may be described as the 'customer accumulator' developed by Cartwright (2000) and reproduced below.

Imagine a situation where there are two shops in a town and each has 100 customers initially. For the purpose of this exercise it is assumed that the total customer base will remain at 200. Let us examine the effect of shop *B* gaining 1, 2, 10, 25 and 50 customers off shop *A* (Figure 9.1).

Shop *A* has lost half its customers but it is now three times smaller and thus perhaps three times less attractive to investors than shop *B*. If we assume for the exercise that each customer generates £10 of profit, the effect of this is shown in Figure 9.2.

Not only is shop *B* now three times bigger in terms of market share, it is three times more profitable and the comparison of profitability is a key ratio in deciding the relative strength and success of organisations.

| Shop A Customers | Shop A Market share | Shop B Customers | Shop B Market share | Numerical difference B − A | Relative size of B compared to A |
|---|---|---|---|---|---|
| 100 | 50% | 100 | 50% | 0 | equal |
| 99 | 49.5% | 101 | 50.5% | 2 | 1.02 |
| 98 | 49% | 102 | 51% | 4 | 1.04 |
| 90 | 44% | 110 | 56% | 20 | 1.2 |
| 75 | 37.5% | 125 | 62.5% | 50 | 1.6 |
| 50 | 25% | 150 | 75% | 100 | 3 |

*Figure 9.1   The customer accumulator* (Cartwright, 2000, with permission).

| Shop A Customers | Shop A Profit | Shop B Customers | Shop B Profit |
|---|---|---|---|
| 100 | £1000 | 100 | £1000 |
| 99 | £990 | 101 | £1010 |
| 98 | £980 | 102 | £1020 |
| 90 | £900 | 110 | £1100 |
| 75 | £750 | 125 | £1250 |
| 50 | £500 | 150 | £1500 |

*Figure 9.2* *The effect of the customer accumulator on profit* (Cartwright, 2000, with permission).

# Lifetime value

One of the important consequences of the consumer revolution has been an increased awareness of the lifetime value of the customer. Repeat business, for the vast majority of organisations, is a key organisational performance measure. It is no coincidence that banks and building societies target students as potential account holders. Whilst they are likely to be very short of money whilst at college or university, statistics show that they are likely to earn higher-than-average salaries later on and, as people are very reluctant to change their bank or building society account, they will become good lifetime customers, any losses that the organisation incurs early on in the relationship being offset by the profits generated by repeat business.

It has been calculated (Cartwright & Green, 1997) that an average person spends, in a lifetime, over £150 000 on motor cars, £25–50 000 on holidays and no less than £100 000 in the supermarket. These figures explain the growth of loyalty schemes in a number of industries. A dissatisfied customer does not leave £30 of groceries at the till, if they never come back some £100 000 of business, according to the accumulator model introduced earlier, goes to a competitor, boosting the latter's market position.

# Customer-driven v product-led

There are two extremes to a relationship with the customer and indeed to marketing as a whole. An organisation which adopts a **product-led approach** develops products and systems that are suited to the organisation. Henry Ford expressed this approach well in the 1920s when he offered customers a Model T Ford in 'any colour as long as it's black.' Such an approach can work in a situation where there is little or no competition and demand exceeds supply. Modern vehicle manufacturers, having listened to their customers, develop a whole range of variations and options around the same model and are thus able to adopt a much more **customer-driven approach**. Whilst it may be initially more cost-effective to produce only one basic model, the modern customer has shown that they wish to make choices. Indeed, as pointed out in *Mastering Customer Relations* (Cartwright, 2000), a companion volume to this book, in the motor vehicle industry, yesterday's options rapidly become today's standard features.

Power steering, air-conditioning, CD players etc. were once highly priced options or only standard on the most expensive top-of-the-range UK car products. By 1999 they were standard on many medium-priced products. The customers had expressed a preference for these items through their purchasing decisions, and the more proactive manufacturers made decisions to offer their mainstream products with such features.

It is not only in terms of the features of physical products that a customer-driven approach is manifested. Service features such as extended opening times (including 24-hour shopping), new means of communications and even the provision of disabled and mother-and-child parking spaces demonstrate a commitment to putting the needs of the customer before those of the organisation, reflecting the fact that it is the customer and the customer alone that directly or indirectly pays the bills and wages of any organisation.

# Added value

Regardless of how a product or service is paid for by a customer, that customer will place a value on it. Payment may be direct, as in most retail transactions, or indirect through taxes, third parties etc. There are many areas of life where customers could actually produce the article or carry out the service themselves but choose not to. It is possible to build one's own car from a kit, to carry out the legal conveyancing of a house and to grow all one's own food. Why don't more people take this approach and save themselves money? The answer is simple; most people do not have either the skills or more importantly the time to do so. It is convenience that forms part of the price.

Customers, in fact, pay for the value that a supplier adds to raw materials or service delivery. By paying a supplier, customer time and resources are released.

Each step of the process of delivering a product/service, be it building a vehicle, processing a loan or dealing with a planning application, carries a skill/time cost and a monetary amount of added value that the customer is prepared to pay. This is known as a value chain, with the costs of the product building up at each step, together with a contribution to the added value. The cost of each step of a process consists of a series of factors based on the costs of materials, time, overheads etc.

Later in this chapter the somewhat complex question of 'who is the customer?' is considered. What it is important to realise is that *every* organisation has customers and that, unless those customers are placed at the centre of an organisation's objectives, they may go elsewhere. Even in a monopoly situation, as discussed in Chapter 12, the customer still has the right not to partake of the product or service. Monopolies rarely last forever and as soon as there is some form of choice, some customers will be lost. If the relationship with the customer has not been at the centre of the organisation's objectives, then there is a danger that there will be exodus rather than just leakage of customers.

For many years, managers have been taught that organisational (and indeed any) objectives should always be written in SMART criteria, i.e. they should be:

- Specific
- Measurable
- Agreed
- Realistic
- Timely (i.e. with deadlines and timescales attached).

Cartwright (2000), in a companion to this volume, suggests that SMART should be amended to C-SMART, with the added Customer-driven being the most important. Unless objectives are rooted in meeting the needs of customers, they will add nothing to the organisation's success or development.

## Grudge purchases

Not all the products or services customers actually need are welcomed by them. It is easy to consider customer needs in terms of the products and services that customers actually enjoy – motor cars, clothes, holidays etc. Successful organisations aim to generate repeat business. Not all organisations, however, wish to use repeat business as an indicator. Surgeons do not want the patient back and the police actually have a reduction in repeat business as an indicator. We all need hospitals and police stations but they are not something that we actively want to participate in. It is, therefore, more problematic to consider those products and services that people actually need but begrudge paying for, so-called grudge purchases. Insurance is an example of a grudge purchase. It is necessary but the costs are often resented. Indeed, if somebody has to make a claim it is because something has gone wrong. Hospital and dental treatment are other examples of grudge purchases, as are home maintenance and essential public services such as prisons and the police force. It might also be considered that undertakers fall into this category – despite the fact that we will all need their services one day, few of us wish to admit it. Astute marketing by the undertaking industry has managed to convince a growing number of people to pre-pay for their own funeral; perhaps this is the ultimate grudge purchase! Even where payment is not direct and the services are funded through taxation, there may still be a resentment to pay. The managers and staff of such organisations have a much more difficult task in developing a meaningful relationship with their customers, most of whom may be very reluctant partakers of the product or service. Many doctors' surgeries, dental practices and local/national government offices have become much more customer-friendly, with appointments being made where possible to suit patients and clients rather than the organisation.

## Who is the customer?

For those working at the front end of a direct selling or service organisation, the above may seem easy to answer – it is the person who is served and who then pays. However, the true picture is more complex yet still easily understood in terms of the concept of a customer chain, each member of which has their own wants and needs. For the enterprise to be a success, all of the members of the chain need to be at least satisfied and preferably delighted.

Firstly it is necessary to differentiate between needs and wants (we have already considered motivational needs in Chapter 3 with the ideas of Abraham Maslow).

A *need* is something that we cannot do without; a *want* is the method by which we would like the need to be satisfied – in many ways a want is a need with added value.

A customer can be defined in simple terms as (Cartwright, 2000):

> One for whom you satisfy a need.

It should also be noted that needs are often very basic and it is wants that grow in importance once basic needs are satisfied.

Unfortunately many organisations seem to believe that the definition above is enough and that all that is required is to satisfy a customer's needs. If you only wish to see the customer once, that may be true, but most organisations want to retain their customers, as discussed earlier, and even if they are only going to deal with that customer once in a lifetime they will still wish for good reports to be given to other potential customers. A funeral director's customer is not the deceased (with whom they will only deal once), but the deceased family and friends upon whom they will wish to make a good impression.

It used to be thought that customers had to be merely satisfied, but in today's competitive world satisfaction is not enough – in order to retain customers they need to be delighted. Needs can be satisfied but to delight a customer it is necessary to understand and then meet their wants.

In the light of the above, Cartwright (2000) further refined the definition of a customer to:

> One for whom you satisfy a need and who you delight in respect of their wants.

Thus there are two main categories of customers – *internal* and *external* – and whilst the latter is important for the final profit and thus often receives the greatest attention, the former add value and have a vital role in quality. The value chain has a customer service chain running parallel to it.

In the vast majority of product/service deliveries, a whole series of people will have added value before delivery to the external customer. A motor car or electronics assembly line gives a clear illustration of how this happens. Each process adds value; a car with no engine is worth less than the one with the engine fitted. Each person or groups of people are suppliers to those next in the process, who are in fact their internal customers.

If a person buys a toy as a birthday present for a neighbour's child – who was the customer, the buyer or the child? It was the buyer's money that paid for the

Person 1 •——▶ 2 •——▶ 3 etc. •——▶ Purchaser •——▶ End User

Internal Customers                                                 External Customers

*Figure 9.3    The customer chain.*

toy but it is the neighbour's child who will (hopefully) be delighted with it. The buyer was a *purchaser* but the child was the *end-user*; the buyer is in fact one back from the end of the customer chain and not the end of it.

The *customer chain* can be represented as shown in Figure 9.3.

It is important to realise that the purchaser and the end-user may not be one and the same, but that there is likely to be considerable feedback between them and good customer care can double the potential for repeat business. The purchaser may come back again for something else but if the end-user is delighted with what the purchaser has provided for them and the purchaser relays a good report on the service they received, then the end-user may also become a purchaser in their own right.

It is easier to see the relationship between internal and external customers and purchasers and end-users in the retail and commercial segments of business than to understand the customer relationships in other areas such as the public service. Who are the customers of the agencies running prisons, is it the prisoners themselves or is it the taxpayers who pay for the service? Other areas of the public sector face the same dilemma and many use the term *client* for the end-user to distinguish the users of a service from those who pay for it.

# Market research

In order to assess and then meet the needs and wants of customers, it is important to find out as much as possible about them. This is usually easier once they become actual rather than potential customers, as a relationship will have been established. Market research is concerned with finding out about the customer, especially their lifestyle, needs and wants. Effective market research ensures that the products and services offered are those desired by the customer. In this way the organisation can become much more customer-driven rather than product-led, an important consideration in a competitive environment.

As the *Mechanical Engineering EDC* wrote in 1971 and as quoted in Wilmshurst (1978): 'One no longer seeks to make decisions solely on the basis of hunch or flair. One now seeks first the facts upon which the hunch, or flair can nourish itself.'

There are four main areas for which organisations make use of market research:

- Findings about new services and products required by the customer
- Indications of the lifestyle trends of the customer base
- Information about the suitability and quality of current products and services

- Information about the perceptions of customers and potential customers in relation to the organisation and the organisation's competitors.

Many organisations contract their market research out to specialist market research organisations.

Effective market research is about asking the right questions of the right people so that only those hunches that meet customer requirements come to market.

There are three 'rights' associated with market research:

- The *right* questions
- The *right* sample of customers/potential customers
- The *right* action following analysis.

Formulating research questions is a skill unto itself. If the researcher uses leading questions (where there is an indication of the answer required) there is a danger that bias may creep in. If the questions are too open, then the subject may veer away from the issue at hand. Yes/No (known as dichotomous questions) can be very inflexible and many researchers prefer to present subjects with multiple choices.

Even if the questions are correct, there is little point in putting them to the wrong people. Effective market research requires a balanced sample of sufficient size to inform the decision-making process. It is important that the sample size ($n$) is not so small as to make the results unrepresentative. Adler (1969) makes the point that even a nation-wide survey in the UK will have a sample size of only 2000 and it is rare for this to rise as high as 5000. Polls related to general elections claim to predict the right result with samples of 2000–3000, although there have been some spectacular unrealised predictions as the true voting intention is only shown in the privacy of the voting booth. This means that the members of the sample need to be chosen with great care if they are to be representative of a large population.

Whilst some surveys may wish to consider the total possible population (say, all of the voters in the UK when a general election campaign is underway), most are concerned with specific populations, e.g. the population that buys chocolate or drinks beer, or drives motor cars etc.

Much market research is conducted using questionnaires. These may be either sent to customers with, perhaps, an incentive for return (entry to a prize draw is a popular incentive) or conducted on the street or in the organisation's premises. The major downside to sending questionnaires to customers and especially potential customers is that the number of returns can be very low, giving a small sample size. If the returns are low, then this can give a very biased sample. Suppose an organisation wished for information about the quality of its products. It is likely that anybody dissatisfied with the product would be more likely to return the questionnaire and thus the sample might show a higher rate of dissatisfaction than was actually the case. Where questionnaires are used on a face-to-face basis, then care must be taken to ensure that there is a balanced sample. Package holiday companies often give out the customer satisfaction questionnaire on the return flight home, when there is little else for the customer to do. These questionnaires often contain extra questions relating to lifestyle, the answers to which can provide the organisation with added details of the customer's lifestyle and a source of income, as such information is very valuable. The answers to these lifestyle questions can then aid the type of social analysis that was the subject of Chapter 3.

One problem with such an immediate customer satisfaction questionnaire is that it provides little time for the customer to reflect on the product/service and may be just a 'happiness sheet' coloured by immediate events and not truly indicative of the total experience, hence the growth in focus groups to be covered in the next section.

## Focus groups

Focus groups have become an interesting method of 'getting close to the customer' as described by Peters & Waterman (1982). Retail organisations and even political parties are using focus groups more and more often to provide in-depth comment regarding their operations and new ideas. Careful chairing of such a group can provide much more detailed information than a questionnaire. The process also links those customers involved into the organisation, strengthening their loyalty. It should go without saying that the comments from such a focus group should always be taken seriously. Experience has shown that such a group can provide valuable information about products and the standard of service, and can also give the organisation a useful sounding board for new ideas.

## Implementing research

Why do customers choose a particular product and service? Customer behaviour often follows a pattern known as AIDA, first introduced in the previous chapter:

- Attention
- Interest
- Desire
- Action.

In order to attract the customer's attention, he or she has to know about the organisation and its products. This may be through advertising but it may also be through less informal means. Once *attention* has been gained then, if the customer feels that the product or service is right for them, their *interest* is stirred. Once somebody is interested they will try to find out more about what is on offer. If they still like what they see and hear, they will begin to *desire* the product or service and that will produce *action* to acquire it for themselves or their client.

From an organisational viewpoint, there are two major problems associated with AIDA:

1. Stimulating demand for one product, service or even supplier tends to stimulate demand for similar offerings across the market. More than one

successful brand advertising campaign has not only stimulated demand for the specific product but at the same time also stimulated demand for competitors' products, and this is possibly unavoidable. Research has shown that those viewing advertisements tend to remember the category of product or service more easily than the actual brand. Once attention and interest have been gained, the person is likely to experience the desire to purchase, so the organisation must ensure that the demand can be met. At the start of the home computer boom in the 1980s, one company stimulated massive interest with their relatively cheap machines. Unfortunately they could not supply enough of them and purchasers had to go elsewhere and, once there, they stayed with the competition. That advertising needs to have integrity should go without saying, and organisations such as the Advertising Standards Authority (ASA) in the UK and similar organisations worldwide take a very dim view of advertisements that are dishonest, misleading or offend public decency.

2. It is very easy to lose a purchase at any stage. If, having gained attention, the organisation is unable to fulfil the customer's service need for information in the *interest* stage, they risk losing him or her altogether. Bad service at any stage after gaining attention can mean a lost customer on a permanent basis. Every expression of *interest* should be treated as a potential *desire* and eventual *action*. Everybody in the value chain should be aware that *desire* without quick fulfilment can fade quickly. This is known as 'Buyer's Regret' in the USA. Once the customer has made up their mind, the longer the wait between order and delivery, the greater the danger that they will have second thoughts. Even asking somebody to wait a few minutes whilst somebody seeks further information or a sample can cause desire to fade and result in a lost customer.

## Product/customer value

An important part of any customer analysis is to predict the products and services that current and potential customers will require. Which products and services should the organisation be concentrating on and which should be discontinued? In sophisticated, global markets, customers are not just buying a car, a television set or an ocean voyage but the supplementary products that surround it, e.g. ambience, service and, of increasing importance, after-sales service. As the goods and services supplied by differing organisations become more and more alike, then it is the supplementaries that affect the final buying decision.

Products and services go through a life cycle from birth to decline and it is important for organisational planners to be aware of this life cycle in order to understand the changing behaviour and preferences of their customers. The implications of the product life cycle were covered in Chapter 2 of this book, as they form an important part of the internal analyses that the organisation must carry out in addition to external scanning.

Life cycles can be short – as in the fashion industry or those linked to other products such as Batman accessories, Power Rangers and the vast range of spin-offs from other films and TV series, or they may be very long – the Boeing 747 and KitKat chocolate bars being good examples.

## Customer behaviour

Loyal customers are obviously very important to organisations as they provide repeat business. However, the effective organisation never takes loyalty for granted and part of its customer analysis must address the question as to whether loyalty is real or in fact pseudo-loyalty, i.e. are the customers in fact hostages (a term explained below) to the organisation. Work by Jones & Strasser (1995) in the USA has considered customer loyalty and in particular why satisfied customers defect. Previously delighted customers do not usually defect unless they cease to become delighted or are even more delighted by the offering of a competitor.

Jones & Strasser have made the point that many organisations believe that if their customer feedback mechanisms indicate satisfaction, then the organisation is in a good position. Their research, however, showed a weak link between satisfaction and loyalty. As products and services improve, then satisfaction becomes in effect the minimum acceptable standard. Jones & Strasser have referred to long-term loyalty and false loyalty, whereas Cartwright (2000) refers to these terms as supra-loyalty and pseudo-loyalty. Many commercial operations have competition curtailed either by government restrictions or by (sometimes illegal) arrangements between the various players. Jones & Strasser have concluded that in the case of monopolies or near-monopoly situations (see Chapter 12), as soon as there is increased competition then the level of satisfaction required to retain previously 'loyal customers' increases. They point out that whilst in monopoly situations it is the customer who has restricted choice, as soon as competition opens out it is the supplier who has only one real choice, i.e. to provide their existing customers with higher and higher levels of satisfaction. The easier it becomes to switch, the more likely it is to happen.

UK banks have made a point of targeting students to open accounts with them, despite the fact that students have little if any disposable income. The fact is that graduates are likely to earn more over their working lives and thus provide more business and revenue for their bank. There has also been a considerable lack of switching of bank accounts. Part of this may be due to loyalty but it has also been relatively complicated to switch banks. Banks are now making it much easier for customers to change to them by easing the complexities that the customer could experience. This is, off course, a two-edged sword. If one organisation makes it easier for somebody to switch from a competitor, its competitors will make it easier for customers to defect to them. Changing one's email provider may require a new email address and people will have to be informed; perhaps it is easier to remain with the current provider. When the UK government deregulated telephones, gas and electricity in the 1990s, the various suppliers made it relatively simple for customers to switch provision. British Telecom, as the UK market leader for telephone services, also made it easy and cheap for defectors to return.

The importance of total satisfaction (or delight) against mere satisfaction was demonstrated by the example of the reprographics giant, Xerox, as profiled by Jones & Strasser (1995). They found that delighted Xerox customers were a staggering six times more likely to give repeat business to Xerox than merely satisfied customers. As it is unlikely to cost six times more to delight a customer than to merely satisfy him or her, then the financial advantages of delighting the customer seem self-evident.

Jones & Strasser have developed terminology for six types of customer behaviour that can be linked closely to the types of loyalty discussed earlier.

## Apostles

Apostles demonstrate such incredible loyalty that it can be described as supra-loyalty (Cartwright, 2000). The apostle is delighted with the service or product and may actually personally identify with the organisation or the product. This is, of course, good news for any organisation. Apostles, in effect, carry out a marketing function for the organisation. They are highly loyal and delighted and they tell their friends and relations.

There are downsides to having too many apostles in the customer base. Their identification with the organisation may be so close that they can come to believe that they are actually part of the organisation. When this happens the distance that should rightly be present in the customer–supplier relationship is destroyed. The apostle can become a nuisance by demanding special treatment and interfering in matters that are really not their concern, such as internal arrangements that have no effect on the customer. There is a delicate balance to be struck by organisations that want the benefits of apostles but must militate against the disadvantages.

The biggest danger associated with the apostle is the tendency to become highly disruptive if dissatisfied. Apostles are paradoxically the most fertile source of the organisation's worst enemy, the terrorist. It is said that 'Hell hath no fury like a woman scorned' but as Cartwright (2000) has pointed out, to an organisation 'Hell hath no fury to compare to a highly dissatisfied apostle'. The dissatisfied apostle does not just feel let down, because of their perceived close link to the organisation they can feel betrayed, and with betrayal may come a wish for revenge and retribution.

Apostles are unlikely to switch suppliers unless they become very dissatisfied, but when they do it will be in such a manner as not to go unnoticed.

## Loyalists

Loyalists form the most important component of the customer base. They are akin to the 'cash cows' defined by the Boston Consulting Group as those products that form the basis for organisational success. Loyalists require less effort on their behalf than do apostles and are very loyal customers, coming back time and again. They tend to be less volatile than apostles and are thus more tolerant of mistakes. They are less voluble in their complaints but that does not mean that the organisation can afford to ignore them. An organisation that loses the support of its loyalists is on the downward spiral to major problems. Loyalists may not make a major fuss if they defect but they will still be lost to the organisation and reluctant to return.

Whilst there might be a certain glamour attached to apostles and their effusive praise of an organisation, loyalists are the true firm foundation for any customer base. Loyalists provide the stability and objectivity required for sustained growth. Loyalists form useful members of focus groups, as they will not be afraid to tell the truth as they see it, but they will be objective in doing so and that will provide useful data for the organisation. Organisations should identify and nurture their loyalists.

Jones & Strasser make the point that loyalists are the easiest customers to deal with. That is true, but customers only become loyalists as a result of high-quality products and services delivered over a period of time and, when there have been complaints, they have been rectified expeditiously.

## Mercenary

Mercenaries are the hardest customers to deal with, as they are basically aloyal. Mercenaries will tend to go for the cheapest or the most convenient option. They are difficult to deal with because they may well be satisfied but they are not loyal. Mercenaries may demonstrate product loyalty but brand aloyalty; they may be brand loyal but have no loyalty to a particular supplier. They may well move from brand to brand or supplier to supplier. If asked why they moved, the answer may be in terms of cost or convenience but it may well be just a desire for a change.

The problem for an organisation is whether to expend energy or indeed money on trying to turn a mercenary into a loyalist. The organisation will need to satisfy the mercenary, as even they will tell people about bad products and services, but unless they are incredibly pleased it may well be that they will continue to shop around. From the organisation's point of view it is important not to pander too much to the mercenary. Too big a discount on the first transaction may well mean that they will always want such levels if they return, but they are just as likely to go down the road and quote your discount to a competitor in the hope that it will be bettered.

## Hostage

Hostages appear to be very loyal but that is only because they have no choice. If a village only has one shop, then it will receive the vast majority of the local trade.

An organisation will not know whether its customers are loyalists or hostages until a competitor or a substitute appears on the scene.

Hostages have no choice. If there is only one convenient shop, one local supplier, one hospital for them to go to, they have no choice but to demonstrate attributes of loyalty even when dissatisfied, hence the use of the term pseudo-loyalty.

The time for an organisation to assess the loyalty and the satisfaction of its customers is not when a competitor opens up but before then. Hostages will leave as soon as they have an opportunity if they are dissatisfied. Even satisfied hostages may leave for a while in order to assess a new competitor. The original supplier will have to hope that the original product/service was of sufficient quality to tempt them back. It is too late to offer discounts and/or enhancements after competition starts. Hostages will ask, and rightly, 'why are you offering this to me now and not before?'

# Defector

Dissatisfy even a loyalist often enough and they may well defect from the organisation. Once a customer has defected and given their custom to another organisation, it may well be difficult to recover the situation.

Organisations need to ensure that complaints are dealt with in an expeditious manner so that any temporary dissatisfaction does not become permanent and thus lead to defection. One organisation's lost customer is a gain for a competitor, with the financial penalties as shown in the customer accumulator introduced earlier in this chapter.

# Terrorist

The terrorist in customer relation's terms is the worst nightmare an organisation can have. Just as the political terrorist acknowledges no rules, neither, it appears, does the customer relation's terrorist.

Terrorists were often apostles displaying supra-loyalty until they were let down and the situation was not recovered. They are not so much dissatisfied with the organisation, product or service as at war with it. They have a desire for revenge and retribution. Many of those who appear on consumer affairs television programmes have been previous apostles. On being let down, they have no problem in letting the world know about it.

The longer a situation remains unresolved, the angrier the terrorist becomes and sometimes their actions may be extreme, irrational and even criminal. The threat of a court appearance for harassment or breach of the peace in respect of their relationship with an organisation may well have an unexpected and negative effect. Court means publicity and by the time a customer becomes a terrorist, putting the problem right is no longer enough, they want to see the organisation humiliated.

As Cartwright (2000) states, the best method of dealing with this type of terrorist is to do what should never be done to a political terrorist – give them what they want and more if necessary and hope that they go away. The organisation will not want them as customers in the future. The organisation should concentrate on cutting its losses rather than trying to win back the custom.

Jones & Strasser's work is useful in that it provides an easy-to-understand explanation of why mere satisfaction is no longer enough to generate loyalty. Loyalty must be earned and should never be taken for granted.

## Summary

Customers are an organisation's most important asset, whether the product or service is one that is desired or a grudge purchase. When an organisation loses a customer, the customer accumulator shows that this is a gain for others within that particular market segment. Customers often follow the AIDA format from initial attention to an actual action, purchasing the product or service. Products and services have distinct life cycles, and decline can be averted by imaginative thinking using new uses, geographic markets etc. Loyal customers may not be as loyal as they seem, as there is a danger that they may be hostages.

## Concepts covered

- Consumerism
- Customer accumulator
- Lifetime value
- Customer-led and product-driven
- Added value
- C-SMART
- Customers
- Market research
- Focus groups
- AIDA
- Customer behaviour
- Loyalty

## Analysis

In carrying out the *customer* analysis in respect of an organisation, the following need to be considered:

1. What is the nature of the customer base?
2. What customer needs and wants does the product/service range meet?

3. What possible products/services developments will meet anticipated customer needs?
4. Where are the current products/services positioned on the product life cycle?
5. Does the hostage concept apply to any of the customer base?

QUESTIONS

1. Why is it important for organisations to develop a customer-driven philosophy as opposed to one that is product-led? What are the advantages of such an approach and are there any disadvantages?
2. Why is it vital for organisations to identify hostages? What can be done to ensure that hostages remain loyal as competition increases?
3. Explain how products and services are positioned within the product life cycle/dynamic product life progression. What steps can organisations take to avert decline? Illustrate your answer with examples known to you.

# Further reading

You are recommended to read *Mastering Customer Relations* by Roger Cartwright (2000) and *In Charge of Customer Satisfaction* by Roger Cartwright and George Green (1997).

# ☑ 10 Legal analysis

*Sources of law – Common law – Statute law – Jurisdiction – Contracts – Consumer law – Codes of practice – Health and safety – Product liability – Employment law – European Social Charter – Competition legislation – European law – Whistle blowing*

> 'Ignorance of the law excuses no man: not that all men know the law, but because 'tis an excuse every man will plead, and no man can tell how to refute him.'
>
> (John Selden 1584–1654)

Whilst the original quote may be considered sexist in today's climate, the term man should be replaced with person, the concept that ignorance of the law is no excuse is still a maxim in the legal system of the vast majority of the world's jurisdictions, including that of the UK.

It is important to distinguish between law and justice. These are words that are often confused and used synonymously. The three main meanings of justice according to the *Concise Oxford Dictionary*, 8th edition, edited by Allen (1990) are (a) just conduct, (b) fairness and (c) the exercise of authority in the maintenance of right. Law is a set of rules put in place by a society and there may be a contradiction between those rules and popular concepts of fairness. Many of the laws of Hitler's Germany were unfair and odious but they were properly enacted laws by a government that could make some claim to have been elected by the democratic process, a process Hitler soon abandoned however. Courts in many jurisdictions have recognised that there is a form of natural justice that all human beings are entitled to, not being tried more than once for the same offence being one of them, but nevertheless justice as the application of authority in the maintenance of right is not necessarily natural justice. Hitler's judges in passing cruel and seemingly irrational sentences for racial transgressions were actually applying the law of Germany at that time.

Linked to legality and justice are integrity and ethics. There has been a recent growth in the developed world in 'ethical investment portfolios' for those who wish to invest their money in organisations that behave in certain ways or refuse to trade in certain commodities, for example armaments, or who will not deal with regimes that are considered oppressive. In order to fully understand ethical changes within organisations, you are advised to read *Managing Values – Ethical Change in Organisations* by Paul Griseri (1998).

Law in the UK is derived from three main sources: common law, statute law and European law (which takes precedence over national law), and falls into two main categories:

- *Civil law*, which is concerned with the rights of people
- *Criminal law*, which centres on the types of conduct that society will and will not tolerate.

In the UK and most other jurisdictions, criminal cases on an issue take precedence over any civil ones. In the famous 1990s trial of the US sportsman O. J. Simpson, a jury found Simpson not guilty of murder after a criminal trial in California. The victim's relatives then instituted civil proceedings against Simpson for damages resulting from the death and won a substantial amount. This happened because the burden of proof is greater in a criminal trial than in a civil one. Perhaps it could only happen in the USA, but the criminal jury found that Simpson had not killed anybody whilst the civil one stated that he had and awarded damages!

Because liberty (and in countries with the death penalty, life itself) may be at risk as the result of a criminal trial, it is important that this comes first before any civil case and/or public inquiry provide too much publicity which can colour a jury's judgement. Different jurisdictions have different rules on pre-trial publicity. There was concern in the late 1990s over the trial in Boston of the British au pair Louise Woodward who was convicted of the 2nd degree murder (later reduced to manslaughter) of Matthew Eappen. Much of the concern centred on the huge amounts of pre- and actual trial publicity, publicity that would not have been allowed in the UK. Whatever the views an organisation or individual may hold about the fairness of the system used in another country, it is for that country to put its own procedures in place and those from outside who seek to work there must make themselves aware of the systems in place.

One of the problems relating to a major rail disaster in London in 1999 was that the calls for an immediate public inquiry over the safety issues could make the bringing of criminal charges for corporate manslaughter impossible, as the publicity generated by the inquiry would make a fair trial impossible. This resulted in no criminal charges being brought.

There have been concerns in the UK over there being both a civil law and a criminal law. Most of this chapter will concern itself with civil law but there are times when organisations, or more correctly those acting on behalf of an organisation, may commit an offence under criminal law. An organisation can be tried in its own right in the UK (and the USA), corporate manslaughter being an example. Fraud is a criminal offence and can be committed by those who seek gain for the organisation as opposed to personal reasons.

# Common law

Common law provides the foundation for UK law. As Montague (1987) has pointed out, the majority of UK rules of law are based on common law rather than by legislation from Parliament. Common law derives from the succession of decisions made by judges, often over centuries. Common law is based on a system of judicial precedent where the decisions made by one judge or by a higher court are used as the precedent for subsequent decisions on future similar occasions. In the UK, the House of Lords is the highest court in the land and thus a decision by the House of Lords binds all lower courts to its rulings. In the UK context, the European Court of Justice, the House of Lords, the Court of Appeal and the High Court are 'superior' courts whose judgements set precedents. Crown courts, County courts, Sheriff's or Magistrates' courts and tribunals are 'inferior' courts whose rulings do not necessarily set a precedent unless upheld by a 'superior' court, usually after a series of appeals to those courts.

As common law is not codified in Acts of Parliament, the concept of reasonableness is key to its understanding. Murder has been an offence since time immemorial but it is only recently that it has formed part of an Act of Parliament. A reasonable person would conclude, so common law has argued, that murder is unacceptable and thus through precedent upon precedent it has always been an offence under common law. In consumer law, reasonableness plays a part when considering the legal rights of a customer.

In the USA, a Federal system is in operation whereby each state has its own set of laws, the Federal Government being involved only when offences legislated under Federal law are involved or when there is a constitutional issue at stake. Surprisingly, murder is not a Federal offence in the USA (unless it involves the assassination of a senior member of the administration) whilst kidnapping is. Each state has its own legislation on murder and indeed some states have the death penalty on the statute book and use it, some have it and don't, and some don't have a death penalty statute. Each US state has its own Supreme Court where the justices can hear appeals. There is also the Supreme Court of the United States whose justices hear cases relating to constitutional matters.

## Statute law

Statute laws are those made by governments and written down. In the UK, it is either the government of the day or an individual Member of Parliament – MP (including Members of the Scottish Parliament – MSPs) who puts forward a new or amended piece of legislation. The process ends when the monarch signs the final bill making it an Act of Parliament and thus law. Between acceptance as a suitable subject for legislation and making it on to the statute book, there is a complex and time-consuming process.

The vast majority of bills are introduced by the government of the day. Whilst there are provisions for individual back-bench MPs of any party to put forward legislation, these are limited. Also limited is the time the government, concerned as it is with passing its own legislation, can allocate to private members' bills. In the case of a government-sponsored bill, there will have been much discussion of the content beforehand.

# Jurisdiction

In these days of global business, legal jurisdiction, i.e. which legal system has jurisdiction over a case, is very important.

In very general terms, the legal system of the country where an issue occurs has jurisdiction over that issue, and it is its laws that will be applied. However, modern business and ease of travel have complicated this basic concept somewhat.

If the matter is a criminal one, in the vast majority of cases the matter will be tried under the legal system of the country in which the offence occurred. In recent times, however, a number of countries, including the UK, have enacted legislation allowing them to try their own citizens for offences committed in other jurisdictions. The two main areas where this occurs (albeit rarely) are war crimes and sexual offences against children. In the case of the latter, a number of countries in the developed world have enacted legislation enabling them to bring suspected 'sex tourists' who it is believed may have committed an offence with a child to court in their own country. The UK is not alone in having legislation on the statute book allowing for the trial in the UK of suspected war criminals who are found to be resident in the UK (after acquiring UK citizenship), even though these offences may have been committed in Eastern Europe during World War II when the accused was a citizen of another country. Up to 1999 there had only been one successful prosecution under this legislation.

If an organisation's employee is arrested for an offence in a country other than that of the organisation's corporate HQ, then that employee will be tried under the jurisdiction of that country and will be subject to the legal procedures and punishment regime of that country. If the employee is a citizen of another country other than that where the organisation is registered, then it will be the diplomatic staff of the employee's country of citizenship which will provide official diplomatic representation. However, a good employer would normally provide legal assistance to an employee who meets legal difficulties whilst on his or her employee's business.

In December 1988, a Pan American Airlines Boeing 747 was blown up over the small Scottish town of Lockerbie. Scotland has its own legal system which operates differently from that in the rest of the UK. As an example, the possible verdicts in a criminal trial in England and Wales are guilty and not guilty. In Scotland there is a third possibility – not proven. Lockerbie is only just over the England–Scotland border a few miles north of Carlisle and thus the investigation was conducted under the Scottish legal system, despite the fact that the passengers and crew were mainly American or English and the aircraft was on a flight from an airport under English jurisdiction (London Heathrow) to one in the USA (John F. Kennedy Airport in New York) and was US built, owned and operated. In due course, two Libyan nationals were accused of planting a bomb in the aircraft and a great deal of diplomatic and political effort was expended to bring them to trial in a manner that would satisfy UK in general, Scottish, US and Libyan sensitivities.

In the Spring of 2000 (as this book was being prepared), the trial of the two suspects opened in an old military airfield in the Netherlands, Libya believing that a neutral venue was necessary for a fair trial. However, in order to satisfy the need to recognise Scottish jurisdiction, the airfield was made temporary Scottish territory. Street names were changed to Scottish ones, Scottish police were drafted in to patrol the interior and Scottish judges were appointed to hear the trial (a jury not being used in this most unusual of trials).

Where organisations operate outwith the jurisdiction of their home country, it is vital that staff are made aware of the legal differences they may encounter. What is not an offence in one jurisdiction may well be in another.

In the USA, the individual states are able to enact their own legislation provided that it does not conflict with Federal legislation. This format has been followed to a degree in the European Union where, as was shown in Chapter 4, European Law is superior to the laws of member states.

This chapter examines a number of aspects of law that need to be included in any analysis of the legal environment surrounding an organisation:

- Contract law
- Consumer law
- Employment law
- Health and safety
- Competition legislation
- European law.

Examples are mainly taken from the UK but mention is also made of European Union and US legislation, the former having its own section in this chapter.

## Contracts

Because of the differences that exist relating to contract law in different countries, this section will deal mainly with the situation in the UK, although it must be borne in mind that Scottish law is slightly different in respect of contracts from the rest of the UK.

The vast majority of civil legal dealings that involve organisations revolve around contracts – they are, together with money for payment, the bedrock of business transactions as they put the relationship between an organisation and its suppliers and customers on a legally enforceable basis.

As individuals, we are all involved in informal and formal contracts, be they contracts to buy and sell houses, credit or hire purchase contracts or contracts of employment. In fact, many of the contracts people enter into do not involve complex legal documents, as there is no requirement for a contract to be in writing. Every retail transaction, for instance, that is undertaken involves a contract.

A contract can be defined as:

---

'an agreement, enforceable by law between two or more consenting parties (who have the right to make such an agreement) which obliges the parties to undertake certain acts which are not indeterminate, trifling, impossible to perform or illegal.'

For a contract to be valid there must be **agreement** about all the important aspects between the parties. The legal term for this is *consensus in idea*. In addition, the parties must **consent** to the contract. If a party were made to sign a contract under duress, then the contract would be invalid. The parties must also wish to be legally bound by the contract. Business transactions are presumed to create legally binding obligations on the parties, whereas domestic situations do not. However, as Cartwright (2000) points out, there has been a growth in pre-nuptial marriage contracts and, if it is shown that the parties intended that these should be legally binding, then they may form valid contracts enforceable at law.

The parties must have the **legal right to make the agreement**. If a person entered into an agreement to sell some goods known to be stolen, then the contract would be invalid as *nemo dat quod non habet*, no-one can give that which he does not have, and possession is not nine-tenths of the law – only the owner of goods can transfer the ownership of them. Young people under the age of 18 in the UK (21 in the USA) are limited in the contracts they can make, organisations may limit which staff may enter into contractual obligations on behalf of the organisation and those certified as insane are forbidden from entering into contracts. Signing a contract whilst under the influence of alcohol or drugs may also affect the validity of the contract.

It is not possible to enter into a contract to commit an act that is **illegal**. Such an agreement is known as *pacta illicita* (an illicit pact). It would be completely unenforceable by law. This is a point that has implications for employment contracts and will be covered later in this chapter.

Contracts should relate to important matters and not be **indeterminate** or **trifling**. A court cannot enforce a contract that is too vague and if, for any reason, the contract becomes impossible to perform, even after it is agreed, then the contract ends. Many holiday contracts include the term *force majeure*, which like Acts of God cannot be covered in a contract. If a hurricane destroys your hotel, you cannot force the holiday company to accommodate you in a hotel that does not exist; careful consideration of the holiday insurance contract is required before purchase, to ensure that cover for such events is available.

## When does a contract come into force?

There are two major parts to the contracting process, both of which have major implications for organisations. The two parts are **offer** and **acceptance**. These must match. In simple terms, organisation *A* offers to sell a product or service to organisation *B* at a price. If *B* accepts, then there is a contract between them (technically in force even if the agreement is only verbal). If *B* is interested but at a lower price, then *B* can make a counter-offer at the lower price. If *A* accepts the counter-offer then there is a contract. If *B* does not accept *A*'s first price and

*A* will not accept *B*'s counter-offer, then there is no contract between them. In retail terms, this is very important. A price on an item in a showroom is not an offer to sell at that price; it is an **invitation to treat**, i.e. for a potential customer to begin to discuss a purchase. There is no obligation on the trader actually to sell at that price. The contractual process only commences when the customer begins the negotiation.

In a similar vein, advertisements are only an invitation to treat, although all such invitations in the UK must comply with the Trades Descriptions Act.

## Withdrawal of an offer

Once an offer has been accepted, it leads to a legally binding contract. Time limits can be put on an acceptance, i.e. the offer is open until such and such a time.

## Acceptance of an offer

Acceptance must be a positive step. It is not possible under UK law to say that 'the offer will have been deemed to have been accepted if we have not heard from you by such and such a date/time'. It is not acceptable in law that the person to whom the offer was made should have to go to the trouble of expressly declining it. Silence is declining, not acceptance, unlike the famous defence by Sir Thomas More when on trial for treason against Henry VIII that 'silence gives consent.'

In cases where offers and acceptance are made by post, which include the majority of commercial contracts, the acceptance is made when it is posted, not when it is received; hence the importance of obtaining proof of posting.

## Tenders

When an individual or an organisation asks for an estimate, they are not actually asking for the work to be done but requesting an offer (a tender). They can then make a decision as to whether or not to accept. If they do accept, then a contract is formed and they are obliged to pay the tender amount and the other party is legally obliged to deliver to the agreed specification for the accepted price.

## Exclusion clauses in contracts

UK common law will accept a clause that is inserted into a contract by one party that seeks to limit their liability for the consequences of a breach of contract or negligence. This is because both parties have agreed to the contract and thus it was open to the other party to object to the clause. However, it has been realised that one party may have more bargaining power than the other and thus the Unfair Contract Terms Act was passed in 1977 and amended in 1995 to redress the balance. However, as early as 1949, courts had been ruling favourably in respect of those who suffered under such unfair clauses.

Many of the cases brought under this aegis have related to tickets with conditions on the back. Airline tickets have a large number of conditions printed on them, often relating to compensation limits in the event of accidents. Eddy *et al.* (1976) have pointed out that US courts have allowed settlements far in excess of the limits because the conditions were not brought to the attention of the purchaser at the point of sale, i.e. when the contract became effective, as discussed earlier. In most of these cases the ticket issuer has been a large organisation and the customer either an individual or a smaller organisation.

In the UK, as in the vast majority of developed world jurisdictions, guarantees for products contain a statement that the guarantee in no way affects the purchaser's statutory rights under their domiciliary jurisdiction. This is because purchasers have protection in the UK under the Sale and Supply of Goods Act (1994) and any clause trying to exclude this protection would be unfair and in fact illegal.

Under the Unfair Contract Terms Act (1977), any term in a contract that attempts to restrict liability for death or personal injury is automatically void. In effect, no individual or organisation can state that they refuse to accept liability for their own actions. Other attempts to circumvent the Act, which will also be declared void, are those that try to restrict statutory rights, e.g. it is a breach of contract law to say that a person cannot take action under the Sale and Supply of Goods Act (1994) as it is the purchaser's right, terms which require the customer to indemnify another person plus terms which impose time limits on complaints unless, in all three cases, the party relying on the term can prove that it was a fair and reasonable term under the circumstances.

It should be noted that insurance contracts and contracts relating to the setting up or dissolution of companies etc. are exempt from the Unfair Contract Terms Act (1977).

## Standard contracts

Except in the case of large orders where a specific contract between the relevant organisations will be drawn up, most contracts between suppliers and customers use some form of standard contract. Car sales, holidays and electrical goods are all dealt with using standard forms designed by the supplier.

Customers receive protection from the fact that it is the supplier who sets up the terms of the contract in the following ways under the 1977 Act, in that any terms that seek to:

1. Exclude or restrict liability for breach of contract
2. Enable a party to render a performance substantially different from that which the customer could reasonably expect

are void unless the supplier can prove that it was reasonable or fair to include the term.

The terms 'fair' and 'reasonable' are open to interpretation. In general, courts will consider the following factors:

- The relative strength of the bargaining positions of the parties to the contract
- Were the goods or services freely available elsewhere?
- Was any discount received by the customer for accepting the term?
- Had the customer previously accepted such terms from the supplier?
- Was this a one-off special transaction?

The 1977 Act states quite clearly that the onus of proof that the term was fair and reasonable lies with the party seeking to rely on the term – usually the supplier organisation.

Amendments in 1995 brought further protection against terms that sought to allow an organisation to vary the price without allowing a customer to withdraw without penalty, terms which tried to stop a purchaser withholding part payment due to a failure to deliver and terms which sought to absolve organisations from the statements of their sales staff. This latter point can have considerable implications for training, as it makes organisations responsible for the actions of their staff in civil, consumer-related matters. Organisations in the UK have always had a vicarious liability for actions by staff where injuries etc. have occurred; they now have such liability for misleading statements.

## The ending of contracts

The vast majority of contracts, whether written or not, come to an end because they are fulfilled to the satisfaction of both parties.

## Breaches of contract

Many breakdowns in customer relations occur when there is a perceived breach of contract by one party or the other.

It is important to realise that these are situations where there was an original intention of fulfilling the contract on the part of the organisations concerned. Where there was no such intention, this is covered by fraud or theft legislation. Any failure to perform can be considered a breach of contract, as can failure to perform within a stipulated time limit. Defective performance of one component of a contract can lead to the aggrieved party rescinding the whole contract provided that the breach is serious.

Whilst no organisation wishes to become involved in litigation, it is a fact of modern life that litigation is becoming more common. It is important to remember that, even in a simple transaction, once payment has been offered and accepted a legally enforceable contract exists. Courts can and do award damages for breach of contract, especially where it can be shown that a financial loss has been suffered.

## Consumer law

In the United Kingdom, the Office of Fair Trading (OFT) has a brief to look after the legal interest of consumers and there are regional consumer councils providing advice and policy suggestions to both the government and the public.

The OFT was set up under a Director General of Fair Trading (DGFT) as a consequence of the Fair Trading Act (1973) which coincided with the introduction of Small Claims Courts. The 1973 Act gave the DGFT powers to identify unfair trading practices and to make recommendations for legislation. The OFT is able to issue notices against organisations who persist in unfair trading, especially where these breach the Trade Descriptions and Sale and Supply of Goods Act (see later). Court action may be taken but of the 400 procedures undertaken by 1986, Montague (1987) reports that few had needed to go to court.

Law is a complex subject. Prior to the growth in consumer rights, although there was protection for consumers, indeed the first Sale of Goods Act in the UK dates from 1893, the maxim *caveat emptor* (let the buyer beware) was usually employed.

In 1965, the American Ralph Nader began to champion the rights of the consumer in the USA. Beginning with an attack on the safety features of US-produced automobiles, his work then went on to look at issues concerning the rights of consumers of a wide range of products. This sparked the formation of a Consumers' Association in the UK, whose magazine *Which?* regularly tested and reported on an increasing range of goods and services. Whilst such organisations were able to raise awareness about price and quality issues, they could not act for individual purchasers. Within the UK, in addition to pressure groups, there exists a network of Trading Standards offices attached to local government.

The following sections consider important pieces of UK legislation specifically designed to protect consumers. The *Unfair Contract Terms Act 1977* has already been mentioned above.

## The Consumer Credit Act 1974

By the 1970s, the purchase of goods on credit was becoming more widespread. In a credit sale, ownership is transferred at the point of the transaction as opposed to hire purchase where ownership remains with the vendor until payment in full is made. The Act set out to standardise the forms of contract that could be made and to introduce cooling-off periods. It should be noted that the protection offered is to the domestic consumer more than to business users of credit. The Act also provides extra protection for those who pay all or part of a transaction by credit card, in effect making the credit card company a party to the contract and allowing the customer to claim off the credit company for cases of poor performance or defective goods.

## The Consumer Protection Act 1997

This Act defines the standards of safety a purchaser is entitled to expect and thus has some commonality with the Sale and Supply of Goods Act 1994, to be covered later. Importantly, it gives wide rights to those injured by a product to pursue claims for damages against manufacturers, importers, suppliers and even those who put their own brand names on generic products.

## Trades Descriptions Act 1968

Often considered a landmark piece of legislation because it attempted to stop growing practices relating to false or inaccurate descriptions of products, the Act regulates the way goods are described to potential customers. The Act deals with three basic aspects of description – claims about the goods themselves, false statements relating to services and incorrect pricing. The Act (section 2) sets out areas that constitute a trade description, namely:

- Physical characteristics
- History
- Quantity
- Size
- Method of manufacture
- Fitness for purpose
- Testing
- Manufacturer
- Use
- Previous ownership.

The Act requires the person selling the product or service (the vendor) to be truthful about these areas. If a box of matches has an approximate number of contents labelled at 100 then, provided that on average there are 100 matches to a box, the Act will have been satisfied. If tests showed that the average was 95, then an offence would have been committed.

Interestingly, availability is not covered by the Act, and thus items advertised in order to 'lure' customers in but which are not available are not covered and nor are the contents of books or CDs where there is clearly a subjective view as to their quality etc. However, if a CD were advertised as being by a band and that band only appeared on one out of twenty tracks, there could well be a case under the Act. It should also be borne in mind that the offence needs to be committed in the course of business and thus purely private transactions are excluded. This has led to a growth in traders attempting to pass themselves off as private sellers using the classified, small advertisement sections of newspapers.

The Trades Descriptions Act carries strict liability in that an offence can be committed even if it is not intended to do so. There is a defence for organisations, however, if a member of staff who should know better carries out an act that renders the organisation liable under the Act. In *Tesco v Nattrass* (1972), a supermarket manager made a false description of a product unbeknown to his employer. He had received proper training etc. and the Court ruled that Tesco were not liable. This case has been used as a precedent to say that there needs to be some proof that the company will not be held liable for false advertising claims if an employee makes a false description.

The Trades Descriptions Act not only applies to goods but also to services. It is an offence (although strict liability does not apply) to make false statements about specified aspects of service. As strict liability does not apply, it is necessary to prove that the statement was known to be false or was reckless, i.e. not sufficient attention was paid to the truth or falseness of the statement.

The Trades Descriptions Act also covers pricing of products and services, which again is related to the truthfulness of statements. Prior to the Act, it was not unknown for companies to make blatantly untrue statements about prices: 'was £50, now £20', when in fact the item had never ever been sold at £50.

Under the Act, where a recommended price is quoted and then undercut, that price must have been in operation. Where a sale price is quoted, then the original price should be shown together with details of where it pertained. There must be evidence that the non-sale price had been applied somewhere within the organisation for at least 28 days over the previous 6 months. If you look carefully at the sale prices in many large retail outlets you will see statements like: '. . . as offered in our Birmingham store for 28 days between August and November'. It is permissible to make a disclaimer for specially acquired products, i.e. those brought in especially for selling at a discount, and this does limit the applicability of this part of the Act.

Pricing, as regards the Trades Descriptions Act, only applies to goods and not to services. Thus an untrue statement claiming that the outlet is closing and this is the last chance to buy would not commit an offence.

Many actions under the Trades Descriptions Act are brought by the Trading Standards Department of local authorities. They have been especially vigilant in the area of counterfeit goods. As designer labels have become more and more popular, so there has been a flood of fakes, often sold in markets. Offering such an item for sale is clearly a breach of the Act, as it is clearly not what it purports to be.

# Sale and Supply of Goods Act 1994

The original Sale of Goods Act was enacted in 1893 in an attempt to codify certain parts of common law. The main aim of the Act was to clarify the rights and responsibilities of the parties involved in the sale and purchase of goods in respect of those areas not explicitly covered by the terms of the contract. The Act was amended in 1979 and again in 1994 when it was re-titled the Sale and Supply of Goods Act. As shown earlier in the section on contracts, there are explicit and implicit terms to a contract. The Act does not forbid any explicit terms. For instance, if a non-working motor car were to be sold, perhaps as a static display, then the fact that it was non-working causes no problem provided that this is stated clearly in the contract. This is of especial importance when dealing with items that are regarded as 'seconds', i.e. usable but with blemishes. If this is not stated then, as will be shown, there is a breach of the Act.

The 1994 Act provides considerable protection for the consumer by stating that: *goods should be of satisfactory quality*. Prior to 1994, the term used was 'merchantisable quality'. The concept of reasonableness has to be applied, and also to the vendor's description of the goods. If they were described as seconds, then it would be unreasonable to expect them to be perfect. If there is a defect, then, provided that the vendor makes the defect clear to the purchaser, no breach of the Act occurs as the purchaser is deemed to have accepted a contract.

The Act specifies five aspects of satisfactory quality:

- Fitness for all the purposes for which goods of that kind are commonly supplied
- Appearance and finish
- Freedom from minor defects
- Safety
- Durability.

Durability is a key aspect that again raises the question of reasonableness. If goods break down after normal use but within an unreasonable time scale, then the Sale and Supply of Goods Act can be invoked. The definition of a reasonable amount of time will vary from product to product. In the white and brown goods markets, i.e. domestic kitchen and entertainment products, there has been much selling of extended warranties over recent years. Manufacturers' guarantees are normally for 12 months. Many extended warranties are sold on the grounds that the purchaser will not be covered for repairs or replacement after 12 months unless they purchase an extended warranty. A washing machine that broke down after 18 months of normal use might well not be covered by the manufacturer's guarantee, but the aggrieved purchaser would most certainly have a case under the Sale and Supply of Goods Act.

The Act makes it clear that the purchaser is entitled to a product that is as near to perfect as possible. Obviously, 100% quality, whilst desirable, cannot be achieved every time and thus there are remedies available to the purchaser should the goods be imperfect in any way.

A key point that relates back to contract law, as covered earlier, is that **the contract is between the vendor and the purchaser and thus the onus for providing redress lies with the vendor and not the manufacturer**. Thus a vendor who claimed that they had to send a faulty item to the manufacturer, or worse, insisted that the purchaser returned the item to the manufacturer, is committing a breach of the Act.

It is not permissible for a vendor to insist that they will provide *no refunds, no exchanges* or *credit notes only*; indeed, signs stating this may constitute an offence under the Act. It is for the purchaser to decide the remedy they require. Provided that the time since purchase is reasonable and that the item has not been altered or had abnormal use then, if they wish for the item to be repaired this should be done free of charge, if they wish for a refund this should be provided, or the item exchanged if that is the purchaser's wish.

The addition of the word 'supply' to the title of the Act reflects the fact that it applies not only to the sale of goods but also to hire and barter arrangements. The law is very clearly on the side of the purchaser. As Wotherspoon (1995) has pointed out in an article, all those involved in selling or supplying goods should be mindful of: '. . . the buyer should receive goods that are of a satisfactory quality.' If they do not, then they can, and increasingly do, sue the vendor.

Many vendors seem unaware of the fact that it is they and they alone who have a contract with the purchaser. If the item is faulty then the vendor may have a case against their supplier, who in turn may have a case against the manufacturer. However, the legal relationship is between adjacent links in the customer value chain.

Should a person receive an item as a present then, according to law, they are not the purchaser and thus any claim has to be made by the person who actually made the purchase. Notwithstanding the above, many retailers will exchange presents, but they are under no obligation to deal with anybody except the original purchaser.

It should also be noted that the cost of the return of faulty goods lies with the vendor and not the purchaser.

Services, as opposed to goods, have been covered in law by the Supply of Goods and Service Act 1982. In receiving a service a customer is entitled to:

- Reasonable care and skill in carrying out the service
- Have the service performed within a reasonable time
- Have the service performed at a reasonable charge if a price was not fixed in advance.

Any materials used in carrying out a service are covered by the same statutory rights as if the customer purchased them personally.

## Consumer remedies

Recourse to law has always been expensive and cost has often been a deterrent to the ordinary consumer taking action. The introduction in 1973 of the first Small Claims courts in the UK made it much easier for actions relating to relatively small amounts to be brought. In the 1990s these courts became part of the new Civil Court in England and the Sheriff Court in Scotland. The amounts that can be claimed are different in England and Scotland and have been increased upwards a number of times since the original £500 English limit in 1973. Without the formality of a normal court and requiring little or no outlay on legal costs by the plaintiff, these Courts have made it much easier to gain redress. In 1999, the total cost to a claimant in England was £150 for a claim of up to £1000 and £180 if the claim was between £1000 and £5000 (the maximum that could be claimed). Where the plaintiff wins the case, the defendant pays these fees.

Larger amounts need to be claimed through the County Court system but with an ever-increasing number of solicitors willing to undertake 'no win–no fee' cases, derived from the contingent approach allowable in the USA, it seems likely that more and more dissatisfied customers may bring legal actions.

It behoves organisations to ensure that they comply fully with the legislation to meet the rights of their customers and to build up relationships such that disputes can be settled amicably without the cost of legal action and the subsequent bad publicity that it can bring.

In 1999, the UK government announced their intention to increase the powers of Trading Standards Officers in a white paper entitled *Modern Markets, Confident Consumers*. Amongst the proposals made were:

- A clampdown on rogue traders, by means of powers to force them out of business
- Additional codes of practice
- Legislation on Internet shopping
- Increased consumer protection.


# Codes of practice and industry arbitration

Many industries have now set up arbitration schemes to resolve disputes without recourse to the courts. The decisions of such arbitration services may be legally binding but customers cannot be forced to use them if they would rather go to court. The arbitration scheme of the Association of British Travel Agents (ABTA) is typical. Their arbitration fee in 1999 was £65 for claims up to £1500, and £112 for claims up to the maximum claim under the scheme of £75 000. In 1998, ABTA handled 18 000 claims, of which 10% went to actual arbitration with the customer winning 85% of these. There is a Chartered Institute of Arbitrators which sets the professional standards for those involved in this work. There are normally time limits on applying for arbitration. As the arbitration service is often linked to a trade association, it is in the supplier's interest to ensure that they have met their obligations, as they may face the wrath of their industry colleagues if they bring bad publicity on the entire industry. Whole sectors have adopted the ombudsman principle, first applied from Scandinavia to the public sector. Banking, insurance and financial services are examples of sectors that have appointed an independent ombudsman (or woman) to rule on disputes.

Following the privatisation of many UK public sector industries in the 1980s and 1990s, regulators were appointed to ensure that consumers received a fair deal. OFTEL (telecommunications), OFWAT (water) and OFGAS (gas) are examples, as are the regulators for the National Lottery, electricity and the rail industry. Appointed through the government, the regulators have the power to penalise unfair practices and monitor standards to see that these are in accordance with the franchise agreements. If they are not, then penalties can be applied and ultimately a franchise could be removed.

# Health and safety legislation

The Consumer Protection Act (1997) and the safety terms of the Sale and Supply of Goods Act (1994) have already been mentioned. Organisations have, however, an obligation under the Health and Safety at Work Act (1974) to look after the health and safety of all on their premises. Anything which puts anybody on an organisation's premises in danger or causes them injury can be dealt with under the Act, and it should be noted that breaches of the Act can lead to criminal charges. Trailing electrical leads, unsafe buildings, slippery floors can all cause injury and it is an obligation placed on both the organisation and its employees to ensure that no-one is put at risk.

# Product liability

Product liability is a term imported from the USA where there have been a number of high-profile financial settlements to customers injured as a result of defective products. In July 1995, General Motors was ordered by a Californian court to pay the sum of $3.2 billion to a family of six, badly burned when a fuel tank on one of its vehicles exploded. The contention was that the company knew that there was a fault and did not issue a recall notice. General Motors immediately appealed and gained a reduction of damages to £750 million but the case shows how careful companies need to be.

Safety is a key aspect of the Sale and Supply of Goods Act and, since 1988, a European Union Product Liability Directive has been in force which allows for action by anybody injured by a defective product *regardless of whether they were the actual purchaser*. A causal link showing that it was a defective product that caused the injury will need to be shown but the Directive shows the importance that is now placed on consumer safety.

# Employment law

Whilst different jurisdictions may apply differing laws controlling the legal relationship between an organisation as an employer and its employees, there are certain broad principles which apply within the developed world. Organisations need to ensure that they are fully cognisant of employment legislation in any jurisdiction within which they operate. For instance, the contract of employment is a much stronger protection to employees in the UK than in the USA, where employment is based on the concept of 'employment at will' and both the employer and employee have the basic right to work together and to part company at any time. This is seen in the lack of notice periods often worked by US employees, who are not tied to the contractual periods of notice of their UK counterparts. However, strong legislation does exist in the USA preventing employees from being dismissed on discriminatory (age, race or gender) grounds. Some states (California is an example) work on the principle of 'good faith' and will protect an employee dismissed without good cause, although other states have rejected this concept.

In the UK, all employees are entitled to a contract of employment that states their duties and working conditions. Whilst there are changes all the time to the details of employment legislation, much of the protection for employees in the UK is derived from the Employment Protection (Consolidation) Act of 1978.

It is not proposed that this section should give details of any particular piece of legislation but rather present the questions that an organisation needs to ask when considering employment legislation in any jurisdiction within which it operates. These are:

• What are the nature and form of the formal contract of employment?
• What legislation exists regarding unfair dismissal?
• What provisions must be made for paid holidays?
• What laws exist relating to hours of work?
• What anti-discrimination legislation is in place?
• What rights do employees have to join (or not to join) a trade union?
• What maternity/paternity rights do employees have?
• What redundancy rights do employees have?

For details of employment law in the UK, you should consult the various leaflets etc. produced by the Department for Education and Employment (DfEE) and available in libraries and JobCentres. These will provide an up-to-date picture. You may also wish to consult *Managing the Flexible Workforce* by Richard Pettinger (1998a), which has an excellent summary of UK employment legislation.

## Trade unions

Whilst the influence of trade unions within the UK (and elsewhere) has declined somewhat over the last few decades, they are still important stakeholders in many organisations. In the UK, trade unions have certain collective bargaining rights; and employees have rights regarding their membership, many of which were enshrined in the Trade Union Reform and Employment Rights Act of 1993 (TURER) which also gave employers rights against unauthorised trade union action and protection from secondary action.

## Holidays with pay

There are very few developed countries that do not provide for holidays with pay for employees. In the UK, the first such legislation was as early as 1938 with the enactment of the Holiday with Pay Act in that year, and holidays with pay are now the norm for the vast majority of UK employees. Indeed, the amount of time given as paid leave has been increasing and, as this has occurred, so have the length of holidays taken, with an increase in the business for those involved in leisure and tourism. In the USA, a two-week Summer vacation with just a few other days during the year is still very much the norm.

## Minimum wage

It was only with the election of the Labour government in the UK in 1997 that a national minimum wage was put into place and this minimum now applies to all employers.

## Working time

Whilst working time (especially for those in hazardous occupations) has long been regulated to some degree, the move from long hours has been slow, especially in the UK where it is claimed workers are employed for longer hours than in other similar economies. Long hours can be dangerous in respect of safety and health, and also productivity and quality can fall if workers are tired. Although accepted later by the UK than the rest of the EU, the Working Time Directive of the European Union now regulates the hours of work for many employees, although they can if they wish work overtime provided there are no safety implications. Many less-well-developed areas are less strict about hours of work, holidays and minimum wages, which has led to the accusation that some manufacturers have exploited less-developed economies in order to escape their national employment rules.

## Discrimination

Nearly every developed economy has some measure of anti-discrimination legislation designed to protect groups of employees. In the UK, it is illegal to discriminate on the grounds of race or gender and this has implications not only for whom is employed but also for remuneration, holidays, hours of working etc. The USA also has a degree of anti-ageism legislation in place. In 1995, UK citizens acquired disability discrimination protection through the *Disability Discrimination Act, 1995*. The Act, which came into force in December 1996, made it an offence for organisations with 20 or more employees to discriminate against those who are disabled but able to carry out work tasks.

## The European Social Charter

As covered in Chapter 4, all EU members have to follow the EU Social Charter, the main items of which are:

- Freedom of movement for workers within the EU
- Protection for employment and pay
- Improvements in living and working conditions
- Adequate social protection and social security
- Freedom to join trade unions etc. (and, of course, the right not to join)
- Adequate and continual vocational training
- Equality of treatment, regardless of gender
- Information to all workers on workplace issues
- Health and safety at work protection

- Access to labour markets for the elderly
- Access to labour markets for the disabled
- Protection for children and young persons at work.

As has already been said in Chapter 4, the last provision was the cause of much concern in the UK media as it was feared that youngsters might be forbidden to undertake paper rounds – this has not proved to be the case but illustrates the 'Europhobia' that occasionally sweeps the UK!

A full explanation of the Social Charter and the implications for organisations can be found in *The European Social Charter* by Richard Pettinger (1998b).

## Competition legislation

Monopolies, covered in more detail in Chapter 12, do not always serve the interests of the consumer. Since the Industrial Revolution it has been recognised that monopolies may pose a threat to trade. Anti-trust legislation in the USA was used as early as 1933 when the US Government forced the break-up of the Boeing Corporation, which then included Boeing Aircraft, United Airlines, Hamilton Propellers and Pratt and Whitney Engines, on the grounds that such a concentration was anti-competitive. In the UK, the DGFT (see earlier) has the power to order an investigation by the Monopolies and Mergers Commission into any organisation that controls over 25% of a particular marketplace. In 1980, the Competition Act was passed which allows for investigations into anti-competitive practices even when monopolies or near monopolies are not involved.

In July 1999, British Airways (BA) were fined £4 million by the European Commission for making what were deemed unfair bonus payments to travel agents. The ruling stated that BA had abused its dominant position in the marketplace contrary to Article 86 of the Treaty of Rome. This was yet another twist to the long saga of BA's bitter rivalry with Richard Branson's Virgin Atlantic, as covered in *Dirty Tricks* by Martyn Gregory (1994).

## Restrictive pricing

The term 'manufacturer's recommended price' used to be found on many, many price tags. With the ending of the Net Book Agreement in 1996, an agreement that fixed the price of books, only pharmaceuticals remained subject to such price fixing. UK and European price legislation bans manufacturers from setting fixed prices. The contract is between the vendor and the purchaser and it is the vendor who should set the price according to the market. The motor vehicle industry and the suppliers of domestic electrical goods have come under investigation in recent years because of concerns that prices might be being fixed at an artificially high level in the UK as opposed to the rest of Europe and the USA.

Governments consider that competition (in moderation) is a good thing and are thus liable to legislate against any practices that restrict fair competition on the grounds that this disadvantages the consumer.

# European law

As stated in Chapter 4, the European Union operates its own Court to uphold EU legislation. The Court not only rules on relationships between member states but also on matters affecting individual and groups of organisations. For example, in 1971 in a judgement concerning road transport, the Court held that the member states no longer had the right to undertake obligations with third countries which affected Community rules, thus establishing that the principle of the Community's powers in the field of external relations must be interpreted in relation to the EU as a whole.

Moreover, when the European Parliament acquired new powers, the Court recognised, before the Maastricht Treaty expressly so provided, that certain acts of the Parliament could be the subject of an action before the Court and, conversely, that the Parliament could challenge acts of the other institutions if they compromised the institutional balance.

The Court has also contributed in decisive fashion to defining the European Community as a community governed by the rule of law, by laying down two essential rules:

- The direct effect of Community law in the member states
- The primacy of Community law over national law.

On the basis of those principles, EU citizens may now rely on the provisions of the Treaties and Community regulations and directives in proceedings before their national courts, and may seek, for instance, to have a national law disapplied if it is contrary to Community law.

The Court has been asked to clarify member states' obligations with regard to the free movement of goods and the establishment of a common market, and to secure the removal of barriers protecting national markets and undertakings and, generally, of all hindrances to trade between member states. Thus European Union consumers may buy in their own country any food product from a country in the Community, provided that it is lawfully produced and marketed in that country and that there are no serious grounds related, for example, to the protection of health or the environment for preventing its importation into the country of consumption. This is the issue that was exercising the minds of the Court and the Commission in 1999–2000, when France and Germany banned the sale of UK beef on the grounds of a health risk due to BSE despite an EU ruling that UK beef was considered safe.

In a 1997 case, the Court found against the French Republic for failing to take the measures necessary to prevent certain French farmers from obstructing the free passage over French territory of agricultural products from other member states.

In a 1998 case directly concerning the health of EU citizens, the Court concluded that national rules which amounted to refusing to reimburse to an insured person the cost of spectacles on the ground that they had been purchased in another member state constituted an unjustified barrier to the free movement of goods. Thus the EU Court has a direct impact upon organisations and is not just an arena for the member states' governments to settle differences.

As regards the free movement of capital and the abolition of restrictions in that connection, the Court has ruled that citizens may export from one member state to another coins, bank notes and cheques without having to obtain prior authorisation. It is within the lifetime of the author that Bank of England permission had to be obtained to take more than £50 out of the UK, so strict were the currency restrictions at the time.

The Court has also fostered freedom of movement for persons, an essential factor not only in the establishment of the common market but also in an ever-closer union among the peoples of Europe.

A European worker who decides to settle in another Community country, and who may at times suffer direct or indirect discrimination, now enjoys the same rights and benefits as regards conditions of work and employment as those given to national workers.

In that connection, the Court has held that a social benefit guaranteeing minimum means of subsistence or a special old-age allowance guaranteeing a minimum income for old people are social advantages to which migrant workers are entitled under the same conditions as national workers. These rulings, coupled with the Social Charter (Chapter 4), mean that EU rules and laws are very important to organisational planners.

The Court has also defined in a number of judgements the extent of the right of the spouse and children of a migrant worker to settle with him or her; in particular, it has stressed that children must not only be admitted to courses of general education and occupational training, but are also entitled to the same assistance as the children of citizens of the State of residence, such as interest-free loans, scholarships and assistance for the rehabilitation of the handicapped. In 2000, this led to concerns in the UK that following the proposed abolition of University tuition fees in Scotland but not in England and Wales, there could be a difference in the way EU and English/Welsh students were treated at Scottish universities, as Scotland and England/Wales are not recognised by the EU as being different countries. A Scottish university could not charge another EU citizen a fee unless they were from England or Wales!

In that context, the conditions of access to vocational training also fall within the scope of the Treaty. In 1985, the Court held that a French student who wanted to study a vocational subject in Belgium should not have to pay a higher enrolment fee than Belgian students.

More recently, in the Bosman judgement (1995), the Court ruled on the compatibility of football federation rules with the principle of freedom of movement for workers. Applying well-established case law, it held that sport at professional level constitutes an economic activity, the exercise of which may not be limited either by rules on the transfer of players or by limits on the number of players from other member states. This has led to the inclusion of an increased number of EU citizens playing in countries other than that of their origin. The reader will have to decide whether this is an advantage or a disadvantage to the game, the playing and watching of which appears to be a passion in all EU countries.

The Court has also ruled on equality of compensation. In a 1989 judgement, a UK tourist who was assaulted and seriously injured in the Paris metro was held to be entitled to the same compensation as a French citizen could expect.

The Court has also had to give judgement on the general rules applicable to freedom of competition. Thus, for instance, the deregulation of air transport was facilitated by the Nouvelles Frontières case (1986), in which the Court held that the rules governing competition contained in the Treaties applied to air transport.

The Court of Justice has stressed the importance of environmental protection, which it has held to be one of the essential objectives of the Community and, as such, capable of constituting grounds for certain restrictions on the principle of the free movement of goods. For example, the Court has accepted (in 1988) that it is lawful for Denmark to impose on distributors of beers and soft drinks an obligation to set up a deposit-and-return system for empty containers, despite its effect on trade between states.

Finally, the important place given to fundamental principles for the protection of individuals in the case law of the Court of Justice must be emphasised. It has been one of the Court's constant concerns to protect the fundamental rights of individuals, and it has declared these to be general principles of law that the Court will apply within the framework of Community law.

Another problem examined by the Court in the context of numerous requests for preliminary rulings has been equal pay for men and women. Since the Treaty of Rome contains a specific provision dealing with that question, the Court holds that no Community or national measure was needed for the direct application of that provision, and that it was the duty of the national courts to ensure that all European citizens enjoyed the benefit of that principle.

The case law of the Court in this area is prolific and has contributed to the equal treatment of women in the workplace. As regards interpretation of the principle of equality, in particular in the context of access to employment, the Court has stated that a national rule favouring women candidates over men is compatible with Community law if it provides for individual examination of each case so that the priority to be accorded to women may be set aside if reasons specific to an individual male candidate tilt the balance in his favour.

In a 1991 judgement, the Court of Justice laid down the principle of State liability for damage caused to individuals by breaches of Community law, giving rise to an obligation to make good such damage. That principle was developed and extended to all cases of infringement and all state bodies responsible for the breach. The Court took the opportunity to set out the specific conditions governing state liability in order to ensure adequate compensation for damage caused and, consequently, effective protection of rights.

An example is concerned with a directive aimed at protecting tourists purchasing package travel. Here the Court held that failure to implement the directive in question constituted a serious breach of Community law, sufficient to give rise to an obligation on the part of the state to compensate consumers who had suffered injury as a result.

## Composition

The Court of Justice comprises 15 judges and 9 advocates general.

The judges and advocates general are appointed by common accord of the governments of the member states and hold office for a renewable term of six years. They are chosen from jurists whose independence is beyond doubt and who are of recognised competence.

The judges select one of their number to be President of the Court for a renewable term of three years. The President directs the work of the Court and presides at hearings and deliberations. The advocates general assist the Court in its task. They deliver, in open court and with complete impartiality and independence, opinions on the cases brought before the Court. Their duties should not be confused with those of a prosecutor or similar official – that is the role of the Commission, as guardian of the Community's interests.

## Jurisdiction

It is the responsibility of the Court of Justice to ensure that the law is observed in the interpretation and applications of the Treaties establishing the European Communities and of the provisions laid down by the competent Community institutions.

To enable it to carry out that task, the Court has wide jurisdiction to hear various types of action and to give preliminary rulings.

## Forms of action

### Proceedings for failure to fulfil an obligation

Such proceedings enable the Court of Justice to determine whether a member state has fulfilled its obligations under Community law. An action may be brought by the Commission, as is practically always the case, or by another member state. If the Court finds that the obligation has not been fulfilled, the member state concerned must comply without delay.

However, if, after new proceedings are initiated by the Commission, the Court of Justice finds that the member state concerned has not complied with its judgement, it may impose a fixed or a periodic penalty.

### Annulment of legislation

A member state, the Council, the Commission and, in certain circumstances, the Parliament may apply to the Court of Justice for the annulment of all or part of an item of Community legislation, and individuals may seek the annulment of a legal measure which is of direct and individual concern to them. The Court may thus review the legality of the acts of the Community institutions. If the action is well founded, the contested measure is declared void.

### Proceedings for failure to act

The Court of Justice may also review the legality of a failure to act by a Community institution, and penalise silence or inaction.

### Actions for damages

In an action for damages, based on non-contractual liability, the Court of Justice rules on the liability of the Community for damage caused by its institutions or servants in the performance of their duties.

### Appeals

The Court of Justice may hear appeals, on points of law only, against judgements given by the Courts of First Instance (whether national or EU, i.e. inferior courts, which all national courts in member states are) in cases within its jurisdiction.

The Court is not the only judicial body empowered to apply Community law. The courts of each of the member states are also Community courts as they make rulings which affect EU citizens and need to apply national legislation which has to fit in with EU legislation.

Being a citizen of the EU confers individual rights on nationals of member states which national courts must uphold.

To ensure the effective application of Community law and to prevent differences between the rules of interpretation applicable in different national courts from leading to different interpretations of Community law, the Treaties provide for a system of preliminary rulings which, while not setting up any hierarchical relationship, has institutionalised co-operation between the Court of Justice and the national courts.

In cases involving Community law, national courts, if in doubt as to the interpretation or validity of that law, may, and in some cases must, seek a preliminary ruling from the Court of Justice on the relevant questions.

Although such a ruling may be sought only by a national court which alone has the power to decide that it is appropriate do so, all the parties involved may take part in the proceedings before the Court of Justice.


## Judgements

The judgements of the Court of Justice are reached by a majority vote. There are no dissenting opinions, and the judgements are signed by all the judges who took part in the deliberations and read in open court.

Whatever the jurisdiction, every organisation needs to ensure that it knows and obeys the law of the land, as stated at the beginning of this chapter – ignorance is not an excuse, hence the need for corporate lawyers who understand both the organisation and the particular jurisdiction.

## Whistle blowing

Although the USA has had legislation in place protecting employees who report their employer for illegal acts, UK employees only received such protection as a result of the Public Interest Disclosures Act of 1998. Under this legislation, an employee cannot be dismissed or disciplined for bringing to the attention of the authorities any action by the organisation that is a breach of the law. This is new legislation and it will be interesting to see how employers receive protection against malicious accusations and, indeed, whether having blown the whistle, the employee would want to carry on with the same organisation. A consideration of the issues involved was published by the Association of College Managers in their October 1999 *Newsletter* (ACM, 1999).

## Summary

All organisations have to operate within the relevant national and increasingly supra-national framework of laws and legislation.

The main areas of analysis concern legislation relating to contracts, employment, health and safety, consumers and competition.

For those operating within EU member states, European law, especially in the fields of competition and the Social Charter, is becoming of increasing importance as European law is superior to national legislation.

Law is a complex subject and interpretation is best left to those who have been professionally trained.

## Concepts covered

- Sources of law
- Criminal law
- Common law
- Civil law
- Statute law
- Jurisdiction
- Contracts
- Consumer law
- Health and safety
- Product liability
- Employment law
- Competition legislation
- European law
- Whistle blowing

# Analysis

In carrying out the *legal* analysis in respect of an organisation, the following need to be considered:

1. What jurisdictions does the organisation operate within?
2. What is the effect of relevant legislation on the organisation in the areas of:
   - Contracts
   - Employment
   - Health and Safety
   - Consumers
   - Competition?
3. What are the penalties for infringing any of the above?

QUESTIONS

1. What are the likely implications of the European Social Charter for organisations operating within the UK, especially in terms of employment rights?
2. Why is a knowledge of the law on contracts vital for any organisation operating within a UK context?
3. 'The consumer is not only morally but also legally king in the UK.' Discuss this statement with reference to the protection given to consumers by the relevant legislation.

# Further reading

You are recommended to read *The European Social Charter* (1998b) and *Managing the Flexible Workforce* (1998a) by Richard Pettinger, *Managing Values – Ethical Change in Organisations* by Paul Griseri (1998), *Mastering Customer Relations* by Roger Cartwright (2000) and *Business Law* by Stephen Judge (1998).

# ☑ **11** Environmental analysis

*Planet Earth – Early environmental warnings – High risk problems – Alteration and destruction of habitats – Extinction of species – Ozone depletion – Global climate change – Medium risk problems – Herbicides and pesticides – Acid rain – Airborne toxins – Water pollution – Low risk problems – Oil spills – Groundwater pollution – Radiation – Thermal pollution – Waste management – Compassionate farming and organic food – Genetic engineering and genetically modified (GM) crops and animals – Cost–benefit analysis and environmental decisions*

As many science fact and fiction programmes and books have stated, we live on a small green planet, the third from our Sun. The planet is 66% water and has an atmosphere that is 80% composed of oxygen. Life forms are based on carbon.

Whilst this book is not the forum for discussing the uniqueness of the planet Earth nor for speculation about other life forms that may or may not exist in the Universe, it is nevertheless a fact that the conditions necessary for our types of carbon-based life forms are likely to be few and far between, so delicate is the balance between an environment that can sustain life and one that cannot. The fear of many environmentalists is that the human species has produced such an impact upon the planet Earth as to begin to upset that delicate balance.

To survive, the vast majority of Earth's organisms need a controlled supply of atmospheric gases (in general, oxygen for animals and carbon dioxide for plants), water and a predictable climate. Green plants (the green is a substance called chlorophyll) take in carbon dioxide and sunlight and use the chlorophyll to convert these to energy, giving off oxygen in the process. Animals take in plant products or the flesh of other animals plus oxygen, and give off carbon dioxide. It can thus be seen that plants and animals need each other, as the former take in oxygen which the latter give out, whilst the latter need carbon dioxide which is the gas that animals exhale. For such reasons is the Amazon rain forest known as the 'lungs of the world' by its inhabitants. Cutting down the rain forests not only causes massive problems with soil erosion but also removes part of the vital mechanism for producing oxygen and removing carbon dioxide from the atmosphere. Carbon dioxide can actually be toxic to animals in too high a quantity, in addition to the fact that we cannot use it for our metabolism.

Fires of any sort also consume oxygen and many of our manufacturing, domestic and transportation processes require heat, thus further depleting the oxygen supply. Provided the Earth's ecosystem does not consume more oxygen than can be replaced by plants nor emit more carbon dioxide than can be absorbed by them, then the system will remain in balance. The concern at the dawn of the 21st Century is that human activity is destroying that balance.

Humans are unique in many ways too complex for consideration here but there are two key aspects to our behaviour. Firstly, we have the intellect to realise what we are doing and to predict its impact on the future and secondly, we are one of the very few species to have inhabited the vast majority of the landmass of the Earth. Human settlements and activities can be found over all parts of the landmasses of Earth with the exception of the most inhospitable. Humans do live high in the mountains of the Himalayas, in deserts and even (as scientific communities) in Antarctica. We are omnipresent on this planet.

Prior to the Industrial Revolution in the early 19th Century, human activity had little effect upon the ecosystem. It is true that humans had domesticated many animal species, were well practised in agricultural techniques and had explored much of the globe, but the environmental impact was negligible. Transportation used horses and sailing ships and thus made use of nature without causing much damage. All was to change and to change rapidly.

From the early years of the 19th Century, the steam engine became the main source of power to be followed by the internal combustion engine at the end of the century, a form of power that is still a mainstay of human activity at the beginning of the 21st Century. Nuclear power (with all its benefits but immense dangers) was developed post 1945. Since then the search has been on for renewable, non-polluting sources of energy, hydroelectricity being among the first, and experiments with wind, wave and tides as energy sources are ongoing. Steam engines initially used wood, which is a renewable resource in the first instance, but were much more efficient with coal, and this led to a vast increase in coal mining in the industrialised world. Coal and oil are non-renewable resources unless one measures over millions and millions of years. Coal and oil are formed from the decay and compression of dead plants over huge periods of geological time. It is only recently that we have begun to realise that our supplies of these products may not available for too much longer and hence there has been considerable effort into finding alternative, renewable sources of energy, preferably ones that have a neutral effect on the environment.

Our knowledge of the impact we are having on the environment is growing all the time, as is the public perception, especially in the developed world, that something has to change. In this book it is intended to treat the environmental issues as a series of questions about key environmental areas. Solutions are not offered but it is hoped that by considering the questions, the reader will seek further, up-to-date information. Whilst neither condoning nor condemning their policies, the Greenpeace Organisation website (details in the Bibliography) is a good place to start, as is the Friends of the Earth website. An Internet search under 'environment' will provide a whole series of relevant websites.

Throughout much of the 20th Century, humans carried on treating the planet in exactly the same way. Natural resources were there to be used and waste could just be put into the ground or poured into rivers and thence the seas where it would disappear. The seas are vast, and the bacteria and plankton in them do a fairly good job of waste management, but it is now clear that the mechanisms are being seriously overloaded.

In 1965, Rachel Carson set alarm bells ringing when she published *Silent Spring*. The book was an exposure of the effects of the indiscriminate use of chemicals and described how pesticides and insecticides were being applied almost universally to farms, forests, gardens and homes with little regard to the contamination of the environment and the destruction of wildlife. She argued that unless it was recognised that human beings are only a part of the living world, our progressive poisoning of the planet would end in catastrophe.

With contributions by J. Huxley and Lord Shackleton (of Antarctic exploration fame), this book could not be ignored. It may have taken some time but the use of pesticides etc. is now vigorously controlled in the developed world, although perhaps less so elsewhere. *Silent Spring* was followed in 1970 by Gordon Rattray Taylor's *The Doomsday Book*, which painted a frightening picture of the years leading up to the Millennium. In 1971, the United Nations commissioned an unofficial report by the Secretary General of the UN Conference on the Human Environment, the report being published in 1972 as *Only One Earth – The Care and Maintenance of a Small Planet* by Ward and Dubos, which made the point that a balance needed to be struck between the two worlds that human beings inhabit; the first is the natural world which is shared with all living creatures, and the second the social and economic world that mankind has created.

Hardly a day seems to pass without there being some dire warning about the environment. In the context of this book, what is important are the steps that individual organisations can take based on their external analysis. In an increasing number of cases there are legal issues to be considered, as governments have legislated for environmental protection. Even where there is no legislation, organisations need to consider the importance of 'green issues' to their stakeholders, especially customers. Whilst developments may be legal, if they are seen as environmentally unfriendly they may have a detrimental effect on the customer base and will thus be counterproductive.

Quoting the Environmental Protection Agency (EPA) in the USA, Sexton *et al.* (1999) list a series of risks faced by the environment broken down into relatively high, relatively medium and relatively low risk categories. The use of the terms high, medium and low refers to the effect of the risks and not to their likelihood. Not all environmental problems are caused by humans. Volcanic eruptions can be devastating to nature and cause pollution and even local climate change. This chapter is concerned, however, with the damage that we can do. The long-term effects of human interference are only just becoming known. Cutting down forests not only depletes the oxygen supply, it can also lead to soil erosion, as can over-farming, and thus create desert-like conditions. Nature can and does recover but it may take a long time and for many species whose habitat has been destroyed the recovery may not come quickly enough. It is only recently that we have begun to realise that bio-diversity is important for all living things, especially for those species at the top of the food chain as we are.

Whilst many issues require concerted sectoral, government or even pan-government intervention and policies, it is possible for one organisation on its own to have quite dramatic effects on, if not the global, then at least the local environment. A major oil spillage from a tanker, although a low risk factor globally, can have a devastating effect on the local habitat and indeed the local economy if holiday beaches etc. are polluted.

The categories quoted by Sexton *et al.* (1999) are listed below.

## High risk

- Alteration and destruction of habitats
- Extinction of species
- Ozone depletion
- Global climate change.

## Medium risk

- Herbicides and pesticides
- Acid rain
- Airborne toxins
- Water pollution.

## Low risk

- Oil spills
- Groundwater pollution
- Radiation
- Thermal pollution.

These will now be considered in turn together with more very important issues:

- Waste management
- Compassionate farming and organic food
- Genetic engineering and genetically modified (GM) crops and animals.

# High risk issues

## Alteration and destruction of habitats

As the human population has grown, so has its ability to transform habitats. Hedges have been removed to aid the mechanisation of farming; forests have been cut down both for wood and to increase the amount of agricultural land. Valleys have been flooded to create reservoirs. Urban areas now stretch for tens of miles in some of the great human conurbations.

All of these actions alter habitats. As stated earlier, over-farming and the removal of trees may lead to soil erosion and the creation of dustbowls as witnessed in parts of the USA in the 1920s. Even the creation of reservoirs, whilst increasing water supplies, can lead to the loss of habitats and may increase the likelihood of earthquakes because of the increased pressure caused by billions of tons of water lying over the underlying rock strata.

Whilst an individual organisation taking a piece of land for building may have only a small effect, the cumulative effect of thousands of developments can be immense. In small countries such as the UK, this may be apparent quite quickly. Anybody flying over the London, Birmingham or Greater Manchester areas at night cannot help but observe, from the lights below, how great is the urban sprawl and how it has eroded the countryside. Hence the setting up of green belts around towns to stop such encroachment and the encouragement given to organisations to develop on previous urban sites (so called brownfield developments) rather than seek new greenfield sites in the countryside.

One of the problems with a greenfield site is that it may require a whole infrastructure before it can be used, so that it is not just a factory that needs to be built but also roads, utility services etc., all of which may cause disruption. Unfortunately, such sites have tended to be cheaper and less congested than those in urban areas, hence the need for financial encouragement to reuse older sites.

In recent years, the environmental lobby has succeeded in halting developments where there are unique species or the site is one of Special Scientific Interest (known as an SSSI in the UK).

The demand for transport links, however, has often taken precedence over any ecological concerns and there have been increasing protests over the destruction caused; the M3 over Twyford Down, the Newbury Bypass and the second runway at Manchester Airport are UK examples that gained considerable publicity. Less well known but of considerable concern is the damming of the Yangtze River in China at the site of the Three Gorges, where vast tracts of land (and settlements) are being flooded. By 2003, there will be a 370-mile reservoir in place serving a major hydroelectric project.

Prior to the early 19th Century, humans made much more extensive use of wood as a fuel and building material than today. Wood is renewable, even if takes some time to grow. There is a story of an early 19th Century British Admiral who always carried a pocketful of acorns which he planted on his travels around England so that the Royal Navy would have a ready supply of oak trees with which to build its ships, showing that concerns about natural resources are not new.

Wood is still a major commodity for building (although not of ships' hulls) and paper etc. Much emphasis is now placed on recycled paper products and producing timber from renewable resources – for every tree cut down, a new one is planted. This is not just environmentally friendly but also presents a good public image. Recycling technology is quite advanced and this book itself is produced on paper suitable for recycling and made from fully managed and sustained forest resources.

Mining, a human activity that has produced vast hills of slag etc., and the similar activity of quarrying have been much more regulated in recent years. The unstable nature of mining slag heaps was graphically illustrated at the Welsh mining community of Aberfan, when a slag tip engulfed the local primary school killing over 100 children and robbing the community of a whole generation. Today the companies involved in these forms of activity are frequently required to landscape the effects of their work and, in doing this, the very plants they use will help stabilise the tip itself.

## Extinction of species

The symbiotic nature of the relationships between species and indeed the aesthetic quality of the vast variety of living things became a buzz phrase in the 1990s under the term *bio-diversity*.

The loss of a species (and many become extinct each year) is not just a theoretical loss. Species depend on each other. The food chain is a complex process and the loss of one link can lead to disastrous effects. If a predator disappears, those it preyed on flourish. The loss of an insect species may seem unimportant but if that insect controlled another, smaller animal that lived on particular crops, then chemical measures which may harm the environment may be needed as a control mechanism. Farmers are re-learning much agricultural folklore and beginning to use natural (and thus much more environmentally friendly) control mechanisms. Nature is actually very good at maintaining natural populations in balance, the system only failing when humans interfere. Many species have quite restricted diets, the Giant Panda and its need for bamboo shoots being a good example. If a smaller species disappears, then those who prey on it may also be threatened. Bio-diversity is in all our interests, not only for the food chain but also for the pleasure that the natural world can provide to human senses.

## Ozone depletion

Until concerns about the ozone layer in the atmosphere entered the public arena, the most that the majority of people knew about ozone was that it produced the faint odour in London tube tunnels caused by associated chemicals. The oxygen we breathe is $O_2$, i.e. two oxygen atoms joined together, whereas ozone is $O_3$, that is three oxygen atoms. Ozone is present in the atmosphere and indeed can be a toxic pollutant. Concern about high levels of ozone were raised by Rattray Taylor (1970) but we now know that the ozone layer in the atmosphere is an important part of the mechanism preventing global warming and protecting living matter from the harmful effects of solar radiation. The huge hole that was reported in the ozone layer from the 1980s onwards has been growing, in part due to the effect of CFCs (chlorofluorocarbons) present in early aerosol containers and refrigeration units which break down ozone.

## Global climate change

Many of the gases emitted by industrial processes contribute to the so-called greenhouse effect of global warming by interfering with the natural climatic mechanisms involving the relationship between the seas and the atmosphere. One of the worst gases is carbon dioxide. This, as stated earlier, is a natural by-product of animal respiration and thus it seems strange that it is a pollutant. However the amount of carbon dioxide produced naturally is absorbed by plants and converted to oxygen. Human industry, however, produces vast quantities of the gas which serve, albeit slowly, to alter weather patterns. Global warming may cause climatic zones to shift and the ice caps to melt at a greater rate. In turn, this may lead to a raising of sea levels and the loss of land. Coastal regions and their cities are thus in some danger!

# Medium risk issues

## Herbicides and pesticides

Provided that they are used in moderation, nature is able to recycle many of the chemicals used in agriculture. However, over-use can lead to dangerous build-ups of toxins in both the soil and water. If these chemicals then enter the food chain, they can have very severe effects. Birds' eggs can be weakened, as was shown by the decline in UK peregrine numbers, and fish stocks may also be affected. Many such chemicals, e.g. Lindane, are now banned in the developed world but may still be in use in less developed areas.

## Acid rain

One of the first noticeable manifestations of environmental pollution was the damage caused to plant life by acid rain. Acid rain contains acidic products from many of the gases emitted as waste products in industrial processes, e.g. sulphur dioxide. Legislation in the developed world has helped halt further damage but acid rain has shown how damaging the uncontrolled release of pollutants can be, as the effects are not localised but carried in weather systems and then deposited as rain. It is salutary to think about the effects on human tissue of these products, given their devastating effect on trees etc.

## Airborne toxins

Many toxic materials can be carried long distances by weather systems, as mentioned above. Thus a local pollution problem may affect huge areas. The incident at the Chernobyl nuclear reactor in the Ukraine in 1986 caused radioactivity to be spread over a huge part of Europe, even affecting Welsh lamb sales because of fears that flocks had been irradiated.

Lead, for long a component of petrol (gasoline), has been a major 20th Century air pollutant suspected of causing medical and behavioural problems in children. This scourge has been alleviated by the use of unleaded fuel, although the other waste products of the internal combustion engines have only been partially reduced by the use of catalytic converters.

## Water pollution

Like oxygen, water is a key requirement for the vast majority of life forms. Water pollution in the developed world became endemic with the onset of the

Industrial Revolution. Waste products were poured indiscriminately into streams, rivers and the sea with little concern for the damage caused.

Not only can such products enter the food chain but also, by depriving the waters of oxygen, they kill marine life and reduce once clear rivers into polluted, slow-moving streams unfit for drinking water. Action in the UK in cleaning rivers has been very successful, with otters returning to the Thames etc. A diverse aquatic lifestyle is normally a good indicator of water quality.

A high standard of drinking water is something those in the developed world have come to take for granted but for much of the world's population it is an unheard of luxury. Dirty drinking-water supplies bring disease in their trail and this can sap the economic vitality from a whole region and cause long-lasting medical problems. Cholera may be unheard of in the UK today but it was the cause of some of the first environmental measures and legislation in the world, as UK cities in the 19th Century were ravaged by the disease.

# Low risk issues

## Oil spills

Oil spills can cause great local damage but fortunately rarely affect huge areas. Nevertheless the costs, both in cash and environmental terms, of clearing up after an oil spill can be huge. The *Exxon Valdez* disaster in Alaska in 1989 not only cost billions of dollars to rectify but threatened the whole of a very fragile ecosystem and challenged the USA's ability to deal with a spill on such a large scale (Sexton *et al.*, 1999).

It is not only the emotive pictures of dying, oil-clogged seabirds and seals etc. that cause the problems, tragic though they are, but the economic implications of an oil spill on to holiday beaches which may destroy the economic infrastructure of the area. Oil is not easy to clean up and its odour can last for long periods of time, rendering beaches unfit for human activities.

## Groundwater pollution

Groundwater pollution is likely to cause only localised problems although if toxins leach into nearby rivers or seep into the water table, then there may be more widespread pollution affecting water supplies. All organisations must ensure that their waste materials cannot run off with rainwater and thus affect wider areas. Many chemicals, e.g. mercury and lead, can be extremely toxic and a number of compounds may be carcinogenic (cancer forming).

## Radiation

Fortunately, with the exception of the Chernobyl incident mentioned earlier, there have been few widespread problems with radiation although there have been some near misses. Problems have occurred with the release of radiation from nuclear plants entering the food chain, strontium-90 being a particular problem as it enters cattle through grass, is then present in milk and can become concentrated in bones.

Radiation (and a number of chemicals called carcinogens) causes cancer and there are currently investigations in a number of parts of the world into clusters of cancer-related diseases near to nuclear installations, childhood leukaemia being a particular concern.

Even low-level radioactive waste as used in medical isotopes must be disposed of carefully. There were cases in the earlier years of the 20th Century of workers developing mouth cancers through licking the paintbrushes used to apply the luminescent dials on watches.

Radiation is always with us, either from space or from radioactive rocks. Granite is radioactive, giving Aberdeen one of the highest background radiation counts in the UK. Radiation also causes genetic mutations and may be part of the evolutionary mechanism. As with many environmental issues, the problems occur when human activity increases the radiation level above the natural background count.

The major problem with radioactive materials is the length of time they remain a hazard. Many of them have extremely long half-lives (the time it takes for radioactivity to halve). The half-life of one isotope of plutonium is a staggering 24 400 years!

## Thermal pollution

Whilst global warming affects all the planet, even local thermal pollution may be a problem in that dangerous gases may accumulate in the atmosphere and if rivers become too warm, they may be depleted of oxygen and life in them may die.

Many of the above problems have their roots in the massive growth of road transportation. Whilst the individual motor car may appear to be insignificant, the energy required to produce and the pollution emitted by millions of vehicles globally adds up to a significant amount.

Governments have begun to take action, examples of which include:

- Lead-free petrol
- Catalytic converters
- Encouragement for recycling
- Increased fuel prices
- Developing electric vehicles
- Public transport improvements
- Increased vehicle taxation.

It remains a fact, however, that huge numbers of individuals and organisations rely on road transport and that any indirect taxation often fails to cut vehicle use if inadequate public transport just means that more has to be paid but vehicle usage is unaltered.

# Waste management

In the early years of the Industrial Revolution, scant regard was given to waste management. In today's more environmentally aware climate, all organisations need to ensure that they meet both legal and moral waste management requirements and that materials are recycled whenever possible. Recycling not only protects finite resources but may also lessen the need for energy. Recycling old cars means less of a requirement for steel, and this in turn means less iron ore needs to be mined and less fossil fuel is needed to convert it into steel. Waste management and recycling are one way in which everybody, whether individually or through their organisation, can assist the environment.

# Compassionate farming and organic food

In the developed world, in particular, recent years have seen a growth in concerns regarding the welfare of farm animals both *in situ* and when being transported, and a public awareness of the benefits of naturally produced organic foods which have been reared or grown without the use of chemicals.

The BSE problems of the 1990s appear to have developed from the methods use to feed cattle (actually feeding them infected material from sheep). Battery chicken production using antibiotics and growth hormones has come under scrutiny, especially as the bacteria that infect the animals appear to develop an immunity to the antibiotics. Customers (at least in the developed world, where there is a choice) appear to be increasingly in favour of naturally produced products.

The problems associated with the possible spread of CJD, the human form of Bovine Spongiform Encephalytus (BSE), a cattle disease that had already caused the UK major economic and political problems in the 1990s, was a matter of grave concern at the turn of the century. Caused primarily by farming techniques, the issue makes a good case study on the need for an environmental consideration to agriculture. Fortunately, fears of a devastating epidemic of human mad cow disease (BSE) appeared to recede in 2000 as scientists reported the first results of research aimed at gauging the scale of the threat, although they warned people not to draw too much comfort from the results of the study into thousands of tonsil and appendix specimens.

The government-funded scientists found no sign of variant CJD among the 3000 samples removed from patients since the 1980s in routine operations. The concern was that had even two or three positive results been discovered, it would have meant possibly thousands of people dying from the incurable disease. However the experts stressed that these were interim findings from an ongoing survey that would eventually examine around 18 000 tissue samples over the next few years.

A huge question mark has hung over the threat posed by new variant CJD ever since the disease was first identified in 1995. Forecasts of the eventual death toll have ranged from a mere hundred or so to several hundreds of thousands, causing a fair degree of public anxiety. Scientists believe most, if not all, cases of infection occurred in the late 1980s as a result of people eating beef contaminated with BSE. Variant CJD is thought to be simply a human version of the cattle disease and has thus crossed the species barrier. After the initial BSE scares, rigid controls introduced by the UK government appear to have kept infected beef out of the human food chain.

Diseases that jump from one species to another often have extended incubation periods. If variant CJD has an incubation period of more than about 20 years, then the cases seen so far could be just the tip of an iceberg as many people might be harbouring the disease without knowing it, and the epidemic could be a time bomb waiting to explode.

By April 2000, there had been 53 confirmed deaths in the UK from variant CJD. One factor which may limit the size of any spread of the problem is the growing suspicion that only certain individuals with a particular genetic make-up are susceptible.

In 2000, the USA began action against the EU over the latter's refusal to purchase animal products that had been reared using growth hormones. EU customers had shown resistance to such products and this led to a minor trade war. Whilst the USA might be able to force EU countries not to ban products, they could not, of course, force customers to buy them. Similarly, whilst the UK could and did take legal action against a French government ban on British beef following the BSE crises, nobody could force a French consumer actually to purchase and consume the product.

## Genetic engineering and genetically modified (GM) crops and animals

Genetic engineering and the cloning of animals made great strides in the 1990s. It became possible to insert genes from other species into agricultural products. Such genes might promote growth or enhance disease resistance. Plant genes could be put into animals and vice versa. Cloning, beginning with a sheep (Dolly) in the late 1990s, gave rise to the possibilities of a limitless supply of organs for transplant using cloned pigs. As each clone is genetically identical to the parent, any defects could be bred out and a pure line obtained. The public, however, particularly in the UK but less so in the USA, became somewhat alarmed at these developments and the government's enthusiasm was seen to wane.

Scientific concerns centred on the introduction of 'foreign' material into an organism and the problems of preventing the spread of pollen etc. By 2000, a number of restaurants, hotels, holiday facilities and food retailers were actively proclaiming that their products did not knowingly contain any genetically modified materials – a clear case of responding to customer demand. Many scientists have continued to insist that such products are not at all harmful but the UK public appears to be somewhat unconvinced.

# Cost–benefit analysis and environmental decisions

Environmental issues often go far beyond the borders of any one country and may be medium-to-long term rather than short-term. In the late 1990s, whilst nearly all world governments recognised the problems of global warming and the need to control the emission of greenhouse gases, when the UK announced major cuts in emissions at the Earth Conference in Rio de Janeiro in 1999, the USA refused to follow suit as did a number of less-developed countries.

Whilst in the medium-to-long term emission limits may be the only answer, it may be hard for a developing country with a struggling economy to adopt costly environmental measures and any limits on industrial output. Global warming may be decades away but a starving population can lead to political and social upheaval tomorrow. Taking anything other than a short-term view requires co-operation and vision.

An organisation may wish to be environmentally friendly but unless others in the sector act with it, it may be placed at a commercial disadvantage. This highlights the need for strong legislation and robust planning procedures to aid organisations in taking the long-term view.

Often the problem is that the benefits are long-term and apply across the board, whilst the costs must be incurred in the short-term and may be borne by a particular sector or even a single organisation. However, if the issue is the survival of the planet and thus the human race, then action is required.

Despite much pessimism, there has been action to cut waste and pollution, and the air is cleaner and fish are returning to many of our rivers. One change has been that the mass of the population in the developed world have a greater awareness of environmental issues and are able to lobby governments and organisations for changes – changes that may not benefit them but will benefit their children and their children's children.

# Summary

Environmental concerns have begun to generate much public feeling. Whilst the problems may be long-term, especially in terms of global warning and radiation, costs must be incurred in the short-term. This means that organisations and governments need to co-operate so that no one organisation or sector becomes disadvantaged. Like the economy, environmental concerns are not limited to one country or region – eventually they affect the whole planet.

# Concepts covered

- The natural environment
- Environmental concerns

- Environmental risk categories
- Types of environmental risks
- Compassionate and organic farming
- Genetic engineering
- Cost–benefit analysis

# Analysis

In carrying out the *environmental* analysis in respect of an organisation, the following need to be considered:

1. How might the organisation impact upon the physical environment?
2. What environmental legislation is relevant to the organisation?
3. How does the organisation deal with waste and toxic products?
4. How much material can and does the organisation recycle?
5. Are there any aspects of the organisation in respect of the environment that may provoke customer concerns?
6. Are there environmental issues that the whole sector must consider rather than just the individual organisation?
7. What effect might global warming have on the operations of the organisation?

QUESTIONS

1. 'Why should I clean up my operation when the factory next door does nothing?' How might you provide an objective response to that question bearing in mind long-term effects and short-term costs?
2. Explain why environmental issues are global rather than local ones, using examples including air pollution, radiation and global warming. Who is responsible for ensuring that action is taken?

# Further reading

You are recommended to read *Better Environmental Decisions* by K. Sexton, A. A. Marcus, K. W. Easter and T. D. Burkhardt (1999).

# ̌  12  Sectoral analysis

*Competition – Cartels and monopolies – Competitive forces – Co-operation within sectors – Differentiation and segmentation – Unique selling point (USP) – Discounting – Branding – Integration*

## Competition

In many parts of the world, the encouragement of competition came to be seen in the 1980s and 1990s as a means of giving customers more choice and protecting them from unscrupulous organisations. The perceived wisdom was that the more players there were in a market, so the more prices would be forced down and quality be driven upwards.

Unfortunately what the politicians enacting much of the anti-competitiveness legislation failed to realise was that increasing the number of players in a market can ultimately reduce customer choice. One of the results of there being a large number of organisations chasing a finite number of customers can be to drive the weaker organisations out of the market, often as a result of take-overs. Unless there is both government legislation and the political will to act on mergers and take-overs (see Chapter 4), the end result can be that a few large organisations come to dominate the market and can in extreme cases actually 'fix' the market to their advantage. The operation of such cartels (technically illegal in the USA and Europe) is covered later in this chapter.

In considering a sectoral analysis it is necessary for those undertaking it to analyse not only the position of their organisation but also that of any actual and any potential competitors. Many business problems occur not because existing competitors were ignored but because not enough account was taken of those who might become potential competitors.

There is competition whenever two or more organisations seek to supply the same product or service to the same individual or group of customers. Competition is all around us. One only has to study any retail shopping centre or high street to discover that similar products or services are available, often at a similar price from a number of suppliers. Chapter 9 stressed the importance of supplementary products such as service in the purchasing decisions of customers, and there is often little save a small difference in price or service to differentiate between the products offered by different suppliers. Indeed, the actual product and price may be identical. Take the case of a chocolate bar sold in any one of a number of supermarkets and smaller retailers for exactly the same price. Cartwright (2000) has differentiated between being loyal to a product, i.e. the person usually buys that chocolate bar, and being loyal to a supplier. Supplier loyalty may be more to do with convenience and standards of service than with product. The product can be bought in any number of outlets but the buyer selects one that is preferred by them.

This chapter will examine the competitive forces acting on an organisation and, as such, draws concepts from the field of marketing.

## Cartels and monopolies

There are fewer and fewer monopolies in the world. Traditionally a monopoly is an organisation that has no immediate competitors. In the past, monopoly status has often been achieved through some form of government intervention, often nationalisation and restrictions on outside imports. The advantage to having monopoly status is that the organisation does not have to compete and for the government concerned it has a major national asset under its control. For that reason strategic industries such as steel, railways, airlines, shipping, telecommunications etc. have been prime candidates for nationalisation around the world. As a spirit of competitiveness went through political thinking in the latter years of the 20th Century, many countries privatised such industries, returning them to the private sector and allowing competitors to commence operations. In the UK there was a wave of privatisations from the 1980s onwards – gas, electricity, water, British Airways, shipbuilding and the telephone network – with many individuals acquiring shares in the new found companies. The protection of national strategic industries using monopoly status has proved difficult to sustain in a global economy. As an example, it may be perfectly possible to set up a nationalised airline but impossible to restrict the operation of competitors from other countries as there are bi- and multi-lateral agreements on operating rights. If British Airways operate a certain number of UK–USA flights then US airlines (which were never nationalised) will have the right to a certain number of flights from the USA to the UK, and thus the customer has a choice and may well exercise it. British Airways proved to be very successful as a private company, gaining considerable market share and a reputation for being a very competent player in a very competitive environment, even though, as Gregory (1994) points out, competitors did not always appreciate the intensely competitive BA attitude. British Telecom is another organisation that, once privatised, became a global player in the extremely lucrative global telecommunications market, proving adept at forging alliances and developing new markets, both geographic and within the UK mobile telephone sector, whilst retaining the original UK customer base.

Other terms that are also used in describing a sector are:

• *Duopoly*: The possession of the delivery of a product or service by only two suppliers, and

- *Oligopoly*: The possession of the delivery of a product or service by a limited number of suppliers.

To give practical examples, as Cartwright & Green (1997) have shown, the bus service in an area may be a monopoly if there is only one operator; if there are two operators it is a duopoly, and if there are more than two but not a large number it is an oligopoly. Monopolies thrive in what have become known as *command* economies, where the decisions about who can supply what are decided centrally, usually by the government. Such systems have been favoured by totalitarian regimes where the political philosophy gives the government considerable control over many, if not all, parts of the lives of its citizens. This is not always a bad thing *per se*, as too much competition can be unhealthy as will be shown later. Amtrak in the USA is an example of a monopoly operating within what is arguably the most competitive and least controlled market in the world. Amtrak, formed as a result of the financial difficulties experienced by US railroads in the 1950s and 1960s, provides all of the long-distance passenger rail transport in the USA, the organisation being formed by the US government to prevent the total collapse of a service that had a large number of suppliers, most of whom were in dire financial circumstances. *Demand* economies, where the market, through customers, decides on the number of suppliers, are more likely to produce non-monopoly situations.

The rail service between Scotland and England in 2000 was essentially a duopoly with two large operators, one operating down the east coast from Edinburgh to London Kings Cross, and one down the west coast from Glasgow to London Euston. The rest of Scotland's passenger rail services remain in the control of a single franchise holder, i.e. a monopoly albeit purely a rail monopoly as there is competition from a number of bus and coach companies. In a similar vein, the long-distance passenger rail companies are subject to competition from coach companies and internal airlines.

The oligopoly situation where there are a few, fairly large players in the market is a common one, major supermarket chains being a good example. The oil industry is another often quoted example with a few very well known names, including Shell, Exxon and Mobil, supplying gasoline products to large areas of the world.

Cartwright & Green (1997) introduced a new concept, that of a *freeopoly*, where there are no restrictions, save those imposed by potential demand, on the number of possible suppliers. They proposed that in a freeopoly where there are no restrictions on the number of potential suppliers of a good or service, the actual number of organisations involved is determined by the number of potential customers and their buying patterns and the relative strengths of the competitors themselves.

Monopolies, duopolies and oligopolies are constrained by the laws of most countries (anti-trust legislation in the USA and the Monopolies and Mergers Commission plus European Union rules in the UK) from fixing prices, although there are frequent complaints in the press that this is not always effective. In 1998, the white goods (washing machines, refrigerators etc.) suppliers in the UK were accused of fixing prices throughout the country, despite the illegality of such actions. In 1999 and 2000, the UK car market came under attack for setting prices at a higher level than in other parts of Europe. The manufacturers responded by claiming that UK taxation policies and the need to build right-hand-drive versions meant higher prices in the UK. As the only short-term recourse, the customer had to buy from abroad, which is quite achievable but less convenient (although it was claimed that some manufacturers placed barriers in the way of those attempting to buy outwith the UK), and sections of the press were demanding UK and EU governmental action.

Where the market is allowed to operate completely unhindered, common sense suggests that if the public will pay $X$ for the product or service from one supplier, they will not pay much more than $X$ for it from another supplier unless there is considerable added value. Thus, within any given area, the price for similar products and services will be roughly the same.

To take an example from fiction (Douglas Adams, 1979, *The Hitchhikers Guide to the Galaxy*), a small town can only support a limited number of shoe shops; the only restriction on that number is the market. Too few and the demand will not be supplied, too many and there will not be enough business to support all the suppliers. Sooner or later the weakest will either close or merge with one of the stronger suppliers. The optimum number is determined by the market. There is as near to true competition as possible. The danger of a monopoly, duopoly or even an oligopoly is that the participants can fix the prices at an artificially high level. In a freeopoly, prices are determined by the market. Most situations tend to evolve away from a freeopoly because of the natural inclination of organisations to grow and merge with or take over previous rivals. In the Adams' scenario, eventually there is one shoe shop too many and this so distorts the economy that the whole planet suffers an economic collapse, as not only do the shoe shops fail but also so do their suppliers, their banks etc.!

In the main, competition increases with the number of suppliers but may then decrease as market forces operate to restrict the number through take-overs and mergers.

The banding together of organisations to influence the market through restricting supply or fixing prices is known as a cartel. As mentioned earlier, restricting such activities forms part of the remit of those responsible for policing anti-trust, anti-competitiveness and merger legislation. Nevertheless, it remains a fact that such cartels do seem to exist. Anthony Sampson (1984, 1993) did much to publicise this issue with his books on the airline and oil industries.

## Competitive forces

The nature of competition can be illustrated by means of the forces acting upon an organisation in a competitive environment. The US management authority Michael Porter (1980, 1985) has produced an extremely useful model, refinements to which have been added by Cartwright & Green (1997).

The model (Figure 12.1) looks at the various forces which act on the organisation and which need to be considered in any review of the sector and the external environment.

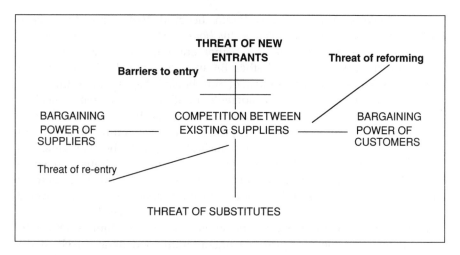

*Figure 12.1  Competitive forces* (adapted from M. E. Porter and refined by Cartwright & Green).

## Competition between existing suppliers

As would be expected, the greatest competition comes between the current players in a particular market. Even where prices are very much the same, there is competition on levels of service, supplementary products and geographic provision. Even the most well-established organisations need to keep a careful eye on the various other players in the market, all of whom may be seeking to increase their market share at the expense of their fellow players.

To ensure adequate market intelligence, a sensible organisation not only samples the quality etc. of its own products and services but also those of the competition. Larger organisations may well employ staff whose main role is, in effect, to spy. A large hotel group once described how their staff, when staying in hotels belonging to other groups, were told to CASE – Copy And Steal Everything; ideas that is, not towels and ashtrays! Airlines, supermarkets, car dealers, clothes retailers, department stores all need to sample the products and services of the opposition. This is not industrial espionage, it is just prudent business as all organisations need to know what their competitors are offering and this forms a key part of any analysis of the external environment.

## New entrants

The provision of some products and services has very high barriers to entry indeed and this may make new entrants very few and far between. You need considerable cash resources to set up a transatlantic airline, as Sir Richard Branson has done with Virgin Atlantic, or to build a new department store etc. Even if the resource barriers can be overcome, the organisation may need to establish credibility in the marketplace and may face intense pressure from existing suppliers. The problems Virgin believed they faced have been analysed by Martyn Gregory (1994) in his book *Dirty Tricks – British Airways' Secret War against Virgin Atlantic*. Whether one concludes that Virgin were a recipient of dirty tricks or whether BA were legitimately defending their markets is irrelevant in the context of this book; what is important is the fact that new entrants have considerable hurdles to overcome, especially if they present an out-and-out challenge to established providers. A new shop opening in competition may produce a price-cutting bonanza for the customer in its initial stages but business needs to be maintained. It takes time to establish a reputation for quality, and organisations need to ensure that there are resources available not just for the initial investment but for the growth phases of the product/organisational life cycles, as covered earlier in this book. A good start but then a failure to develop because of under-investment can have long-lasting repercussions, as customers (and staff) lose confidence in the ability of the organisation to maintain itself in the marketplace.

Large organisations often have the resources to enter a new market by buying up an existing player. Whilst this strategy may seem attractive, the buying organisation may not have the expertise, culture and knowledge to operate successfully in that particular market environment. Peters & Waterman (1982), in their book *In Search of Excellence*, talk about successful companies 'sticking to the knitting', i.e. staying close to what they do well. In the 1920s, automobile makers like Ford believed that it would be relatively easy for them to enter the aircraft making business, but found it wasn't; Ford only made one major product, the Ford Trimotor, which was only moderately successful. They then left the market to those who understood it and never returned; the skills required for plane making were in fact very different from those needed for the automobile industry. On the other hand, Disney have proved quite adept at moving into new markets where these are complementary to their main market; in addition to the theme parks, they operate hotels, retail outlets both within and outside the USA and even a cruise line, the latter building on the Disney recipe for inclusive entertainment. The Disney Cruise Line has received good reviews by those such as Ward (2000) who analyse the cruise industry and allocate ratings to the various products offered.

In the past there had been a perception that certain sectors of business were immune to the threat of new entrants. Government provision and services in the UK were believed to have little or no private sector competition save at the margins, but experience with privatisation and market testing in the UK has shown that even those services previously supplied by national and local government can be entered by the private sector, e.g. refuse/garbage collection, school meals and social service provision. Many areas of defence operations, especially those connected with servicing of equipment and the supply of ancillary services such as catering, can be managed and resourced from the private sector, once any security issues have been addressed.

# Substitutes

Cartwright & Green (1997) have pointed out that after World War II there was intense competition between the various US railroads operating trans-continental services, and between the shipping companies operating on the lucrative North Atlantic routes between Europe and North America with the introduction of new and more luxurious tonnage. However, when Boeing introduced the 707 jet airliner into commercial service with Pan Am on 26 October 1958, the writing was on the wall for both the railroads and the shipping companies. The shipping companies were actually no longer in the shipping business and the US railroads were no longer in the railroad business; they were in the business of mass transportation over a long distance, and the new jet airliners could do the job much faster – a classic example of substitution. The shipping companies looked for new markets within the cruising market but ships designed for the 'liner' trade were not really suitable for the vacation market and many of the companies collapsed and their vessels were laid up (Cartwright & Baird, 1999). The railroads could not compete at all and eventually, in 1971, all long-distance passenger trains in the USA came under the Amtrak banner, as mentioned earlier, and the passenger route network was cut severely.

By re-assessing their business, the railway companies in the USA and Europe are now in a position where they can challenge the airlines on short-haul routes by the introduction of new technology. The flight from London (Heathrow) to Paris (Charles de Gaulle), previously one of the most pro-fitable scheduled airline routes, takes a mere 35 minutes but the airports are a long way from the city centres and there is considerable time taken to check in, especially for passengers with baggage. *Eurostar* trains using the Channel Tunnel complete the journey in 3 hours, city centre to city centre. In a similar vein, by using newer equipment Amtrak have gained 33% of the market share between Washington DC and New York by offering city centre to city centre in just over 3 hours' service. It is perhaps not surprising that London Heathrow only received a direct rail service from Central London after the opening of the Channel Tunnel.

Substitution can involve collaboration. Railways will never cross the Atlantic and the introduction (not before time) of a rail link from Central London to Heathrow Airport (as covered above) in 1998 is an example of how the two modes of transport can complement each other when they are not in a competitive situation.

On a national scale, the UK government has been attempting to convince car drivers to use substitute forms of transport, buses etc. in order to relieve city centre congestion and to reduce vehicle emissions. The slowness of many to switch is indicative of the fact that a substitute must be at least as efficient and convenient as the original product. Until the public transport system can reach the same level of convenience as the car or is much cheaper to use, drivers may decide to stay with the familiar.

# Re-entry and re-forming

These are additions to the original model and were first postulated by Cart-wright & Green (1997) as examples of two additional threats to the competitive equilibrium.

## Re-entry

Organisations that were in the marketplace but have left it may still possess expertise in the particular area of operations. There may be 'memory of the organisation' held by customers. Such organisations may decide to re-enter the market. Major airlines re-enter geographic markets they have vacated, usually having left a small office or agency in the area so that they can re-enter and re-establish their position very quickly.

Re-entry is more likely where there are fewer problems about buying expensive plant or where the organisation can use its cash resources to buy out one of the remaining suppliers; or, as in the case of the airlines quoted above, they already possess all the necessary hardware (or can charter spare capacity), and all they need are landing slots and to reactivate their airport and agency operations.

Business operations have become very fluid in recent years, and vacation and re-entry may well become much more common. There is a danger that customers may become confused by such comings and goings and thus an organisation would not be advised to make a habit of leaving and re-entering a particular market too often.

## Re-forming

Re-forming occurs according to Cartwright & Green (1997) when a competitor moves out of the market but sells on its expertise and plant to another company, who can then take their place in the competitive situation without the major barriers to entry that would normally occur. The British P&O Group were able to become a major player in the US cruise market by their purchase of Princess Cruises in 1974. The Princess brand has grown considerably since then and this has allowed P&O to maintain the number 3 position in the cruise industry despite considerable competition, in addition to giving them a major share of the US market which is by far the most lucrative in the industry.

When analysing the state of competition, organisations are well advised to consider whether any of their competitors are vulnerable to such a take-over by an outsider, who will more than likely bring considerable resources to bear in order to increase the market share gained as a result of their acquisition.

By acquiring a place in the marketplace in this manner, the purchasing organisation nullifies any of the new-entry problems as they acquire expertise, hardware and most importantly an existing customer base.

Carnival (the world's largest cruise company) started with one ship and now controls whole sections of the marketplace through its acquisition either entirely or as a major stockholder of Cunard, Holland America, Seabourne, Costa etc., as well as its original operation. In nearly all cases, Carnival, by not changing the name or the nature of the product of the companies it acquired, also retained the loyalty of their customers. Carnival and its market position will be discussed later in this chapter when considering segmentation and differentiation, where the company is a good example of how organisations position themselves in a competitive marketplace.

## Bargaining power

Depending on the monopoly–freeopoly situation, suppliers and customers have varying degrees of bargaining power, less at the former end of the continuum, more at the latter.

In general, a supplier will wish to supply the minimum acceptable (note the use of the word 'acceptable') quality at the highest possible price, whilst the customer wants the highest possible quality at the lowest possible price. This is a version of the supply and demand effect introduced in Chapter 5.

If the supplier has a monopoly, they can demand a higher price as the customer has nowhere else to go but organisations should be aware of the danger of new-entrants and substitutes, as discussed earlier. Monopolies can be broken overnight. In a free market economy there is a point of quality for any product or service below which a customer will not drop, regardless of the price.

The more potential suppliers of goods and services to an organisation there are for a given product or service, the more the organisation itself can force the price of supplies down and the quality up. Conversely, the more competitors an organisation has, the more likely it is that its prices will need to come down, whilst its quality of output needs to be as high as possible.

A trend in recent years has been for organisations to develop closer relationships with their suppliers, offering them training and making them a full part of the manufacturing/service/delivery process. This has advantages for both sides, in that the supplier has greater guarantees of work, but conversely they can become tied to the fortunes of the contracting organisation. They have in fact become an integral part of the organisation's value chain.

## Co-operation within sectors

Notwithstanding competitive forces, there are compelling reasons why even in the most competitive market, its members need to undertake a degree of co-operation.

The first such reason is that many things that will be bad for an individual organisation will be bad for others in that market. Eddy et al. (1976) make the point that aircraft manufacturers and airlines are loathe to criticise their competitors after an accident, on the grounds that, however competent, well-managed and safety oriented an airline is, it could happen to them in the near future. A disaster that happens to one airline also has spin-off effects through cancelled bookings on others; that is a fact of human nature. Eddy and his colleagues point out that nearly every airline disaster results in cancellations on other airlines the next day.

Secondly, many large projects may be beyond the capabilities of a single organisation. A number of organisations may agree to co-operate on a particular project, share the lessons learnt and divide the profits between them, but to compete in other areas. An organisation may even agree to produce products for a rival if it is believed that the marketplace can produce the required demand. There will normally be a *quid pro quo* that says: 'if we produce this for you using our spare capacity, will you produce another product for us using your spare capacity?'

Thirdly, the competitors in a sector may work together to repel a new entrant or defend against a substitute product. This is in all their interests, although it may bring charges of cartel forming as happened in the airline industry with regard to new entrants on the North Atlantic route in the 1970s and 1980s.

Whilst competition can be cut-throat, it is often not in the interests of organisations in the sector to see others go to the wall. If an organisation does fold, the lack of confidence generated can have repercussions for all members of the sector and thus they may help rescue the situation, normally gaining something themselves, often a part of the other organisation, in the process.

## Differentiation and segmentation

To attract customers to a product or service, an organisation has to offer them something that its competitors don't. To survive, each organisation needs what Porter (1985) has described as *competitive advantage*, and one or more *unique selling points* (USPs), i.e. those things which only that organisation offers and thus the things that distinguish it from other organisations offering similar products and services.

Many USPs do not remain so for long, as competitors can see the advantage and may decide to expend resources to match the original USP. One well-known USP was that of a retail chain that would exchange goods bought at one store at any other branch, or provide a refund irrespective as to whether it was the actual purchaser making the request. This was of major benefit to those who had received unwanted presents. Under UK contract law, an exchange or refund only needs to be given to the actual purchaser and not to a third party. Such exchange/refund policies are now practised by a large number of groups.

Geographic location can be a USP; a hotel with its own moorings on the banks of the River Thames is able to offer a USP to its customers, especially those owning or hiring boats on the river. A restaurant at the top of the highest building in a city is able to offer the USP of an unequalled vantage point. The largest cruise ship in the world is able to offer this cachet as a USP but only so long as it is the largest, and the trend has been for ships to become bigger and bigger. In 1969 the famous *Queen Elizabeth 2* was the second largest passenger ship afloat and the fifth largest ever built. By 1999 it was the thirty-third largest. Nevertheless, because of its special standing in the mind of cruise passengers, it still had the USP of being the *QE2*, an indefinable but highly marketable USP. The *QE2* was not the largest, not the fastest and not the most luxurious, but when Cartwright & Baird (1999) studied the industry it was the ship most mentioned as 'I would love to take a trip on the *QE2*' by UK actual and potential cruise goers. This section will draw heavily on the shipping industry (especially the cruise segment) because, firstly, this is an area that the author has analysed in some depth and, secondly, it provides excellent examples of differentiation, segmentation, integration and branding.

A USP is, in effect, an organisation's monopoly.

There are two basic ways to obtain competitive advantage:

- Offer a similar product to your competitors but offer it cheaper – *cost*
- Offer a similar but different product – *differentiation.*

# Cost

Cost is an important component of any product. Chapter 5 introduced the types of costs faced by organisations and the manner in which the actual price of a product or service is a function of the costs of production/delivery.

An important point to make at the beginning of this discussion on the marketing concepts to consider when analysing an organisation's environment is that there is a continuum of cost positioning. It is possible to make £100 profit by selling 100 products with a profit of £1 each or one product with a profit of £100. The former is known as high volume–low margin and the latter as low volume–high margin. The Ford Focus is an example of the former, a Rolls Royce of the latter. Organisations normally compete with those in a similar position along the continuum.

It is an axiom in management accounting that fixed costs must be met if any business is to be a success. Fixed costs are those costs that the organisation will incur even if it has no customers. Every product or service should contribute to the fixed costs of heating, lighting, rents, administration, marketing etc., because those have to be paid however many or few products or services are actually delivered to customers.

No enterprise goes into profit, or in the case of a public sector organisation leaves a deficit situation, until the overall revenue income is at least equal to the overall fixed costs, a position known as breakeven. Provided the organisation has enough cash or credit to meet its recurring expenditure, it can avoid a cash flow crisis and carry on trading.

There is obviously a minimum price that any organisation can charge for its products or services. This is the breakeven cost where all of the fixed costs of the organisation as allocated to that product or service are met, and the variable costs associated with the production or delivery of the product or service are also covered. At this point there is no profit or surplus.

Competition on costs is complicated by the need to maintain quality. Customers may wish to pay a low price but the bargaining power part of the Porter model (see earlier) suggests that they will always wish to have an acceptable level of quality. Thus there becomes a lower quality limit below which an organisation cannot drop and this, in effect, sets a limit on any cost reductions unless gained in such a manner as to leave quality unaffected. Fortunately for organisations, there are strategies that can be adopted to cut costs without diminishing quality.

One of the comments often to be heard during any consideration of the sector during an organisational analysis is 'how can they do it at that price?', i.e. how can a competitor undercut others in the sector with a seemingly similar product? There are a number of ways, one or a combination of which may be used at any time:

● Reduce waste
● Reduce staff costs
● Lower quality
● Reduce margins
● Make a deliberate loss.

If the final category appears strange – all will be revealed later.

## Reduce waste

In any process, whether it is manufacturing or service delivery, there is waste. The waste may be actual material or it may be viewed in terms of wasted time that has to be met through the wage bill. Locating a manufacturing facility close to the sources of raw materials and component suppliers can reduce the costs of transportation. As was shown earlier in Chapter 1, where the supply of materials for the Boeing 777 was examined, this is not always possible, as the organisation will want to obtain the best deals in terms of price and quality it can from suppliers. If the best supplier is in Japan whilst the organisation is in Seattle, then so be it. However, the costs associated with such decisions need to be written into the costings for the operation. There may be other factors, such as a wish to co-operate with another organisation or even another country, that mitigate against transportation costs.

Wasteful practices tend to creep up on organisations. In a booming economic climate or a time of low-cost raw materials, eliminating waste may not seem important. It is possible that the measures needed to become more efficient may have significant short-term costs, e.g. new machinery. If the economic climate becomes less favourable and margins grow tighter or competition increases, then these short-term costs may need to be incurred to achieve longer-term efficiencies.

## Reduce staff costs

Staff costs can form up to 80% of the total costs of an organisation. However expensive the equipment used in an organisation is, the most expensive commodity is nearly always people. Modern technology, as discussed in Chapter 7, can dramatically reduce the number of people required for a particular task.

Some organisations have saved on staffing costs by moving their operation to a lower wage economy. India, with a large number of well-educated people with high levels of technical/computer literacy but with lower wages than Western Europe or the USA, has been used by a number of organisations as a base for data processing. Information can be downloaded using standard communications technology, processed in India and then fed back. Whilst such developments benefit the employment statistics in India, they may of course lead to job losses elsewhere; there are very few gains in the world of business without somebody suffering a degree of pain.

## Lower quality

The importance of maintaining quality has already been stressed. The important point is that an organisation must maintain an acceptable quality – acceptable that is to the customer. Customers will not want to pay for quality in excess of their requirements. They may accept it if there is no cost, but this is rarely the case.

This book also introduces the slightly different concept of 'a waste of quality'. There is anecdotal evidence that when Ford analysed the famous Model T it was found that however old the vehicle was when it was scrapped, the kingpins were normally in first class condition. Henry Ford did not consider that this was a reason to congratulate the engineers: the kingpins were over-engineered, the quality standard was too high. In the 1980s, the term 'planned obsolescence' came into vogue in the car industry. Parts should be engineered for the anticipated maximum lifetime of a vehicle. Indeed it may well be to a manufacturer's advantage not to over-engineer. Sabbach (1995) makes the point that one of the reasons for the rise in price of jet engines has been the lack of follow-on sales. Earlier-generation engines needed replacing more often than the current generation and thus the sale of an engine to an airline meant a series of follow-on sales. The latest engines last far longer in service and thus there are fewer opportunities to make further sales to the same customer. In the airline industry, safety is paramount and thus one of the disadvantages of a more reliable engine is that it will cost more, not because of the manufacturing costs *per se* but because the engine supplier needs to make the bulk of their profit on the first sale, as there will be less likelihood of follow-on sales.

## Reduce margins

In a monopoly situation, margins can be as high as the market will bear. In a competitive situation, it may be necessary to reduce margins to gain competitive advantage. This often starts a price war as players make a reactive reduction in their margin. This is clearly an untenable situation in the long-term, as eventually one player will reach the zero margin position where no profit is made. This is one reason why cartels are formed to try to control prices and to hold them at a level that is acceptable to all the members of the cartel. Whilst, as stated earlier, such tactics often fall foul of the law, it is not in the customer's interest for organisations to make a loss. In the private sector this will drive them out of business and thus reduce choice, and in the public sector the taxpayer ends up making good any deficit.

In order to clear old stock it may be acceptable to sell it at no or a very reduced margin. There are considerable costs in terms of space and insurance in carrying stock, and thus old stock may be disposed of not in order to make a profit but merely to clear space and save on insurance costs.

## Discounting

The use of the '*SALE*' as a means of encouraging spending and reducing the levels of old stock has been practised for many years. The latter years of the 20th Century have seen a growth in the use of discounting as an almost permanent feature of business operations. Discounting is virtually a permanent sale where customers can nearly always achieve a price less than that quoted. Dickinson & Vladimir (1997) and Ward (1999/2000) have commented on the effects of discounting on service levels within the cruise industry where the practice is endemic. They claim that discounting can act so as to lower standards. There is in fact less money available to the organisation if the majority of customers are paying a discounted price. A customer looking at a 1999 brochure which quoted prices of £3095 for two weeks in the Mediterranean would expect standards commensurate with that price. The fact that the customer (and any others) could purchase the cruise for £2270 using a combination of early booking and travel agent's discounts does not mean that they would expect a diminution of service by the 27% discount gained (Cartwright & Baird, 1999). The organisation has to try to maintain a £3000 level of service on an income of £2270. This might suggest that the original margins were too high or that the organisation never expected to make them anyway. This can cause a problem in that customer expectations may have been raised to an unrealistically high level and the short-term gain may be negated because of a loss of repeat business.

## Make a deliberate loss

It may sound strange to talk of making a deliberate loss as a business strategy but there can be short-term reasons for doing so. One relates to tax advantages and is outwith the scope of this book. The second is concerned with the concept of a 'loss leader'. A loss leader is a product or service that is deliberately offered at a loss in order to entice customers. There are three major types of loss leader – those that entice the customer in and then use the opportunity to sell unrelated products; those that sell the core product at a loss and then sell supplementary products, enhancements, training etc. at a profit; and those that offer the basic product model at a loss but then use sales technique to persuade the customer to upgrade to a more expensive, profit-generating model. A basic car model may be offered at a low price but in the knowledge that whilst this may elicit interest in a potential customer, experience shows that they will want more than the basic model, for which the price will be higher.

# Segmentation

Within any cost grouping there are a number of ways a company can differentiate/ segment its products. These can relate to the provision of supplementary products or services, they may be centred on the customer base or they may be based on brand names. Many people are loyal to a particular brand and this brand loyalty (Cartwright, 2000) can be very strong. It is not unusual for the same product to be sold under a different brand name in different parts of the same organisation. There are electrical stores in the UK that sell similar products under differing brand names in their stores – the stores being part of the same group but with different store brand names.

To illustrate branding in more detail, an example is taken, as explained earlier, from the cruise industry – probably the fastest growing commercial operation in the UK in the late 20th and early 21st Centuries.

Carnival Cruises, the largest cruise company in the world, consists of a series of brands, each targeted at different segments of the market. Cartwright & Baird (1999), in their study of the cruise industry, postulated that within the customer base there were in fact customers whose motivation for taking a cruise differed. Some went for the social aspect, others for the ports of call, still others to relax etc.

Carnival commenced operations with one ship, the *Mardi Gras*, in 1972 and by 1999, by expanding the original Carnival brand and by acquiring other companies, Carnival was clearly the market leader in terms of number of ships and market share.

|  | STANDARD | PREMIUM | LUXURY | NICHE |
|---|---|---|---|---|
| UK MARKET | Share in Airtours/ Direct Cruises | Cunard | Cunard | |
| N. AMERICAN MARKET | Carnival Costa | Holland America | Cunard Seabourne | Windstar |
| EUROPEAN MARKET | Costa | | | |

*Figure 12.2   Branding of Carnival Cruise products* (taken from *The Development and Growth of the Cruise Industry,* Cartwright & Baird, 1999, with permission).

In order to satisfy the needs and wants of as many of the above as possible, Carnival operate a series of different companies, each targeted at different needs and different price groups from the standard to the luxury as shown in Figure 12.2.

By using a series of brands – Carnival itself, Cunard, Costa etc. – the organisation is able to appeal to a very wide customer base both in terms of price and lifestyle. There are in fact separate US, UK and European markets, and Carnival has a presence in each. There is also a growing Far Eastern market and Carnival explored entry into this market in 1998 but decided not to proceed at that time.

Soap powders, chocolate bars and electrical goods are all branded. Many may be made by the same manufacturer but are designed to appeal to different segments of the market.

A recent phenomenon has been that of **generic products**. A manufacturer, say in Korea, may make a series of identical products which have the brand attached when they arrive in the country of re-sale. Many brown goods (televisions, hi-fis, computers etc.) are made in the same factory and then have a 'brand' attached by the retailer.

Segmentation applies to the manner in which the marketplace is divided up. In Chapter 3, the various socio-economic groups in the UK were introduced. Each of these forms a different segment of the marketplace for a particular class of product or service. Newspapers are a single business sector but one that is divided up into a series of segments: broadsheets, tabloids etc. Publishers usually have a different title to meet each market segment, sometimes titles from the same publisher taking completely opposing views on issues. The car market is similarly segmented with a manufacturer such as Ford offering products for a number of market segments. For success, it is important that organisations offer the right product to the right segment, and that means understanding the behaviour of that segment.

It is possible that a similar product but with a different brand name may be offered to different market segments, washing powders being a good example: there are only a handful of manufacturers worldwide but a plethora of different brands catering for different social and geographic segments. Segmentation can be applied to the vast majority of products and services – holidays, kitchen appliances, confectionery and magazines are just a few examples of where similar products may be offered to different segments under different names.

# Integration

One of the most important ways that an organisation can grow is by integration either horizontally or vertically. It is essential that organisations are aware of the growth strategies of their competitors.

## Horizontal integration

Organisations that are growing by horizontal integration expand outward by developing competitive brands, complementary products and by-products (Johnson & Scholes, 1993). Whilst it may seem paradoxical for an organisation to develop competitive products, it is not an unusual strategy. The car manufacture VW deals in its own brand but also that of Skoda and Seat. This allows penetration into different geographic and social group markets. Carnival, as mentioned earlier, have been very successful in developing a range of seemingly competitive brands but which, on closer examination, actually complement each other. More elderly holiday makers who might well feel out of place on a Carnival ship, noted as they are for a younger clientele, may well be very happy with the ambience on a Holland America Line vessel. As both brands are owned by the Carnival Group, they complement each other. The way in which Carnival have also acquired brands in different price segments allows their customers to trade up as their disposable income increases without being lost to the group.

## Vertical integration

Johnson & Scholes also refer to this as forward and backward integration. In this form of growth, the organisation acquires or develops other parts of the supply chain. Package holiday companies in the UK have acquired travel agencies (backward integration) and airlines (forward integration) in order to provide a more complete package to their customers and at the same time take greater control over the supply chain. Such integration can be a cause of concern in that only the organisation's products are promoted in shops that to the outsider are unconnected to the core business, and this may be an area investigated by government agencies keen to promote competition.

An organisation that is buying into other areas of the supply chain may present a threat to others already competing in that area, and thus the analysis of such developments forms an important part of any consideration of the external environment.

# Summary

This chapter has looked at the sector within which an organisation operates, concentrating on the competitive forces that act on the organisation. Cartels and monopolies were described followed by a discussion on competitive forces and the work of Michael Porter. The importance of some form of co-operation within sectors was considered and the chapter concluded by examining how organisations can grow using differentiation and branding to meet the needs of differing market segments and integration.

## Concepts covered

- Competition
- Cartels and monopolies
- Competitive forces
- Co-operation
- Differentiation and segmentation
- Unique selling point (USP)
- Discounting
- Branding
- Integration

## Analysis

In carrying out the *sectoral* analysis in respect of an organisation, the following need to be considered:

1. What business is the organisation actually in?
2. What sector of the environment (public, private, voluntary) does the organisation belong to?
3. Who are the main competitors?
4. What USPs do the organisation have?
5. What USPs do competitors have?
6. Is there a danger of substitution?
7. Is there a danger of new entrants?
8. Is there a danger of re-forming?
9. Is there a danger of re-entry?
10. Is there collaboration between competitors?
11. Does branding have implications for the organisation?
12. Is the organisation growing and, if it is, how is this happening?

QUESTIONS

1. Explain why too little competition may be bad for the customer but so might too much. What is the role of government in regulating competition?
2. Taking a sector of business you are familiar with, show how the amended Five Forces model can be applied to competition. Ensure that you take into account new entrants and substitution.

3. How can organisations grow using integration? Give examples of how a single organisation can cater for different market segments. You should ensure that you cover the importance of branding as part of your answer.

# Further reading

You are recommended to read *Competitive Strategy* (1985) and *Competitive Advantage* (1980) by Michael Porter for a full analysis of competitive forces within the marketplace.

# ▪ ∨  13  Future trends and cases

The following case study on the introduction of new ships by both P&O Cruises and Festival Cruises in the late 1990s and early 21st-Century is designed to show how all of the aspects of a SPECTACLES analysis come together to form a coherent whole, albeit from a position of hindsight. The cruise industry has been chosen firstly because it has been a recent area of study by the author, and secondly the huge sums involved leave little room for errors in analysis or planning. As such, it is a worthy sector to conclude this book.

Firstly the facts are presented and then, in the concluding part of the chapter, the context is set into various components of a SPECTACLES analysis.

## P&O Cruises – *Oriana* and *Aurora*/Festival Cruises – *Mistral*

In 1999, the author of this text and his colleague Carolyn Baird published the first comprehensive, academic text on the cruise industry, an industry that has been growing at a phenomenal rate. Whilst the reader may believe that this is an industry whose customers are the rich, this is far from true and cruising is being actively advertised as a vacation experience for families in a wide variety of income brackets.

The following is adapted from their text (with permission) to show how the industry and two organisations within it have analysed the external environment and made massive investments at what they believe to be the most appropriate time. As such, the study has social, political, economic, cultural, technological, aesthetic, customers, legal, environmental and sectoral aspects, making it a useful means of bringing together all the areas covered in this book.

### Note on the size of ships

In order to have a common denominator when discussing the size of ships, this case study uses Gross Registered Tonnage (GRT), often written as tons, *but* GRT is not a measure of weight but of capacity and is the total enclosed volume of the ship in cubic feet divided by 100. The word tonnage comes from the mediaeval 'tun' meaning a barrel. This is the normal method of describing the size of a merchant vessel and is in accordance with the International Convention on Tonnage Measurement that came into force on 18 July 1982.

A comparison of the *Olympic* of 1911 and her ill-fated sister ship, *Titanic* of 1912, shows an example of how this is used. Although almost identical, *Titanic* had the forward part of A-deck enclosed and thus the GRT figure of 45 224 for *Olympic* increased to 46 328 for *Titanic*.

Adding an extra deck with enclosed spaces can therefore dramatically increase the GRT. When the *Norway* (ex *France*) had two decks added during her 1990 refit, her GRT increased from 66 343 to 76 049.

The size of warships, on the other hand, is measured by the amount of water they displace (known as the displacement) on Archimedean principles.

As over two-thirds of the world's cruise ships operate in the US market and North America still uses feet and inches, most measurements are given in feet, with the metric equivalent in brackets if appropriate.

## The cruise industry

Cruising can be described as a multi-centre holiday where you take your hotel with you from centre to centre, and for nearly 7.8 million people in 1998 (Ward, 1999) this was a type of holiday for which they were prepared to pay not inconsiderable sums of money. As a vacation package, cruising is nearly always at the top, in terms of cost, of the particular holiday price sector being considered by the customer. There are 'cheap' cruises but they are cheap compared to other cruises, not in comparison with other holidays in that particular sector.

According to the Maritime Evaluation Group, in 1998 nearly 7.8 million people worldwide undertook a cruise, the 1996 figure being 7.2 million, with that for 1992 being 5.4 million, an increase of 44% over the 7-year period. By nationality, the figures are even more interesting, as shown in Figure 13.1.

Any UK sector that is achieving an annual growth rate of 27% is well worth studying!

The US market comprised approximately 64% of the total market in 1996, although this was down from 79% in 1992. The figures are affected by the fact that it is the US market that is growing slowest of all.

It is no surprise to those who have followed the market that, since 1992, Airtours and Thompson Holidays have entered the UK cruise market with the use of three vessels each, whilst P&O increased their UK capacity by 82% between 1992 and 1997 with another new vessel, the 76 000 ton *Aurora*, commencing operations in 2000.

| Nationality | 1992 | 1998 | Annual % increase |
|---|---|---|---|
| USA | 4 250 000 | 5 050 000 | 3% |
| UK | 225 000 | 650 000 | 27% |
| Germany | 190 000 | 283 000 | 7% |
| Canada | 150 000 | 250 000 | 10% |
| Japan | 20 000 | 225 000 | 146% |

*Figure 13.1  Increase in cruise passengers 1992–98* (source: Maritime Evaluation Group (Ward, 1999)).

Similarly, there has been an increase in the number of vessels dedicated to the Japanese and German markets, the former showing the most potential for growth, followed by the UK market.

Clearly, 7.8 million cruisers (the title given to those undertaking a cruise) will inject considerable sums into the industry and thus the market is very competitive. It is, however, as will be shown later, a market that is showing increasing signs of both vertical and horizontal differentiation, as described in Chapter 12.

The reasons behind the degree of investment to meet an expanding customer base are worthy of study. Whilst most of the industry's growth in the 1970s, 1980s and early 1990s had been in the US market, the numbers in Figure 13.1 show that there are healthy UK and generic European markets, and this case study on P&O and Festival is based on companies that have decided to expand in these particular markets.

## *Oriana/Aurora* – P&O Cruises

The 69 000-ton *Oriana* which entered service in the Spring of 1995 was unique in that she was the first vessel built specifically for the UK cruise market. Earlier vessels for the UK market had originally been designed for the liner service, had been displaced by air transportation and had then been modified for cruise operations.

In 1974, P&O Cruises, the UK Cruise operation of P&O, had refitted the 45 000-ton *Canberra* as a full-time cruise vessel. Built in 1960, the *Canberra* and her 1959 cousin the 42 000-ton *Oriana* launched by the Orient Steam Navigation Company, which merged with P&O in 1960, were designed for the UK–Australia liner service. By 1973, large passenger jets had decimated the liner trade and the ships commenced cruising, mainly in the Pacific and Caribbean but without much success. *Oriana* spent much of her time in the Southern Hemisphere before being sold to Japanese interests as a floating tourist centre in 1986, but *Canberra* was allocated to the slowly re-emerging UK market where she built up a loyal following. In 1972 'The Great White Whale' as the Royal Navy nicknamed her was hastily converted to a troop ship to carry 3 Brigade, comprising Royal Marines and elements of the Parachute Regiment, to San Carlos Water in the Falkland Islands. Equipped with extensive medical facilities and helicopter landing pads, *Canberra* was in the first wave of the assault to recapture the Falkland Islands from the Argentineans. Despite her conspicuous white appearance (she was never repainted grey) and her vast bulk, she was not hit despite intensive Argentinean Air Force activity having spent three nerve-wracking days in a confined anchorage.

The British public had watched as *Canberra* had sailed out of the Solent on 9 April 1982 and they had cheered when she returned undamaged; the ship had entered the history books and possibly the psyche of the nation. The *Queen Elizabeth 2* also sailed to the South Atlantic, but later and only as far as South Georgia where she was considered safe, but *Canberra* went into harm's way. At that time, the *QE2* was regarded as the flagship of the British Merchant Marine and the government were unwilling to risk losing her (Hastings & Jenkins, 1983). She transferred her troops to *Canberra* and the ferry *Norland* on 28 May, and *Canberra* went back to the war zone.

*Canberra* became a quintessential British experience. Douglas Ward, writing in 1994, said: 'This ship provides a cruise vacation package in very comfortable, though not elegant, surroundings, at an affordable price, in good British floating holiday camp style, but with every strata of society around you' (Ward, 1994).

By 1987, *Canberra* had captured 20% of all cruises sold in the UK (many UK cruisers undertook holidays on US market vessels, including those of Princess Cruises, the US arm of the P&O operation) and a massive 45% of all cruises that originated in UK ports (Cartwright & Baird, 1999). Despite the fact that she still had many inside cabins, no balconies and a proportion of cabins without en suite facilities, *Canberra* was still holding market share well into the early 1990s with regular 60% repeat business.

As a brand, P&O Cruises was launched in 1988 based on *Canberra* and the smaller 29 000-ton *Sea Princess* (later renamed *Victoria*). Also in that year, P&O decided to investigate either a new running mate or a replacement for *Canberra*. As it turns out, *Canberra* operated for a short period with the new ship, *Oriana*, before being replaced by the 63 500-ton *Star Princess*, transferred from the Princess operation and renamed *Arcadia*. There was nothing intrinsically wrong with the *Canberra* product other than she was an old ship that had seen much service. P&O Cruises were keen to retain the success of *Canberra* and went to great lengths to analyse why the ship had such a loyal following.

UK cruisers have different preferences from their transatlantic brethren. Robert Tillberg (a well-known and respected cruise ship designer) spent a considerable amount of time both on board *Canberra* and out and about in 'Middle England' finding out what people wanted. One of his discoveries was that UK cruisers prefer more smaller and intimate public rooms than those from North America – an example of Organisational Body Language in action. *Canberra* was a ship with a large number of smaller public rooms rather than the larger spaces found on US market ships. Barr & York (1982) have described this factor of *Canberra's* success as 'disaggregation of space'. Tillberg and P&O also realised the importance of the 'comfort factor', comfort in this case being psychological; *Oriana* would have a semblance of *Canberra* in her appearance. The inset lifeboats and twin funnels were very characteristic of *Canberra* and a similar approach was taken for *Oriana*, although there was a single funnel cunningly fashioned to give an impression of two merged funnels. A cruiser transferring from *Canberra* to *Oriana* would begin to feel at home even seeing the ship from the main road leading to Southampton Docks.

The current generation of P&O Cruises and Princess ships could not be described as lacking in elegance (see the Ward quote about the *Canberra* earlier in this case study). Even a proportion of the Princess ships operated by P&O for the US market are sufficiently 'British' as to attract a loyal UK and Canadian following.

The author has sailed on both *Victoria* and *Oriana* and had the opportunity to visit them when berthed together in Barbados. He described *Oriana* as a 'swanky'

London hotel with the West End and art galleries on the doorstep, whilst the *Victoria* is nearer to one of the elegant country house venues in the Scottish Highlands; but both have a British atmosphere that seems to strike a sympathetic chord with many UK cruisers who find some of the newer US market mega ships rather too 'glitzy' for their tastes (Cartwright & Baird, 1999). It was this 'Britishness' that P&O Cruises wished to capture for their new ship.

The decision to order a new vessel is not one that P&O could take lightly. Although the UK market was growing in the late 1980s, it is a sobering thought that whereas a new ship for the US market needs to capture a mere 2% of that market, a new P&O vessel for the UK market would have to assist in retaining *Canberra*'s massive share once she was retired plus gain 10% on her own merits.

Planning for the new ship started in 1988. Certain key parameters in the design became clear very early on:

- The vessel needed a shallower draft than the *Canberra* in order to allow her to visit an increased number of ports.
- She needed to be fast. Designed for the UK home market, many of her cruises would be Southampton–Southampton, and yet Italy and the Eastern Mediterranean were popular UK market destinations so she would need to be able to get there and back within the traditional British 14–16-day holiday period, which would mean a service speed of 24 knots compared with the 19.5 knots of P&O Princess's 70 000-ton *Crown Princess* and *Regal Princess*, both ships being intended for the US market, including the Caribbean.
- The ship would need the 'disaggregation of space', i.e. smaller public rooms to cater for British preferences rather than the larger ones preferred by Americans.
- There would need to be a wide range of cabin options, again to cater for the UK market where many families are happy to cruise in 3- or 4-berth cabins.
- As British cruisers apparently sunbathe more than those from North America, generous open deck space would be required.
- As world cruises are an important January–March part of the P&O Cruises portfolio, the vessel must have a beam of no more than 34.2 metres, the maximum permitted for the Panama Canal.
- The vessel must be environmentally friendly to meet both regulations and the increased environmental awareness of customers.

Initial designs were put out to tender in December 1989 but none of the twelve tender bids could meet P&O's budget. *Oriana* was only one of a number of large cruise ship projects being undertaken by P&O at the time. The company was investing heavily at the time, as Figure 13.2 shows.

This represents a combined Gross Registered Tonnage of nearly 968 500 and, based on the figure of $4000 (£2500) per ton, a conservative investment of $3 874 000 000 (£2 421 250 000). This is in addition to P&O's ferry and deep sea container operations although, as we will show when examining market share, P&O are only number 3 in the market behind the various interests controlled by Carnival and Royal Caribbean.

| Name | Company | Market | Size (GRT) | Capacity | Year |
|---|---|---|---|---|---|
| Oriana | P&O Cruises | UK | 69 000 | 1975 | 1995 |
| Sun Princess | Princess | US | 77 000 | 1950 | 1995 |
| Dawn Princess | Princess | US | 77 000 | 1950 | 1997 |
| Grand Princess | Princess | US | 104 000 | 2500 | 1997 |
| Sea Princess | Princess | US | 77 000 | 1950 | 1999 |
| Aurora | P&O Cruises | UK | 76 000 | 2000 | 2000 |
| Ocean Princess | Princess | US | 77 000 | 1950 | 2000 |
| Sister to Grand Princess | Princess | US | 109 000 | 2500 | 2001 |

*Figure 13.2    P&O/Princess new cruise ship building 1989–2001* (Cartwright & Baird, 1999).

Any organisation making this type of investment needs to be very confident about interest rates and the amount of disposable income their potential customers will have at their disposal, in addition to predictions about the price of fuel oil etc.

*Oriana* was put on hold until September 1990, by which time only two shipyards were in a position to bid for a revised, slightly smaller than originally intended, design. Unfortunately, the three UK yards out of the original twelve were not interested and eventually the German yard of Meyer Weft in Pappenberg, Northern Germany, was able to produce an acceptable design at a price that met the P&O budget.

Soon the detailed design of *Oriana* was underway. Much of the detailed design used the same technology as that employed by Boeing for the 777 airliner, namely CATIA (Computer-graphics Aided Three-dimensional Interactive Application) and EPIC (Electronic Pre-assembly In the CATIA), which allowed a three-dimensional computer model of the vessel to be constructed and to check for interference between components, i.e. two components trying to occupy the same space (Sabbach, 1995). Both Boeing and Meyer Weft used computer technology to make the design and building processes more efficient.

The basic statistics of *Oriana* and her recent near sister *Aurora*, introduced in 2000, are as shown in Figure 13.3.

It can be seen that in the 5 years between *Oriana* and *Aurora*, it was believed that UK tastes had progressed to require more facilities with balconies, which is one of the major differences between *Oriana* and *Aurora*. Whilst the former only had balconies in suites and staterooms (i.e. cabins with separate sleeping and sitting areas), *Aurora* had the majority of her outside accommodation with balconies. In fact, *Oriana* has 13% of her accommodation with balconies compared to 43% on *Aurora*.

Internally the ships have similar facilities with the exception of a business centre and alternative dining facility on *Aurora*, again mirroring changed customer demands.

On completion, *Oriana* boasted the largest swimming pool afloat (one of three on the ship) and an unrivalled set of public rooms for a mainstream cruise liner. Douglas Ward (1999), described *Oriana* as:

|                                              | Oriana            | Aurora            |
|----------------------------------------------|-------------------|-------------------|
| Gross Registered Tonnage                     | 69 153            | 76 000            |
| Crew                                         | 760               | 850               |
| Passenger capacity regular                   | 1 760             | 1 874             |
| Passenger capacity maximum                   | 1 975             | 1 950             |
| Passenger space ratio, regular               | 39                | 41                |
| Passenger space ratio, maximum               | 35                | 38.4              |
| Passenger decks                              | 10                | 10                |
| Cabins (comprised of)                        | 914               | 934               |
| Penthouse suites                             | 0                 | 2                 |
| Suites with balcony                          | 8                 | 10                |
| Mini-suites with balcony                     | 16                | 18                |
| Staterooms with balcony + sitting area       | 94                | 96                |
| Staterooms with sitting area, no balcony     | 66                | 0                 |
| Outside cabins with balcony                  | 0                 | 288               |
| Outside cabins                               | 410               | 242               |
| Inside cabins                                | 320               | 279               |
| Wheelchair accessible cabins with balcony    | 0                 | 8                 |
| Wheelchair accessible cabins without balcony | 8                 | 14                |
| Length                                       | 260 m (853 ft)    | 270 m (889 ft)    |
| Beam                                         | 32.2 m (105 ft)   | 32.2 m (105 ft)   |
| Draft                                        | 7.9 m (26 ft)     | 7.9 m (26 ft)     |
| Service speed                                | 24 knots          | 24 knots          |

*Figure 13.3*   Oriana *and* Aurora *statistics* (Cartwright & Baird, 1999).

'. . . thankfully, quite conventional, and is evolutionary rather than revolutionary. Capable of speedy, long distance cruising. Has the largest stabilisers of any ship, covering an area of 231 sq. ft. She is a ship that takes *Canberra*'s traditional appointments and public rooms and adds more up to date touches, together with better facilities and passenger flow, and a feeling of timeless elegance.'

*Aurora* has received similar descriptions.

Both ships are aimed at the upper end of the UK 'traditional' market and their fixtures and fittings reflect that. As part of the design, cabins are more 'seagoing' than they would be on a US market ship, again an example of Organisational Body Language. Indeed Princess Cruises, the P&O US operation, refer to all cabins as 'staterooms'; P&O Cruises reserve the stateroom tag to a particular grade of higher-priced cabins – Britons appear to like the word cabin. There are more cabins with baths and showers on *Oriana* and *Aurora* as opposed to the trend towards showers only in most US market accommodation, reflecting a cultural difference between UK and US tastes; 40% of *Oriana*'s cabins have baths compared with less than 4% on the *Dawn Princess* class. Again reflecting social and customer trends, there are nearly three times as many wheelchair-accessible cabins on *Aurora* than *Oriana*.

Accommodation on board ships is smaller than that in landside hotels, yet careful use of colour and design by Petter Yran, the architect responsible for cabin design, has given an impression of spaciousness. There are seven major types of accommodation on *Oriana*, ranging from 4-berth inside to suites. Another first for *Aurora* is the provision of coffee-making facilities in all cabins, reflecting the almost universal provision of this feature in most hotels. In common with all new cruise ships, all accommodation has en suite facilities, meeting a social and customer requirement that has grown considerably in recent years, factors of sociological and customer analysis that any organisation in the tourism business needs to be aware of.

The use of wood within the accommodation has been extensive and this utilisation of a traditional material with modern moulding and fire-retardant techniques has allowed P&O Cruises to re-introduce the traditional opulence associated with the first-class accommodation of the liner trade to the whole of their customer base, a trend which is being followed by the Princess operation and other cruise operators. As land-based package holiday hotels have improved their accommodation, so must the cruise operators follow.

Myer Weft assembled both ships in their huge erecting hall, sections being put together in one part of the shed and then craned into position like a gigantic construction kit, the maximum weight of any one section being limited to 600 GRT, the combined capacity of the two main cranes. The hall is 370 m long and over 100 m wide, an area equivalent to six soccer pitches, a large building indeed. The first part of the keel of *Oriana* was laid on the huge floor on 11 March 1993. A total of 14 444 tons of steel was erected in the building of *Oriana*. As mentioned earlier, computer design played a major role in ensuring that the various subassemblies fitted together perfectly and that the holes for pipe runs etc. were all in the right places.

Between March 1993 and the floating out of *Oriana* on 30 July 1994, equipment and fittings arrived from all over Europe: engines from Germany, crockery from Staffordshire, stabilisers from Scotland, galley equipment from Poland, bathroom units from France, lifeboats and tenders from the Netherlands, swimming pool equipment from Denmark, cutlery from Sheffield, gas boilers from Wakefield – the list seems endless. All of the equipment had to be fitted in according to the carefully prepared plans.

*Oriana*'s funnel was too large to be fitted inside and thus the ship was floated out into daylight firstly on 30 July 1994, and finally on 7 January 1995 the funnel was fitted and final fitting out and finishing commenced.

Robert Tillberg made extensive use of lightweight materials for the upper parts of the ship to reduce topweight, the aim being to create 'glass walls'. As Tillberg has stated (P&O, 1995):

'. . . a window is a hole in a wall in which you put glass but on *Oriana* they really are glass walls, which give unrestricted views.'

The techniques to do this are relatively new and they allow designers much more latitude and creativity.

UK cruisers like to attend a proper theatre rather than the show-lounge concept prevalent on ships for the US market. To place a 'West End'-style theatre on *Oriana*, needing as it did a large room unsupported by pillars, gave the designers headaches but was eventually solved by strengthening the surrounding areas, giving *Oriana* the first proper sea-going theatre.

It took the tugs, one of which had to be craned from the bow to the stern of *Oriana*, over four hours to gently manoeuvre her stern out of the building dock after it had been filled with 132 700 cubic metres of water (838 000 full bathtubs); *Oriana* was afloat.

When later that month *Oriana* sailed for her sea trials, it was necessary to dredge the River Ems, something that has to happen each time a large ship is launched at Pappenburg, as the river is normally only 6.8 m deep and *Oriana* draws 7.9 m when fully loaded, and even empty was far too deep for the 40 km of river. Not only had the Ems to be dredged but a railway bridge had to be dismantled to let the ship pass, a similar process being required for *Aurora*.

Extensive sea trials took place in the North Sea and, in March 1995, *Oriana* was handed over to her owners, and the Red Ensign of the British Merchant Marine was raised for the first time.

In April 1995, following an impressive naming ceremony by Her Majesty Queen Elizabeth II at Southampton, *Oriana* sailed on her maiden cruise and provided a large increase in available berths for the UK cruise market, increasing the P&O Cruises potential UK market by over 80%. *Aurora* arrived in Southampton in April 2000 to be named by the Princess Royal, with her maiden cruise being in May 2000.

*Canberra* was not withdrawn until the Autumn of 1997 and was immediately replaced by the *Arcadia* (ex *Star Princess*), with no decrease in available berths.

*Canberra's* last cruise was considerably overbooked and crowds lined the entrance to Southampton to mark the last arrival of the ship that had heralded the rebirth of the UK cruise industry and had become almost a national institution. *Canberra* was not sold on to another operator, she sailed later in 1997 for Pakistan and the ship-breakers. Had she been refitted and sold, there was always the likelihood that in the short-term, her loyal following may have gone with her.

*Oriana* has proved very successful indeed, bringing a new era of cruising to the UK market. As mentioned earlier, elegance is an important factor for the market segment that *Oriana* is designed for, and elegant is an apt description of the ship. Whilst not as 'glitzy' as many of the new builds for the US market, there is a timeless feel about *Oriana*. The ship looks and feels British, an important comfort-zone factor when marketing the product.

P&O Cruises commissioned a complete art collection for the *Oriana*, all of the works from UK artists. No fewer than 2882 pictures plus ceramics and sculptures were commissioned, more than are found hanging in the National Gallery in London. P&O Cruises actually sell a full catalogue of the art collection on board and it is more than a day's work to wander around the ship looking at each item.

With the *QE2* effectively under US ownership from 1998 (following the acquisition of Cunard by Carnival) and marketed heavily towards the US customer, *Oriana* was fast becoming the UK flagship, although *Aurora*, due to debut in May 2000, may take over this mantle, as indeed might the new proposed *Queen Mary* for Cunard.

In April 1997, P&O Cruises ordered a new 76 000-ton vessel from Meyer Weft to be named the *Aurora* and due to debut in May 2000. The ship will be a larger version of *Oriana* with enhanced facilities, including a conference room and a business centre but still designed for the UK market.

The philosophy behind *Aurora* gives a good indication of P&O Cruises' thinking about the UK market, and reprinted below is an interview conducted by the editor of *The Dawning of Aurora*, Kay Davidson with Gwyn Hughes, the Managing Director of P&O Cruises, about the reasons and planning behind the decision to spend £200 000 000+ on another new vessel. The interview was first published in *The Dawning of Aurora*, a series of pamphlets being sent to P&O Cruises 'POSH' Club members (loyal customers) as the building of the ship progressed, and which not only provides information about the ship and the company but invites customer views to be submitted. *Aurora* is likely to be very successful if the 11 000 expressions of interest as early as Summer 1998 for the maiden voyage in May 2000 was any indication.

(The interview below was reprinted in Cartwright & Baird, 1999, and items in italics added by the authors to aid understanding, with the permission of Cartwright & Baird.)

# The beginning of *Aurora*

Ordering a new ship is not a decision that any shipping line takes lightly. It represents massive investment – £200 million in the case of *Aurora* – and there has to be confidence that enough people will wish to take cruise holidays over the life of the ship. And as the life of a ship exceeds 30 years, the predictions have to be accurate.

*Kay Davidson conducted the following interview with Gwyn Hughes, Managing Director of P&O Cruises, to find out some of the reasoning and planning behind the building of Aurora.*

**Q. *Aurora* is to be delivered in Spring 2000. Why then – why not earlier?**
**A.** It was of paramount importance that the success of *Oriana* was ensured before we brought another new ship into the fleet. The retirement of *Canberra* last year [*1997*] meant that we needed to bring another first class ship in as soon as possible; the length of time that it takes to build a new ship meant that *Arcadia* [*ex Star Princess*] was by far the best option open to us at that time. Demand for quality cruises is rising steadily and so we are confident that we are introducing *Aurora* at the right time.

**Q. Do you feel that P&O should have ordered *Aurora* at the same time as *Oriana*?**
**A.** Hindsight is a wonderful thing! Yes, in the light of *Oriana*'s success, we could have taken the plunge and ordered two ships but at the time it was more sensible to act with caution.

**Q. When was *Aurora* first mooted?**

**A.** We always have plans for new ships on the drawing board. Plans were made early in 1997 after *Oriana*'s first two seasons.

**Q. Are there plans for a sister?**

**A.** As I said, there is a constant planning process in place. It is worth remembering that order books in the major shipbuilding yards are virtually full for the next two years.

**Q. Did P&O Cruises consider taking another of the Princess Cruises' ships and refitting it as they did with *Arcadia*?**

**A.** Princess' business is expanding as rapidly as our own and they need all their current ships for their expansion plans. In addition, building a new ship will allow us to incorporate all the latest developments in shipbuilding. This means that *Aurora* can bring world-class facilities such as round-the-clock dining to the British Cruise market.

**Q. Will the British Cruise market absorb this increase? Especially in the light of increased choice now available to those wishing to take a cruise holiday?**

**A.** We are confident that *Aurora* will be just as successful as our other ships. The growth in the popularity of cruising remains very strong and the type of ships that P&O has means we are in the best position to fulfil British demand.

**Q. What does this development mean for *Victoria*?**

**A.** *Victoria* is an exceptionally popular and highly individual ship. Her presence in the fleet is assured for years to come.

**Q. Will *Aurora* be British registered?**

**A.** As with our other ships, it is our intention that *Aurora* will be registered in Britain.

**Q. Where will *Aurora* be based?**

**A.** Southampton is the homeport for P&O Cruises.

**Q. Many people might have expected you to call the new ship *Canberra*. Why is this not the case?**

**A.** That name is still clearly associated with one particular vessel that has not been out of service for very long. We know that there are many strong – and happy – memories of *Canberra* and we would not wish to cause confusion by giving another ship the same name so soon.

**Q. Why build *Aurora* in Germany at Meyer Weft?**

**A.** Prior to any decision, yards with the appropriate competencies were reviewed – both in the UK and worldwide. Meyer Weft built a very fine ship in *Oriana* and as *Aurora* is a development of *Oriana*, it was clearly of benefit to build her at the same shipyard. Meyer Weft have a very impressive record as one of the world's leading cruise ship builders; they have great technical expertise in building new-generation cruise ships and can deliver both on price and on time.

**Q. In a nutshell, how will *Aurora* differ from the other ships in the fleet?**

**A.** That's hard to summarise in a few sentences! *Aurora* will incorporate all the latest features introduced into new vessels worldwide plus a number of other innovations. As I mentioned earlier, she will have 24-hour dining as part of an extensive range of dining options, and other examples include an indoor/outdoor swimming pool and unsurpassed children's facilities. This will make her a very forward-looking ship with a particular ambience. We are confident that the other ships will maintain their own unique appeal and we will maintain our investment in all the ships and their onboard services so that we continue to offer the highest levels of passenger enjoyment.

(Reprinted by permission of P&O Cruises.)

P&O obviously believe in the continuing growth and viability of the UK market and it is an interesting reflection of that market that their repeat passengers identify so closely with the company and its vessels as to be interested in the technical progress of building etc.

*Aurora* arrived in Southampton in April 2000 and from the outset is was clear that she was an evolution of the *Oriana* concept. *Aurora* has alternative dining venues, more balconies, two huge penthouse suites and a business centre. As such, she brings UK cruising into line with that offered to the US market.

Despite all the technological advances, *Aurora*'s maiden voyage could have been a public relations disaster for P&O. During her naming by the Princess Royal, the bottle of champagne not only failed to break but fell out of its cradle and into the water. This is regarded as a very bad omen by sailors. Eighteen hours into her maiden voyage, a bearing overheated and the ship had to return to Southampton, with the subsequent abandonment of the cruise. As there can only be one maiden voyage, this was a considerable disappointment to those on board.

P&O recovered the situation brilliantly by not only refunding all fares but also offering another cruise at no cost. In this way the situation was recovered and as an organisation they were seen to be doing right by their customers, turning a potential disaster into a customer relations' triumph.

## *Mistral* – Festival Cruises

The launch and naming of a new ship is always an exciting and emotional affair for those involved. The naming of P&O's *Oriana* in 1995 involved Her Majesty the Queen, the band of the Scots Guards, the choir of Westminster Abbey and the Bishop of Winchester, pomp and circumstance at its best. However, in the days when mega-ships of 100 000 GRT are taking to the seas, the launch of a medium-sized liner might not seem a fitting case study to examine the impact of the external environment on an organisation.

*Mistral* (48 000 GRT), however, may well be an important milestone in the history of the cruise industry and together with *Oriana*, a worthy example of how all the external factors can come together to give a window of opportunity to a proactive organisation as they were the first ships to be built to cater for, respectively, the UK cruising market and the generic European market. As has been shown throughout this book, the North American and UK markets have been well served in recent years by a growing number of cruise vessels designed to cater for their specific needs; other European nationalities have been less well served. As well as the UK market, there have been German and Italian sectors in addition to small French operations, but other than the predominantly Italian MSC (Mediterranean Shipping Company) cruises, European union has not been evidenced within the cruise industry.

Festival Cruises was founded by George Poulides in 1993 (Ward, 1998) whose operations had previously owned *The* [sic] *Azur* (14 717 GRT ex *Eagle*) which had latterly been under charter to Chandris. The vessel, built in 1970, had been converted from a P&O cross-channel car ferry to a cruise ship in 1981 (Kludas, 1992) and had gained a good reputation, especially among UK cruisers, for inexpensive cruises. The ship is the largest that can pass through Greece's Corinth Canal and this was a marketing USP for her owners. The *Azur* was joined by *Bolero*, 16 107 GRT (ex *Starward*), originally one of the earlier NCL Miami-based cruise liners. Known in Europe as Festival Cruises, the operation was marketed in North America as Azur–Bolero Cruises (now being known as First European Cruises) and gained good reports from Ward (1997, 1998, 1999) for a modestly priced product delivered well, but without the facilities normally to be found on the current generation of vessels, especially those for the US market. A third ship was acquired in 1997 with the purchase of the *Flamenco*, 17 042 GRT (ex *Southern Cross*, ex *Starship Majestic*, ex *Sun Princess*, ex *Spirit of London*), originally ordered by Kloster but purchased whilst building by P&O in 1972.

At this point, Festival appeared to be a small operation using vessels primarily displaced from the US market and operating in the lower-to-middle range of the Standard product segment.

A prediction as to the future development of Festival might have suggested that they would either acquire more older ships or that they could be vulnerable to a take-over by a larger operator, perhaps one of the new UK entrants to the cruise industry. It would have been hard to predict that they would charter the *Bolero* to the UK package holiday company of First Choice from the Spring of 1999 and that they would also introduce a brand-new 47 900 GRT vessel, move themselves into the top end of the Standard market and perhaps knock on the door of the Premium categories.

In early 2000 not only did Festival announce the building of more new vessels but P&O attempted to acquire the Festival operation, although this fell through. P&O has, as explained, decided to float their cruise operations as a separate business on the London and New York Stock Markets, and acquiring Festival would have added a new, European dimension to their operations.

*Mistral* had been laid down, unnamed, for another cruise company. The builders were to be Chantiers de l'Atlantique in France, the same yard that built the *Norway*, ex *France* – still the world's longest passenger ship. The incomplete vessel was acquired by a group of French investors and placed on long-term lease/charter to Festival in 1997 (Ward, 1999) at a very early stage in construction and named *Mistral* with a debut date of July 1999.

As soon as Festival acquired the hull, still in its early stages of building, the design philosophy was to build a ship that would appeal to a generic European market, providing a high-quality cruise experience at affordable prices and with a European ambience.

Whilst Festival as a company is a newcomer to the market, its principals have been in the ship owning market for over fifty years and thus they have a body of knowledge upon which to base their design philosophy.

January 1999 saw a major political change in Europe. In addition to enlargement of the European Union (EU) throughout the late 1990s, 1999 saw the first group of countries including France, Germany and Italy (but excluding the UK) embark upon monetary union with the introduction of the 'euro', as covered earlier in this book. The idea of a common European identity was gaining ground, although more slowly than many of those committed to a united Europe might have wished. The European cruise market was still delineated into nationality-based sectors.

Industry experts in the USA have commented that many of the ships operating in the European cruise market were older vessels displaced from the North American market. The only really new vessels that had been built exclusively for European-based cruisers were a few smaller German vessels and *Oriana* plus *Aurora* (see earlier) for the UK market.

*Mistral* is one of the first ships built for the European Standard or Premium markets to include balcony cabins (others being *Oriana*, *Aida* and the later *Costa*), now a feature of nearly all new builds in the North American market.

Based on full occupancy of the 4-berth cabins and two sharing the other accommodation, this gives *Mistral* a normal cruising complement of 1232 on a 47 900 GRT hull, although it must be stressed that according to Festival's brochure, all of the 2-berth cabins can accommodate a third or fourth cruiser. This brings the maximum possible occupancy up to 2275 but it is highly unlikely that every cabin would be occupied by a family to its fullest extent, and Festival have informed us that the maximum number of berths to be sold will not exceed 1580. These figures put the *Mistral* in line with other companies moving up-market but with, according to Festival, cabins that are above average size for Standard products.

Passenger accommodation has been kept away from the main nightlife areas of the ship as a matter of policy.

As another deliberate policy, no suites are available, the space they would have occupied being used to increase the number of mini-suites with balconies available, as these have a greater appeal to European passengers.

Décor, especially artwork, is of a general European ambience and the library includes volumes in the main European languages.

Language is a problem on multi-nationality ships, Ward (1999) commenting upon the number of announcements needed in order to relay information to all cruisers. To militate against too many announcements in differing languages, Festival developed an interactive, fibre-optic, in-cabin TV system to relay much routine information.

The naming of decks and public spaces reflects the generic European concept of the ship. The decks are named *Paris*, *Rome*, *London*, *Berlin*, *Brussels*, *Athens*,

*Cannes* and *Madrid* respectively, whilst there is a Mayfair Lounge, San Marco Room, L'Etoile Restaurant, Richelieu Library and Caffè Grecco etc. – truly European!

All outside cabins have picture windows, there are no portholes in passenger cabins and with mini-suites closely resembling the superb examples on *Oriana* both in size and layout, the accommodation should join that on *Oriana* and *Aurora* in setting a benchmark for the European market.

In 1998 the currency on board Festival ships was the Italian lire but with the introduction of the eurozone, Festival decided to adopt the euro as the shipboard currency on its vessels, although holidays will still be booked and paid for in national currencies, especially in the UK where Festival have a growing market. Given that the ship is registered in France, indeed she is one of the few, if not the only, cruise ships registered in France, use of the euro might be a useful way of avoiding any 'national preferences'.

*Mistral* will also be one of the first (*Edinburgh Castle* introduced the trend in Europe) vessels, including *Aurora*, for any purely European market to offer alternative dining, with the Rialto Grill being available as a matter of course to mini-suite customers and at a supplement to all others. In this, the ship follows the precedent of the *QE2* where different restaurants are used for different cabin grades.

*Mistral* operates a series of 7–12-day Mediterranean itineraries based on Venice, Genoa in the Summer and Autumn (including Lebanon and Syria) and then crosses to the Caribbean for the Winter, offering 7-day figure-of-eight cruises based on Martinique or Guadeloupe (French Islands – French ship), bringing two new base ports into the area.

Fitting neatly into the price bracket between the Standard products of Thomson and Airtours and the Premium P&O product, in addition to offering a 'national' ship for the French market, *Mistral* seems to be well placed within the marketplace.

The decision to move to the upper end of the Standard product is deliberate policy by Festival and the research for this book suggests that there will be market share to be captured from those cruisers trading up from other Standard products, plus new cruisers who wish for a product that is linked less directly to the package holiday sector.

The importance of ships like *Mistral*, *Oriana* and *Aurora* is that they bring cruising for the European market more into line with the facilities offered by companies operating in the North American market. Cartwright & Baird's (1999) UK research sample were of the general opinion that having cruised on a North American market upper-range Standard/Premium vessel, the offerings in terms of facilities of many of the European market companies in the Standard range were considerably inferior.

Whilst still a relatively young company, Festival intend to enter the 21st Century with five ships (including *Bolero* on charter to First Choice) and were certified to ISO 9002 (Quality Assurance) in 1994 and the International Safety Management Code (ISM) in 1994/95, the first cruise line to be certified for both areas.

The *Mistral* offers cruising for the smaller European markets, including the Netherlands (although many Netherlanders still use Holland America, despite the company being owned by Carnival), Belgium, Spain, Portugal etc. in addition to the UK, French, German and Italian markets. This gives the company the whole of the EU as a marketplace – the trick will be to convince each national group that they are not a minority. In that respect the success of *Mistral* may well be closely linked to the progress of closer European unity.

Whilst competitors may not always welcome a new player into the marketplace, the advent of a new upper-range Standard product for the European market can only drive up standards overall. Given the pan-European nature of the *Mistral* operation, it is likely that the ship will serve to introduce new people (and nationalities) to cruising, thus increasing the overall European market.

Cruising is one of the fastest growing business sectors, with ships costing upward of £200 000 000 each to build and commission. Proper analysis of the external environment is thus vital when spending such huge sums of shareholder money.

The following section fits the relevant segments of the cruise into the components of the SPECTACLES analysis, shown as bullet points as a means of showing how important the analysis is.

# P&O Cruises/Festival SPECTACLES analysis

## Social

- Cruising becoming seen as a more family-oriented type of holiday
- Increases in leisure time
- More older people with disposable income
- More sophisticated customer behaviour requiring alternative dining etc.
- Foreign holidays becoming the norm rather than the exception in Europe
- Safe way to travel
- Allows holidaymakers to remain within their comfort zone by serving familiar food, entertainment etc.

## Political

- *Mistral* reflects EU ideals
- More areas of the world becoming safer and more welcoming for travellers, e.g. Lebanon and Syria
- International regulations rendering older ships obsolete
- P&O commitment to keep its ships under UK registry
- Use of euro by Festival as on-board currency

## Economic

- Increases in disposable income
- Discounting has brought prices down

## Cultural

- *Oriana* and *Aurora* allow UK travellers to remain within their cultural comfort zone
- *Mistral* has a European ambience
- Holidays abroad have become a European cultural norm

## Technological

- Building techniques have allowed new forms of accommodation, e.g. balconies
- Modern ships have less draught and can thus reach smaller, more interesting ports
- Good safety record for the industry
- Ease of arranging flights to and from ships – often charter flights organised by the cruise company
- Cashless cruising using EPOS (Electronic Point of Sale) linked to an on-board credit account

## Aesthetic

- All three ships look like ships – an important aesthetic point
- Use of OBL by the companies
- Use of art etc. on board

## Customers

- Growing customer base with new customer segments
- Maintains customer comfort zone
- High-quality service
- Allows customers to travel in safety

## Legal

- Increasingly difficult for older ships to meet safety and environmental legislation
- Holidays with pay a legal right in Europe

## Environmental

- New ships are environmentally friendly

## Sectoral

- Busy sector with a need to introduce new products to keep up with competition

The above are just a few of the factors that have led to these multi-million pound investments.

Whatever business an organisation is in, be it a corner shop, a university or a cruise line, it cannot ignore its external environment. That environment is becoming more and more complex as time goes on and thus the importance of effective external analysis cannot be emphasised enough.

# ■ ⩔  Bibliography

Abercrombie N & Warde A (1992) *Social Change in Contemporary Britain*, Polity Press

ACM (1999) *Managers at Risk*, Association of College Managers, Edition 91, October

Adams D (1979) *The Hitchhikers Guide to the Galaxy*, Pan

Adler E (1969) *Lectures in Market Research*, Crosby Lockwood, London

Aldrich D F (1999) *Mastering the Digital Marketplace*, Wiley

Allen R E (ed.) (1990) *The Concise Oxford Dictionary*, OUP

Ardrey R (1967) *The Territorial Imperative*, Collins

Argyris C (1960) *Understanding Organisational Behaviour*, Tavistock Institute

Barr A & York P (1982) *The Official Sloan Ranger Handbook*, Ebury

Bernstein C & Woodward B (1994) *All the Presidents Men*, Touchstone

Bowen D (1999) *The Daily Telegraph Electronic Business Manual*, Net Profit

Brassington F & Pettitt S (1997) *Principles of Marketing*, Financial Times/Pitman

Browne D J (1989) *Economic Theory and Practice*, Edward Arnold

Carson R (1965) *Silent Spring*, Harmondsworth

Cartwright R (2000) *Mastering Customer Relations*, Macmillan – now Palgrave

Cartwright R & Baird C (1999) *The Development and Growth of the Cruise Industry*, Butterworth Heinemann

Cartwright R & Green G (1997) *In Charge of Customer Satisfaction*, Blackwell

Cartwright R, Collins M, Green G & Candy A (1993) *In Charge – Managing People*, Blackwell

Cartwright R, Collins M, Green G & Candy A (1994) *In Charge – Managing Yourself*, Blackwell

Casserley H C (1980) *The Observer's Directory of British Steam Locomotives*, Warne

Chapman C (2000) *How the Stock Markets Work*, Century

Clancy T (1998) *Death of Honor*, Putnam

Clutterbuck D & Goldsmith W (1984) *The Winning Streak*, Orion

Clutterbuck D & Goldsmith W (1997) *The Winning Streak Mark II*, Orion

Clutterbuck D, Clark G & Armistead C (1993) *Inspired Customer Service*, Kogan Page

Davidson M & Cooper C (1992) *Shattering the Glass Ceiling*, Sage

Davie M (1986) *Titanic – The Full Story of a Tragedy*, Bodley Head

de Jonge P (1999) whiteknuckleride@amazon.com, *Daily Telegraph Magazine*, 21 August, pp. 38–46

Dickinson R & Vladimir A (1997) *Selling the Sea*, Wiley

Donald D (ed.) (1999) *The Encyclopaedia of Civil Aircraft*, Aurum

Eddy P, Potter E & Page B (1976) *Destination Disaster*, Hart-Davis

European Union (1998) *EC Directive 93/104 Concerning Certain Aspects of the Organisation of Working Time*, Brussels

Fayol H (1916) *General and Industrial Administration*, translated from the French by C Storrs (1949), Pitman

Foot D K & Stoffman D (1999) *Boom, Bust and Echo 2000*, Macfarlane, Walter & Ross

Gardiner R & Van der Vat D (1995) *The Riddle of the Titanic*, Weidenfeld & Nicolson

Grant A (1991) *The American Political Process*, Dartmouth Publishing

Gregory M (1994) *Dirty Tricks – British Airways' Secret War against Virgin Atlantic*, Little, Brown & Co

Griseri P (1998) *Managing Values – Ethical Change in Organisations*, Macmillan – now Palgrave

Hackett, General Sir John *et al.* (1978) *The Third World War, August 1995 – A Future History*, Sidgwick & Jackson

Hailey A (1975) *The Moneychangers*, Souvenir Press

Hall S (1995) *Rail Centres – Manchester*, Ian Allan

Handy C (1976) *Understanding Organisations*, Penguin

Handy C (1978) *Gods of Management*, Souvenir Press

Handy C (1989) *The Age of Unreason*, Business Books Ltd

Hastings C, Bixby P & Chaudry-Lawton R (1986) *Superteams – A Blueprint for Organisational Success*, Gower

Hastings M & Jenkins S (1983) *The Battle for the Falklands*, Michael Joseph

HM Government (1974) *Consumer Credit Act 1974*, HMSO

HM Government (1997) *Consumer Protection Act 1997*, HMSO

HM Government (1995) *Disability Discrimination Act 1995*, HMSO

HM Government (1973) *The Employment Protection (Consolidation) Act 1973*, HMSO

HM Government (1973) *Fair Trading Act 1973*, HMSO

HM Government (1974) *Health and Safety at Work Act 1974*, HMSO

HM Government (1938) *Holiday with Pay Act 1938*, HMSO

HM Government (1999) *Modern Markets – Confident Consumers*, HMSO

HM Government (1994) *Sale and Supply of Goods Act 1994*, HMSO

HM Government (1982) *Supply of Goods and Service Act 1982*, HMSO

HM Government (1993) *Trade Union Reform and Employment Rights Act, 1993*, HMSO

Hubbard R G (1997) *Money, the Financial System and the Economy*, Addison-Wesley Longman

Jefkins F (1980) *Public Relations*, Macdonald & Evans

Johnson G & Scholes K (1993) *Exploring Corporate Strategy*, Prentice Hall

Jones T O & Strasser W E Jnr (1995) 'Why satisfied customers defect', *Harvard Business Review*, Nov–Dec, pp. 88–99

Judge S (1998) *Business Law*, Macmillan – now Palgrave

Keegan J (1998) *The First World War*, Hutchinson

Kludas A (1992) *Great Passenger Ships of the World Today*, Patrick Stephens

Lewis R D (2000) *When Cultures Collide*, Nicholas Brealey

Lynn M (1995) *Birds of Prey*, Heinemann

Lynn J & Jay A (1989) *The Complete Yes Prime Minister*, BBC

Marston J E (1979) *Modern Public Relations*, McGraw-Hill

Maslow A (1970) *Motivation and Personality*, Harper & Row

Mintzberg H (1983) *Structure in Fives: Designing Effective Organisations*, Prentice Hall

Montague J (1987) *Business Law*, Chambers

Morris D (1969) *The Human Zoo*, McGraw-Hill & Jonathan Cape

Morrison A M, White R P & Van Velson E (1994) *Breaking the Glass Ceiling*, Addison-Wesley

Nugent N (1995) *The Government and Politics of the European Union*, Macmillan – now Palgrave

P&O (1995) *Oriana, from Dream to Reality*, P&O Cruises

Pascale R T & Athos A G (1981) *The Art of Japanese Management*, Simon and Schuster

Peters T (1987) *Thriving on Chaos*, Alfred A Knopf

Peters T & Waterman R (1982) *In Search of Excellence*, Harper & Row

Pettinger R (1996) *Introduction to Organisational Behaviour*, Macmillan – now Palgrave

Pettinger R (1998a) *Managing the Flexible Workforce*, Cassell

Pettinger R (1998b) *The European Social Charter – A Manager's Guide*, Kogan Page

Porter M (1980) *Competitive Advantage*, Free Press

Porter M (1985) *Competitive Strategy*, Free Press

Pugh D (ed.) (1971) *Organisational Theory – Selected Readings*, Penguin

Quinn J, Mintzberg H & James R M (1988) *The Strategy Process*, Prentice Hall

Rattray Taylor G (1970) *The Doomsday Book*, Thames and Hudson

Rolt L T C (1955) *Red for Danger*, Bodley Head

Sabbach K (1995) *21st Century Jet – the Making of the Boeing 777*, Macmillan – now Palgrave

Sampson A (1984) *Empires of the Skies*, Coronet

Sampson A (1993) *The Seven Sisters – The Great Oil Companies and the World they Made*, Coronet

Sexton K, Marcus A A, Easter K W & Burkhardt T D (1999) *Better Environmental Decisions*, Island Press

Smithers A (1997) *Vocational Qualifications – What Went Wrong?* Paper to the TES Conference, Perth, 18 April

Stoppard M (1980) *Miriam Stoppard's Healthcare*, Weidenfeld & Nicolson

Taylor F W (1911) *Principles of Scientific Management*, Harper

Trompenaars F (1993) *Riding the Waves of Culture*, Economist Books

Trotter W P (1975) *The Royal Navy in Old Photographs*, Purnell

Trudgill P (1975) *Accent, Dialect and the School*, Edward Arnold

Urwick L (1947) *The Elements of Administration*, Pitman

Ward B & Dubos R (1972) *Only One Earth*, André Deutsch

Ward D (1994, 1997, 1998, 1999, 2000) *Berlitz Guide to Cruising and Cruise Ships – 1994/1997/1998/1999/2000*, Berlitz

Ward G, Burns R & Burns K (1990) *The Civil War*, Knopf

Weihrich H & Koontz H (1993) *Management – a Global Perspective*, McGraw-Hill

Wilmshurst J (1978) *The Fundamentals and Practice of Marketing*, Heinemann

Winder D (1999) 'On line banking', in *PC Pro*, Issue 57, July, pp. 206–218

Wotherspoon K R (1995) 'The Sale and Supply of Goods Act 1994', *Journal of the Law Society of Scotland*, March, pp. 88–91, Law Society of Scotland

# Useful web pages

http://www.europa.eu.int/en/comm/eurostat/facts/wwwroot/en/index.htm
(European Union statistics)
http://www.foe.org      (Friends of the Earth)
http://www.greenpeace.org      (Greenpeace)
http://www.scotland.gov.uk      (Scottish Executive)
http://www.scottish.parliament.uk   (Scottish Parliament)
http://www.statistics.gov.uk      (UK Government Office of National Statistics)
http://www.open.gov.uk      (UK public sector information)
http://www.odci.gov/cia/publications/factbook/index.html
(World Factbook – CIA/USA)

# ◤ Index of names

Abercrombie N   50, 62
Adams D   228
Adler E   177
Aldrich D F   136, 143
Allen R E   186
Ardrey R   8
Argyris C   3
Athos A G   126

Baird C   14, 97, 118–19, 238, 239–40, 244
Bezos J   138–9
Blair A   50, 136
Bowen D   136, 143
Branson R   26, 33, 229
Brassington F   157, 161
Browne D   103
Byng J (Admiral)   9

Carson R   214
Cartwright R   4, 12, 14, 16, 24, 28, 30, 34, 41,
   44, 46, 94, 97, 118–19, 130, 146, 147, 150,
   151, 153, 158, 162, 166, 168, 169, 171–2,
   174, 175, 181, 184, 185, 211, 227–33, 238,
   239–40, 244
Casserley H C   129
Chapman C   113, 114
Clancy T   96
Clutterbuck D   7, 170
Cooper C   50

Darwin C   56
Davidson M   50
Davie M   121, 169
de Jong P   138–9
Dickinson R   238
Dubos R   214
Dunne J   3

Eddy P (et al.)   19, 31, 89, 105, 159, 233–4

Fayol H   9, 11
Foot D J   58–9, 62

Gardiner R   121
Goldsmith D   170
Grant A   88, 91
Green G   12, 14, 15, 30, 34, 41, 44, 94, 118,
   150, 151, 153, 162, 173, 185, 227–33

Gregory M   28, 204, 226, 230
Griseri P   186, 211

Hackett J   65
Halley A   109
Handy C   22, 25–8, 44, 51
Hastings C (et al.)   18
Hastings M   2, 60, 160, 247
Hegel G W   19
Hitler A   186
Hubbard R G   94, 100, 108, 109, 110, 114

Jay A   47
Jefkins F   158
Jenkins S   2, 60, 160, 247
Johnson G   38, 115, 117–20, 128, 241
Jones H (Colonel)   3
Jones T O   180–4
Judge S   211

Keegan J   1
Koontz H   127

Lewis R D   122, 128
Lynn J   47

Malthus T   56–7
Marston J E   157
Maslow A   45–6
Minkin B   21
Mintzberg H   10–12, 22, 93
Montague J   187–8
Moore J (General, Sir)   2–3
Morris D   8–9, 57
Morrison A (et al.)   50

Nugent N   91

Pascale R T   126
Peters T   11, 51, 120, 170, 178, 230
Pettinger R   7, 76, 91, 202, 211
Pettitt S   157, 161
Pope A   31
Porter M   228–33, 243
Pugh D   4

Rattray Taylor G   214
Rolt L T C   49

# ☑ Index of subjects